THE
PSYCHOLOGY
OF
ATHLETIC
COACHING

J. W. MOORE
Southern Connecticut State College
New Haven, Connecticut

Burgess Publishing Company

426 South Sixth Street • Minneapolis, Minn. 55415

Physical Education Consultant to the Publisher:

ELOISE M. JAEGER
Chairman, Department of Physical Education for Women
University of Minnesota

GV711
M64

Copyright © 1970 by Burgess Publishing Co.
All rights reserved
Printed in the United States of America
Library of Congress Catalog Card Number 72-101711
Standard Book Number 8087-1346-9

Second Printing 1970

TABLE OF CONTENTS

261647

INTRODUCTION

The purpose of this book is twofold: (1) to show how certain guides for teaching and learning may be applied to the coaching of sports, and (2) to point out the relationship of meaningful learning to successful athletic coaching.

Meaningful learning is that type of learning in which the student sees some function in the material to be learned, in which there is an interrelationship of factors, and in which the learner's efforts are directed toward the discovery of the interrelatedness of those factors. This book attempts to point out ways and means by which the knowledges and skills of athletes may be organized into meaningful material so as to facilitate learning by the player.

Adherence to sound methods of instruction based on accepted theories of learning is an important factor in teaching (coaching) success. There is no guarantee that a team will win all its games because the coach is a good teacher. However, the coach can be reasonably sure that his players will be able to perform well if they have been taught the sport through a system which adheres to sound principles of instruction. Learning a sport can be expected to take place if the coach sets the stage for learning, orients the learner in terms of what the learner is supposed to accomplish, plans for the continuous improvement of the player, strives for cooperative group action, recognizes individual differences, and shares the evaluating process with his players.

Chapter I introduces coaching as a profession, carried on by educators possessing positive personality traits, guided by a philosophy, and accepting responsibilities toward individuals and factors connected with the job. The importance of proper organization and planning is stressed and the basic concepts of successful teaching and coaching are covered. The coach's responsibility to others is pointed out. Moreover, the need for proper organization and planning are covered. The next six chapters are devoted to the application of psychological concepts to the coaching of sports. They are the core of this book. It is in these chapters that we point out the methods of improving the performance of athletes through a better understanding of the factors affecting teaching and learning in athletics.

Chapter VIII discusses the common problems connected with the operation of sports programs outside of the actual teaching. Some of them necessitate an understanding of the proper function of agencies directly or indirectly influencing the operation of a sports program. Conditioning the athlete for competition programs of development and the latest information regarding nutrition, tobacco, alcohol, and drugs, and their effects on athletic performance are covered in Chapter IX.

Test questions covering factual material and discussion questions dealing with concepts are included at the end of each chapter.

The author wishes to express his appreciation for the efforts of Don Tonry and Irving Leveton for their artistic contributions and to Ruth DiLeone for her patience and professional job of typing.

Chapter I
COACHING AS A PROFESSION

"A good coach is a good teacher,
a great coach is a good teacher and good organizer."

THE PHILOSOPHY OF COACHING

General opinion among educators indicates that athletic coaches should be judged the same as other members of the faculty. They are expected to be highly qualified technically in their sports specialty and should possess personal and professional qualities characteristic of all teachers. Moreover, like all teachers, coaches will develop a philosophy regarding their work. A person's philosophy is the way in which he views things, events, relationships, and the values he sets upon them. Hence, one individual, for example, might set a high value upon gaining wealth and a very low value on gaining friendships. Such is his philosophy of life, and his actions will reflect that philosophy. Any man who hopes to achieve a high quality of practical success should base his activity on a firm foundation of sound theory, and no theory is worth formulation unless it includes all the available suggestions of everyday practice. The great pragmatizer is always a theorizer, and the great theorizer is always a practical man.

Just as any department of an educational institution is expected to operate within a philosophy in harmony with that of the entire institution, so each division of a department should carry out its activities in a manner in keeping with the educational philosophy of that department. In some institutions, athletics operate as an independent enterprise, but in the majority of schools and colleges athletics are included as a part of the physical education department and administered like other divisions of the department. One means of operating within a sound philosophy of athletics would be to conduct the program of athletics as an intrinsic part of the educational curriculum and as a facet of the physical education program, completely budgeted like other educational programs, with no pressure placed upon the instructors and coaches to produce winning teams, and with athletic competition considered as an advanced

1

phase of the physical education program designed to meet the needs and interests of the more highly skilled student.

If athletics are regarded as a part of the physical education program of a school or college, it seems proper that the philosophy of any coach should be in harmony with the educational philosophy of the physical education department. The most sane attitude toward athletics is that the coaches consider the athletic program to be an educational program. The most widely accepted objectives of education are those that may be reached as readily through a physical education program, including athletics, as through a teaching program in any other subject.

As stated above, a person's philosophy is the way in which he regards things, events, relationships, and the values he sets upon them. A coach's philosophy, then, will be the way he regards his sport, the problems connected with it, and the importance he places upon those problems.

For example, what degree of value does he place upon each of the following? Does he consider the following limited list of problems of competitive sports to be of greater or lesser importance? Which will overshadow others?

Winning or losing
Personal contact with his players
Rapport with the academic faculty
Relations with the alumni
Relations with the public
Relations with the press, radio and T.V. personnel
Health of his players
Careful planning for best use of time
Improvements of teaching techniques
Wide open or conservative type of play
Physical conditioning of players
Moral and ethical conditioning of the players
Business management of the sport
Budget limitations
Emotional control during games
Relations with officials
Offense or defense

He will be motivated to act on his problems in accordance with his attitude toward them. Some will receive little thought and effort because he feels that they are not important. The meeting of other problems receives much thought, time and effort. A coaching philosophy then is really a collection of attitudes toward the problems of coaching. Two coaches may think alike with respect to the importance of physical conditioning and yet be poles apart in their attitudes toward offense and defense. One football coach will select his best players and devote the majority of his time to molding them into a strong defensive unit. The other coach will select his best players for offense, and the greater part of his coaching time will be spent on developing the offense. Another example can be seen in basketball coaches, some of whom stress deliberate play-situation offensive patterns as opposed to the coaches who believe strongly in a fast-moving, free-lance method of scoring.

To determine the philosophy of a coach, we must examine his attitudes toward all the factors or problems connected with his job. If it is possible to classify a coach as a particular philosophical type, it is because his attitude toward certain of the problems causes him to stress the solution of those problems.

To many people, the chief problem of a coach is to win more games than he loses. Therefore, they interpret his total philosophical makeup according to his attitude toward winning or losing. This is an important enough factor to cause us to denote a separate section to it in this book. However, a more accurate analysis of philosophy would be gained from knowing how a coach felt toward everything connected with his job.

To better understand a coach's philosophy, one might observe the conduct of his players. Their style of play, the condition of their uniforms, the respect shown officials and opponents, the language used, their stamina in the late stages of the game, their conduct off the field, their ability to withstand game pressure, their scholastic standing in the school, and the attitude of the student body and faculty toward the team are just a few of the indicators of a coach's philosophy. They will show whether or not the coach considers the acquisition of character traits (outcomes) to be important. One study of the attitudes of the faculty of a large eastern university toward the intercollegiate athletic program indicated that the majority of the faculty felt that the favorable outcomes of sports participation were being realized by the athletes. It can be taken as a vote of confidence in the philosophies of the coaching staff.[1]

The emphasis placed on factors other than victory in games in this section is not meant to minimize the importance of coaching to win. Any meeting billed as a contest is expected to determine a winner. Being able to win graciously is as much a virtue as losing with good grace. A reputation for being a good loser often is built upon a

---

[1]E. Gross and M. Torback, "Are Intercollegiate Athletics Worth While?", *Athletic Journal*, Vol. 26, No. 6, September 1955, p. 26.

habit of losing. Coaches and athletes who lack confidence in their ability to win should not compete. Coaching to win will be covered in another section of this book.

A coach's philosophy might be based on the coach's belief in the social, emotional, moral and character-building outcomes of athletics. Years of associating with many coaches in various sports leaves one with the impression that practically all of them are driven by a high resolve. They love their sport, enjoy the task of working with young athletes, and feel that they are helping to mold fine character. Love of their sport and devotion to it seems to be characteristic of those who have spent many years in the profession. The development of proper attitudes based on educational philosophy early in a coach's career will probably do much toward the acquisition of a healthy philosophy of coaching.

PERSONALITY TRAITS OF COACHES

The usual definition applied to the term personality is a list of qualities or characteristics that distinguish one person from another. Each trait is supposed to be established well enough within a person's behavior so that it will be quite apparent. A person may display many traits during his life situations, but some of them will dominate. These often will be the characteristics by which the individual is identified. His behavior indicates the quality of his physical, mental, emotional, and social health. Heredity, physical factors, and social and cultural factors affect the degree of their development. Heredity traits are transmitted from parents to their offspring through genes found in the chromosomes of the sex cells. From them, a person is endowed with such identifying features as the size or shape of his body, facial features, intelligence. He may also inherit a special capacity for artistic, mechanical, or athletic ability. The physical factors affecting personality development are the central and autonomic nervous systems and the ductless glands of the endocrine system. Emotions and our physical reactions to our emotions indicate the effect of our autonomic nervous system on our behavior. Hormones from our ductless glands may affect our growth, energy, alertness, and maturity. Social and cultural factors include the environment in which a person lives and his interaction with people in that environment. We are partly products of our experiences within our environment. Society has already established rules of behavior, and the individual is expected to adjust to those rules.

As a result of those experiences and adjustments, he will acquire knowledge, assume attitudes, establish values, and develop habits. The sum total will be his personality.

It is extremely important for a coach to establish his self-image. This means that he should understand himself. His strengths, weaknesses, motives, desires, and drives should be clear to him, and he must learn to live with them. This is not to imply that he should never consider changing. Personality development is dynamic rather than static. It never stops. Changes can take place at all stages of life. Some traits and characteristics may dominate a personality in early years and disappear with age and maturity. To establish his self-image and understand himself better, a coach might use a self-evaluation test to determine the degree to which he possesses traits that are considered to be socially desirable and technically necessary for success in athletic coaching. We offer the following:

Leadership—inspires followership without question or hesitation.

A sense of humor—sees the funny side of a situation even if it momentarily runs counter to his objectives. Is quick with a witty remark.

Friendliness—readily accepts people for themselves, not for what they can do for him. Is pleasant to all who approach him. Outgoing and warm.

Forcefulness—always regarded as the "boss-man." Makes believers out of skeptics. Dynamic, take-charge type of person.

Good appearance—always dressed appropriately. Is neat clean, always shaved, exhibits proper posture.

—Honesty—can be relied upon to do the right thing at all times. His teams play by the spirit of the rules.

Industriousness—works hard at his job and gives out with his best effort.

Reliability—meets his responsibilities squarely and accomplishes the task if it is within his power.

Emotional stability—does not possess a "short fuse." Remains calm but determined under stress, setting a proper example for players, other coaches, and spectators.

Loyalty—recognizes his responsibility to his employers and others. Stands by them in controversies.

Persistence—has a high degree of psychological endurance commonly classified as stick-to-it-iveness.

Responsibility—is ready to accept blame when things go wrong. Does not shift the blame to players or assistant coaches.

Ambitiousness—has a felt need to succeed. Almost overpowering will to win, to be the best.

Creativeness—has original thoughts. Constantly thinking of newer and better ways of doing things.

Optimism—recognizes the seriousness of problems, but has enough confidence in himself, his associates, and the team to prohibit worry and pessimism.

Integration—well organized. Plans for every contingency. Dislikes surprises.

Understanding—is reasonable in his demands. Realizes that they have limits to their ability to cooperate and produce.

Cooperation—readily adjusts his problems to harmonize with those of his associates. Known to be ready to "go the extra mile."

Culture—attuned to the activities of a twentieth-century American. Has interests and knowledges in fields other than sport. Effective speaker free from gross grammatical errors.

Self-discipline—is mentally tough. Intolerant of poor, shoddy work on his own part. Keeps himself in good physical condition through a regimen of work, rest, and play.

Trust—assumes that he will receive the type of treatment from others that he gives to them. Gives opponents and officials the benefit of the doubt. Confidence in the integrity of those with whom he comes in contact.

The list by no means exhausts the list of traits usually associated with a proper personality for coaching, but it gives a good insight into the behavior patterns of successful coaches. If one should indulge in self-evaluation using those traits as criteria, he could arrive at a score but, without knowing the degree to which the good coaches possess the various traits, he would have no basis for comparison. What he would accomplish, however, is an awareness of his own traits and a realization that a large majority of them are useful to some degree.

We have been considering the positive characteristics of good coaches. It seems obvious that the converse of these qualities would indicate the negative type of personality. It is important for an athletic coach to be aware of some of the behavior traits that invariably spell failure in the profession. The possession of any one of the following would not prohibit success unless it was outstanding (example—persistent intoxication), but combinations of the bad traits lessen one's chances of success proportionately.

The following are considered poor traits for athletic coaches:

Sensitivity to criticism—a thin skin will result in a frequently bruised ego causing many unhappy moments.

Disloyalty—on the part of an assistant coach, it is cause for dismissal. Because it is a two-way street, the head coach must set a proper example in order to expect loyalty from others.

Emotional instability—a display of temper and acts of anger indicate immaturity. Unfortunately, it sometimes appeals to the adolescent mind resulting in imitation.

Overly critical—it is especially bad when it is exercised on a sensitive individual before teammates and/or the public.

Laziness—will result in a shoddy-appearing squad. It takes time and effort to teach proper techniques necessary for a good performance.

Poor discipline—is usually due to a failure to bring the squad to the point of self-discipline. Because they lack the feeling for self-discipline, the team members create incidents which violate the coach's rules.

Intemperance—a weakness for liquor will bring about a loss of respect by the players. Pity may prolong the agony of failure, but failure is inevitable. Drinking is not the answer to problems. They are always there when the individual becomes sober.

Selfishness—approaching every problem with the thought of protecting oneself regardless of other people will build up resentment. When such an individual finds himself in need of friends, they are usually not available.

Worry—carrying his problems within himself for twenty-four hours a day. It is usually caused by the failure to take positive steps to solve the problems. A mental and physical breakdown could result.

Discourtesy—coaches need to be ever conscious of public relations. Discourteous behavior will tarnish his public image and lose friends for his program. Courtesy must be accorded without discrimination to people in all social strata.

Aloofness—some great coaches have been austere and outwardly cold on the athletic field, but they have not been insensitive to the problems of people around them.

Vulgarity—is usually a defensive mechanism against some other type of personal inadequacy. It is never attractive to normally sensitive people. It is inexcusable when practiced before young people.

The implication found in the two lists should be clear to athletic coaches. Possession of positive traits enhances one's chances of success, while the negative traits lessen the chances. As previously stated, personality is not static, but dynamic. People change with maturity, but the change may be too slow in the case of athletic coaches. A change in *habits* must be preceded by a change in *attitudes*. In the discussion of coaching philosophy, it was pointed out that coaches looked upon the factors connected with their job as important or unimportant, necessary or unnecessary, desirable or undesirable. The factors are his problems. His attitudes have affected his behavior toward the problems, resulting in positive or negative behavioral traits. Happy is the coach who finds himself scoring heavily on the positive side. For the coach whose score is largely in the negative column, a decision should be made. If he feels that a readjustment of attitudes and behavior is called for, he should initiate the change. If these habits are long ingrained, it will take time, effort and self-discipline. The coach must decide whether the satisfactions gained from improved behavior are worth the effort. They usually will be.

RESPONSIBILITIES

Athletic coaches, besides being expertly trained in their special field, should present evidence of education and competency equivalent to academic teachers in order to be bona fide members of high school and college faculties.

The privileges of faculty rank for the coach bring with them responsibilities toward the student, department, and institution, as well as responsibilities directly related to the athletic program. The coach cannot ignore the demands which all these responsibilities put upon his time and interests. His attitude toward the total educational program of his institution will largely determine the esteem in which he is held by his colleagues and may, in the long run, be an important measure of his worth to the college or school and community.

The coach is expected to be concerned about the physical, social, mental, emotional, and moral development of his players. All teachers have opportunities for guidance, and coaches may be called upon to act as faculty advisors for athletes and nonathletes among the student body. It has long been recognized that coaches and physical education teachers have excellent opportunities for guidance in three vital areas of character development due to the learning situations in athletic activities. These areas are personal guidance, social-emotional guidance, and moral-ethical guidance. The coach as a teacher can assist an athlete in the solving of personal problems involving adjustments to school environment, personality development, scholastic standing with emphasis on graduating with his class, development of habits of healthful living, development of proper attitudes toward cooperation, self-sacrifice, honesty and extra effort, and socially acceptable behavior on and off the field. Needless to say, one of the most important attitudes to be instilled is that toward study. If an athlete with a questionable record of scholastic achievement is admitted to college, invariably he will become a scholastic problem unless the coaches establish a strict regimen of study hours. Tutorial help will be needed to supplement the efforts to keep the boy eligible. Most academic failures in college can be traced to bad study habits established in high school. It behooves high school coaches to spot the youngsters with study faults early in their careers and do their best to correct them. This is one of the extra responsibilities which a high school coach should accept. The gratitude of parents and the young athlete when he is accepted into a college and makes good will be ample pay for the coach's effort.

A boy will be aided in his physical development if he is a participant in a well planned training schedule which takes into consideration his age and organic power. Frequent rest periods should be provided during workouts, and coaches must be alert for signs of fatigue. A physical examination at the start of the season and before a boy is readmitted to the squad after an illness or injury is a wise precaution. The coach should always abide by the team doctor's decision in matters dealing with fitness for play. Every boy who is a member of the squad is entitled to good, safe equipment whether he is a star or a lowly scrub, and coaches of contact sports should check each boy's uniform to make sure that his protective armor is suitable. An insistence on proper hygiene among squad members will aid in reducing the cases of infection which often plague teams.

Although all teachers are supposed to feel a responsibility for the whole development of the student, some authorities feel that the coach has more influence on the lives of pupils under his care than any other teacher in the school system. Often the coach is a boy's hero, the man he looks up to and worships. No matter how much pressure is brought on a coach to produce winning teams, every boy who has played for him should be a better gentleman as a result of his experiences. It is from these experiences that the outcomes of sports are expected to be achieved. Much of the learning acquired by the students comes as a result of observation and imitation of the coach. The coach has but little private life, if it may be called that, and his conduct is always expected to be above reproach. His speech, walk, dress, and mannerisms will be copied by the youths who look to him for leadership.

Although at times he may doubt it, a coach or teacher does not work alone in meeting the needs of students. A coach has the cooperation of other teachers, administrators, the school nurse, the school doctor, and the home. The coach or physical education teacher can help the student develop confidence through skills and opportunities for leadership. A student seeking assurance should receive encouragement and praise to foster achievement. If a boy is seeking assurance, a coach can build within that student the necessary skills and attitudes, so that the boy may receive the recognition and esteem of his peers in wholesome and acceptable ways. Thus, a coach should recognize and accept a responsibility for working with students on and off the field, finding causes of undesirable behavior and replacing the causes with skills, knowledges, confidence, and abilities so that each student may grow and develop to his maximum.[2]

To the Department

The place of athletics in education is designated as part of the volunteer program in the curriculum of physical education. A desirable practice would be for all coaches to be members of the physical education staff and, as such, to assume certain responsibilities toward that department. Any coach who has the interest, training, and ability to teach health and physical education courses and otherwise assist in the work of the department should be a better varsity coach, granted, of course, that he is not overburdened during the season in which he is head coach.

A coach may be selected because of his proficiency in intercollegiate or professional athletics or because of his record as an interscholastic or intercollegiate coach. But to be of greatest service to the department in which he is going to work, the coach should also qualify as a teacher. A new coach should bring to the department an educational attitude, a spirit of cooperation, an interest in and an enthusiasm for physical education.

In a democratically administered department, all persons concerned with a problem help to formulate a plan for meeting the

[2]George F. Anderson, "Psychological Aspects of Teaching Physical Education," *Journal of Health, Physical Education and Recreation,* 21:152, March 1950.

problem. The director or administrating officer of the department carefully weighs the evidence on all sides and makes his decision, which then becomes the departmental policy. A coach should accept his responsibility for sharing in the formulation of plans. He should voice his opinions regarding departmental matters whenever he is called upon to do so. Once a decision has been reached and a policy established, the coach, like all other teachers in the department, should abide by that decision.

One coach may wish to gain for his sport all the financial support possible, but the departmental budget should be divided equitably, and that particular coach should not insist on a budget which will force a curtailment of the other sports programs. Moreover, he is expected to stay within his budget when one is established, in order to save himself and the director of the department much embarrassment.

With few exceptions, most schools and colleges are pressed for playing space to accommodate physical education classes, intramural programs and varsity athletics. Here again, the coach is expected to recognize the value and needs of the other activities by restricting his demands to the minimal.

Varsity coaches often display a lack of interest in the regular physical education classes as well as in the intramural programs. This indicates a poor professional attitude on the part of any member of a physical education teaching staff. The rank and file of students lack the necessary skill to place them on varsity teams. They would improve their skills if given some individual attention instead of being neglected or treated with patronizing superiority. Modern physical education programs stress sports and physical fitness activities. The physical education instructors are expected to know something of many sports and be expert in a few of them. It is highly probable that the instructors could improve the performance of the majority of class members if they would strive with the same amount of energy that they devote to the varsity teams. To be a good physical education teacher involves, among other factors, being prompt to class, being properly attired, having equipment and supplies ready, offering expert instruction, being present for the entire period, and evaluating the progress of class members. Concentration, enthusiasm, and interest in the physical education class activities equal to that shown on the varsity field would raise physical education to a place of high esteem with the students and institutional administration and enhance the prestige of the staff.

The varsity coaches should never set themselves apart from the other physical education staff members. The coach's problems are better comprehended by his fellow workers who often have had experience in competitive athletics. They are likely to be sympathetic toward the troubles of the coach who, in turn, should understand and respect the educational contributions of his non-coaching colleagues. Coaches are physical educators, and no physical educator can become an integral part of an educational institution if he fails to cooperate fully with his professional colleagues.

Coaches sometimes ask to be excused from the regular salary scales of their colleagues, feeling that the risks involved in the profession of coaching deserve more adequate compensation than that of general faculty members. Many school systems offer extra pay for coaching sports. It is usually prorated on the basis of responsibility, with the head coaches receiving more than the assistants. Often the sports themselves carry a degree of importance, and we find football and basketball coaches being paid more than coaches of such sports as golf, tennis, and swimming. This is not standard throughout the United States, because in some areas a sport such as wrestling and hockey will be held in higher esteem than basketball. There are good arguments for and against the practice of extra pay, but the trend seems to be in favor of the practice. When such a policy is established, it seems only fair that the extracompensated coach be willing to carry a normal teaching load during the regular school day.

Tenure is a desirable feature of any coaching position and, if coaches can qualify themselves academically for faculty rank, it would seem wise for them to accept a lower salay with the permanency of tenure than a special contract and higher salary without tenure. The American Football Coaches Association has a standing committee studying tenure plans for football coaches.

To the Institution

Certain responsibilities to the institution in which he works should be recognized and accepted by the football coach. The privilege of faculty rank carries with it the responsibilities of additional thought and service to the institution beyond that of teaching and coaching. The coach who has prepared himself for the field of education should be willing to assume his share of committee responsibilities in the solving of institutional problems. Coaches might well serve on such standing committees as curriculum, admissions, institutional development, public relations, orientation and guidance, social affairs, library, and student activities.

A high school coach's educational training should fit him for broad service within the school and community, as well as for the specialized service connected with his particular sport. His duties should include such items as membership on regular school committees and attendance at teachers' meetings. He will find, in addition to his coaching duties, that he must accept a share of the responsibility for the following: working with supervisors, improving the curriculum, directing extracurricular activities, academic advising, promoting pupil progress, participating in administration, improving community life and practicing public relations. So that he may render the utmost good, the coach should familiarize himself with the total organization and instructional scheme of the school. With this knowledge, he can be of great help in organizing a curriculum which gives proper emphasis in each area.

Institutions of learning gain prestige through activities apart from athletics, and the fortunes of their athletic teams do not dictate the success or failure of their academic programs. An athletic team is only one activity in the broad educational offerings of an institution, and it should be regarded as such by all concerned. If a coach should attempt to place it in any other category or to gain unwarranted prestige for his program to the detriment of other courses, he would serve to create antagonism toward himself and the department. An inescapable fact that the reputation of the coach as a man and a teacher will reflect on the institution he represents; and he should see that the effect of his sport on the school or college is a favorable one.

The soundness of an athletic program is affected by certain administrative policies common to all institutions of higher learning. These concern admission, retention, and curriculum. Like all faculty members, the coach has the responsibility of supporting these policies. He will make no attempt to have admitted an athlete who clearly has not met the standards for admission, nor will he plead that a boy be retained in college whose academic record indicates his inability to do college work. Moreover, a coach should not insist that an athlete follow a curriculum other than that set for his major course of study in order that he remain eligible, or that he escape a late-afternoon laboratory course. Policies established for all students apply to athletes, and a coach who attempts to circumvent them degrades his profession in the eyes of his faculty colleagues.

A coach should approach his tasks as an educator not as a hired professional. Matters concerning his sport or any other part of his work should be discussed directly with officials of the institution, rather than with an alumni committee or group of businessmen who are interested in promoting a sport at the institution.

The late Herman Hickman, coach at Yale University, described his relations with the alumni as "an attempt to keep them sullen but not mutinous." However, alumni groups should not be ignored altogether. High school and college athletics greatly need the sympathetic understanding, good will, and loyal support of the alumni.

A coach must maintain friendly and cooperative relations with the institutional administration and with the faculty. His attitude toward the administration should be frank, polite, and agreeably self-reliant. The coach's feeling toward the institution should be the same as that expected of all teachers. Any faculty member should not overestimate his own importance; nor should he resent justified and well intended suggestions or criticisms from his administrative superiors.

Tuss McLaughry, a fine coach and long-time Secretary of the American Football Coaches Association, once summed up the responsibilities of the football coach in terms which still seem appropriate for all coaches:

> Whether or not intercollegiate football performs its duties toward the player and is kept in its proper place depends largely on the coach. It is within his power to make football a worthwhile sport to all concerned or to degrade both players and the game and bring disrepute on the college which he represents. His value to the university is dependent on how well he can handle his responsibilities, which are to teach football technique to his players, to develop strength of character when weak traits are apparent, and in general handle these boys of an idealistic age the way he would want his own boy to be handled, regardless of how much pressure is on him to win. He should encourage study, and should show to the administrative officers that he is not only interested in winning football games, but will wholeheartedly cooperate in the whole process of education. ...The coach's value to the whole community, the way he handles his everyday affairs, aside from his influence and ability to win a fair percentage of games, is what makes him valuable to a university and on this alone will he be judged.[3]

To the Staff

The size of a coaching staff varies with the size of institutions and, in some cases, with the degree of importance granted to the sport. Whether a coach has one assistant or many, he must accept a patriarchal attitude toward those who serve him. He must be as much an inspirational leader to his staff as to the players, for he will put greater demands on them for time, effort, self-sacrifice, and loyalty. These are the common elements forming the framework of a fine coaching staff.

[3]D. O. McLaughry, "The Relationship of Football to a Physical Education Program," *37th Annual Proceedings of the College Physical Education Association,* 1933, p. 52.

Esprit de corps will evolve only if it is cultivated by the head coach. The high morale, characteristic of successful coaching groups, comes about as a result of a program of training and development designed to bring out the best performance by each coach. Members of the staff are usually selected for certain strengths or teaching skills. When they produce in better than ordinary fashion, they should be commended. Individual efficiency and extra effort should always be recognized.

A necessary virtue for an assistant coach is loyalty, but it is a "two-way street." A man cannot *demand* loyalty, he must *command* it through his relations with his subordinates. These include:

Fair and equitable treatment for every staff member.

Never shifting the blame for defeats onto the assistants, even though the weakness may obviously be in the area for which one assistant is largely responsible.

Making every effort to secure for his assistants the best possible salaries and fringe benefits to make their living easier.

Being willing to strongly support the candidacy of one of his assistants for a head coaching position for which he is qualified.

Making clear to the assistants the limits of recruiting practices as defined by the NCAA or Regional Conference and never placing them in positions which may induce them to violate the rules.

Determining the strong and weak points of each assistant so that the strengths may be used to good advantage and the poorer traits concealed until they can be modified through personal effort by the assistant.

The coaching staff is the official family of that particular sport. As a family, they must work harmoniously, respecting each other, giving of themselves, directing all efforts toward the common goal of success for the head coach and his program. Such spirit must be founded on faith and confidence in the head coach. He must deserve it before he can command it.

To the Sport

With very few exceptions, the coach has been an active player in the sport he coaches, usually, with better than average success. He may have been blessed with a fine neuromuscular system, but more often his success was due to long hours of practice, a strict regimen of training, and a willingness to sacrifice either time or pleasure to become a good performer. The satisfactions derived from participation might be a feeling of physical well-being, a sense of accomplishment, the joy of competition, or just plain fun. Certainly, the coach will attribute other learnings or even qualities of character to his sports experiences. As a result of his contact with the sport, he will develop a genuine affection for it.

A coach should feel a responsibility for improving his sport. This may be done in several ways. The rules governing play are changed frequently because some coaches feel that a change would benefit the game. Rule changes are suggested by coaches to make a sport more exciting, or more challenging, or safer for the players. The coach should be a creative and thinking person with a flair for experimentation. New and better techniques are products of the fertile minds of coaches resulting in more interesting games and improved performances. In spite of the nostalgic reminiscing of veteran coaches, the fact remains that modern athletes are outperforming those of the previous generation.

The game itself may be degraded by thoughtless indiscretions on the part of coaches. Having a team play in a ridiculous manner or deliberately foul in order to embarrass officials or opponents is one method of showing indifference toward one's responsibilities.

Players should be made to believe that sports participation is a privilege, not a right. It is true that the athlete qualifies for his right to compete by conditioning himself physically as well as developing skills. However, there would be no competition if the sport or game *did not exist*. It is the sport that offers opportunities to the young athlete to gain the beneficial outcomes of athletic competition. It may include the opportunity of getting a college education which, in turn, may open many doors to future successes following graduation. The coach should instill in the mind of the young athlete the attitude that he owes to the game his best effort at all times. Not to play the game honestly, winning or losing in accordance with the fortunes of sports, should be unthinkable. When athletes are admitted to college without proper credentials, receive financial aid over and above that allowed by regulations, and retain eligibility despite poor academic records, they are bound to acquire the impression that their talents have been purchased. If an opportunity is offered them to use those same talents to control the scoring in a contest, it doesn't disgust and anger them as it would a boy who is a legitimate scholar athlete. Sports provide much to those who would compete, but they deserve the best efforts of the competitor.

THE COACH AS AN ORGANIZER

In the early history of secondary and intercollegiate athletics, the toil of the coach could almost cease with the closing whistle in the final game of the season. Sports were strictly seasonal, not only in interest for players and spectators, but also in work and responsibilities for the coach. This situation is no longer true. Today the coach is employed on a year-round basis, and much of his time is spent in carrying out tasks which are considered a part of the sports program. These changes in the characteristics of the job are due to several factors:

the increasing complexity of the games requiring more time to be spent in planning;

an emphasis on winning resulting in a constant search for talent;

an increase in interest among students, resulting in larger squads;

the wider use of teaching materials, such as movies, field equipment, and other aids;

the strengthening of eligibility standards, requiring closer supervision of the academic work of players;

the increased cost of personal equipment, requiring thoughtful study of the merits of the various items, and of the needs of the squad, and the budget;

a new emphasis on speed and deception in sports, such as football, requiring more time to be spent in practice.

It has already been pointed out that the coach should possess competency in handling curricular and extracurricular responsibilities characteristic to all teaching personnel. In addition, he should have an understanding of the special problems involved in coaching an athletic team. Not all of the problems and tasks facing a coach are found on the playing field, gymnasium, or pool. The daily workout plan, the selection of assistants, the creation of a schedule, the purchase of equipment and the final preparations for games are a few examples of his problems. All of them are important aspects of coaching and require thoughtful consideration and careful planning by the coach.

An efficient coach is constantly searching for materials and methods which will not only make his job a little easier but also insure his doing a better job of coaching. He may secure the services of one or several assistants, and he may acquire much equipment, and have many resources at his disposal. No single element guarantees success. Winning coaches have operated with one assistant, small squads, and a minimum of equipment. Conversely, poor teams have been turned out in institutions which are blessed with the needed resources. How well the coach organizes the elements at his command largely will decide the success of his program. The organizing process will involve everything from the use of psychological principles of learning to planning the opening play of a game.

As in all educational planning, the focal point of attention should be the individual player. The coach should bear in mind that boys do not compete because they are forced to do so or to satisfy the needs of a coach. They play because they want to do so and to satisfy their own needs and interests. When the coach organizes and plans his sport program, he should design it to contribute to the growth and development of the player.

The remainder of this chapter is made up of a four-part treatment of the tasks facing the coach. The first three parts deal with tasks apart from actual teaching and learning which are important aspects of the coach's job. They are discussed under yearly planning, day-by-day planning, and planning for the game. The fourth part covers organization for learning in which the coach plans his teaching and learning situations in accord with certain concepts of learning.

PLANNING

Yearly

Although the greatest part of actual coaching is done during a single season of the year, the other periods of the year find the coach actively engaged in related activities extremely important to the success of his program. The following will serve to indicate the types of problems he will face. Of course, many of these problems will be shared with other members of the athletic department and, if attacked cooperatively, they will be solved with far more ease than if they were left to one individual.

Selection of assistants—The selection of assistants and scouts is one of the most important of the coach's problems, for the men who work with him can make or break him. The selection of these men should be based on the same factors which apply in the selection of any teacher. Experience, coaching success, education, knowledge of the game, intelligence, and personality should all be considered in determining choices. Every head coach in a college should have at least two assistants, and the optimum number will be determined by the size of the squad and the extent of the program. Generally speaking, the larger the number of coaches, the more specialized can be the training program. If the number of assistants is limited, the head coach should endeavor to have a staff whose members are qualified to coach at least one division or phase of the sport as a specialty but who understand the total problem of molding a team.

For example, some of the sports assistants would break down like this:

COACHING STAFFS FOR VARIOUS SPORTS

Sport	Small High School	Large High School	Small College	Large University
Football	1 Head Coach 1 Backfield Coach 1 Line Coach	1 Head Coach 1 Backfield Coach 1 Line Coach 1 Defensive Specialist 1 JV Coach	1 Head Coach 1 Backfield Coach (Offensive) 1 Line Coach (Offensive) 1 Line Coach (Defensive) 1 Defense Coordinator 1 Freshman Coach 1 Assistant Coach	1 Head Coach 1 Offensive Line Coach 1 Offensive End Coach 1 Offensive Backfield Coach 1 Defensive Coordinator 1 Defensive Line Coach 1 Defensive Secondary Coach 1 Freshman Coach 1 Backfield Coach 1 Line Coach 1 Free-lance Assistant
Basketball	1 Head Coach 1 Assistant	1 Head Coach 1 Assistant 1 JV Coach	1 Head Coach 1 Assistant 1 Freshman Coach	1 Head Coach 1 Assistant 1 Assistant 1 Freshman Coach 1 Assistant
Baseball	1 Head Coach	1 Head Coach 1 Assistant	1 Head Coach 1 Assistant 1 Freshman Coach	1 Head Coach 1 Assistant 1 Assistant (Pitching) 1 Freshman Coach

COACHING STAFFS (Continued)

Sport	Small High School	Large High School	Small College	Large University
Track	1 Head Coach	1 Head Coach 1 Assistant (Field events)	1 Head Coach 1 Assistant (Field events)	1 Head Coach 1 Assistant (Field events) 1 Assistant
Swimming	1 Head Coach	1 Head Coach	1 Head Coach 1 Assistant (Freshman Coach)	1 Head Coach 1 Assistant 1 Freshman Coach
Soccer	1 Head Coach	1 Head Coach 1 Assistant	1 Head Coach 1 Assistant 1 Freshman Coach	1 Head Coach 1 Assistant 1 Freshman Coach
Wrestling	1 Head Coach	1 Head Coach	1 Head Coach 1 Assistant (Freshman Coach)	1 Head Coach 1 Assistant (Freshman Coach)
Gymnastics	1 Head Coach	1 Head Coach	1 Head Coach 1 Assistant (Freshman Coach)	1 Head Coach 1 Assistant (Freshman Coach)

Naturally the number of assistants for a sport would be limited by budget and other factors, and a sport that could offer the maximum number of assistants as they have been listed would be richly endowed. Hence, a head coach might have to settle for less than the number indicated here. Assistants should not become specialized to the point where they lose sight of the whole picture but should be able to recognize that other elements contribute to the building of a complete team. Differences in personality types are desirable, for they tend to balance one another. The staff members should be able to work together harmoniously and exude an air of unity of purpose which will be "caught" by the squad. Loyalty is a quality of character which is a must for all assistants. A good head coach will encourage his assistants to give vent to their creative urges and to speak their minds in staff meetings, but when once a decision has been reached each member must abide by that decision and defend it to those who might question it.

The selection of assistants may not be an annual problem for most head coaches, since they are inclined to retain those whose help they value. Assistants do move on to more lucrative positions, however, and a head coach should not retard the professional progress of his staff members.

In high schools, the assistant coaches may be selected by a school board or some other authority. Often the head coach has no choice in the matter because the assistants are picked mainly for their ability to teach subjects other than football. The head coach is then faced with the problem of teaching his system to his assistants so that they in turn can teach it to the players. In a very small high school, a head coach may have only one assistant or he may have to do the entire job himself.

Scouts, too, must be selected by the head coach. Scouts are those who observe the opponents in action and report on their strengths and weaknesses. They also may offer suggestions for successful action against the opponents. These men may be professional scouts who have had a long career at this phase of the game, or they may be members of the coaching staff. Their comprehensive reports on the coming opponents aid in the selection of objectives for the practice sessions prior to the games. Scouting is accepted as a legitimate part of modern sports, and the coach should take pains to see that each of his opponents is observed in action by a competent operator whose report will serve to forewarn the team as to what awaits it.

Budget—The head coach should have a good idea of the amount of money needed to carry out his program. He can get this information from the financial records of previous years. In most democratic organizations, he will be allowed to submit a budget which will be acted upon by a committee within the athletic department. In other instances, the Athletic Director alone will approve or disapprove the budget. The proposed budget will be added to those of other sports and the total amount submitted to the financial committee of the administration. The approved amount will then be allocated to the various sports by the committee within the athletic department. Because of his desire for an ample budget, the coach may often be chagrined at the amount allocated to him. However, when it is apportioned on an equitable basis, he should accept the decision of the committee. Accurate records of all expenditures should be kept, and the coach should be aware of the state of his budget at all times. Careful planning is necessary to anticipate the needs of his program, so that the end of a fiscal year will find a balance between expenditures and the budget for his sport. When equipment is bought in large quantities, money can be saved by requiring competitive bids from firms selling the equipment.

Equipment and facilities—Closely related to the problem of budget is that of equipment. The cost of personal and field equipment has risen sharply in recent years, making it imperative that coaches be extremely careful in the purchasing and care of athletic gear. Most coaches advocate the use of separate equipment for games and practices, and this adds to the quantity which must be kept on hand. The selection of such items as wearing apparel and protective armor should be left to the head coach, who usually will ask for opinions from his assistants, the trainer, and players. Quality should always be considered. This is not always indicated by price. Some studies have brought to light that certain principles should be observed in the purchase of athletic equipment, in order that the best value can be obtained for the money expended.

The care of equipment is also a problem which the coach will face. An equipment manager who understands his duties and is willing to work at the task of repairing, checking, and issuing equipment will save many dollars as well as headaches. The coaches should cooperate by instructing the players in the art of caring for equipment, especially when it is wet. Equipment should be cleaned and repaired after each season and again following any off-season practice. The coach should examine the equipment before and after this operation and use the information in making up his budget. A running inventory should be maintained by the equipment manager.

Facilities for games will not always have to be arranged by the coach, because the athletic director or faculty manager will assume most of the duties, but practice space will always be a problem for the coach. Probably he never will be satisfied with what is available and constantly will be requesting additional playing space for his program. The coach should guard against becoming unreasonable in these demands, for the available space must be divided equitably with the other sports in the intercollegiate and intramural program. The playing surfaces should be kept in as good condition as possible, and the coach can act as an advisor to the groundskeeper or to anyone in charge of that operation. As a program specialist, the coach should have available any information needed to create and maintain good playing surfaces.

Schedule and travel—Schedules may be made up from one to three years in advance. All coaches are vitally interested in this problem, and many of them shoulder the complete responsibility for forming their schedules. In some schools or colleges, the director or faculty manager of athletics is obliged to make the schedule, but in practically all cases the coach is given the right to approve or disapprove proposed opponents. Where conference rules determine the opponents, the dates of games or the place of certain opponents on the schedule are of vital importance, and again the coach's wishes are granted whenever possible. The coach would like to have his traditionally difficult games spaced; so he intersperses games with easier opponents to afford his team a chance to relax and rest. He realizes that it is well nigh impossible to keep a team at a physical, mental, and emotional peak over a prolonged period. Another item to be considered is the amount of travel required for a schedule. If long distances are to be covered, it involves much planning for transportation, meals, and housing accommodations. Time lost from classes will have to be made up, and excessive absences from class are a peril to the scholastic standings of the players. The coach should try to minimize these problems.

Off-season practice—The coach does most of his experimenting during off-season practice. He hopes to settle in his mind the type of offense and defense best suited to his material and to decide on the personnel of his first and second teams. Planning for the off-season practices will take up a great deal of the time of the coach and his staff during the intervening months, but intensive work will not start until the players report. Thereafter, the coach should meet with his staff daily, and go over reports of of the previous day's practice, and discuss the progress of the squad toward its objectives. Motivation is a great problem during off-season practice, because the players do not have a schedule to which they can look forward. Intersquad games serve to kindle interest among the players, and they also offer a good learning medium because they are actually game situations.

The day-to-day planning should be as intensive as planning during the regular season. The practice sessions themselves will contain more individualized work periods than those of the regualr season because they will be devoted more to learning, while the regualr season practices will stress improvement of technique already learned and coordination of team effort.

Off-season practice should never be prolonged to the point where it prohibits the players from participating in other varsity sports. Here again, philosophy plays a major role in determining which sport has a priority on the athlete's time. Some institutions decree that the sport in season has first call, while in others, where athletic scholarships are in vogue, a player must report for the sport which has subsidized him. Some coaches excuse a boy from off-season practice if he is a starter or sure point-winner in another sport in season. The athlete's scholastic ability is sometimes a factor, and a boy may be persuaded to report or not for a second sport according to his ability to maintain proper grades while competing.

Guidance of players—Much of the coach's time will be taken up with guidance and counseling among students. The rapport between the coach and his players is ideal for this type of work and has been recognized by authorities. Personal problems of all types may confront the coach in the course of a year and he must be able to offer wise counsel to those who appeal to him for aid. The coach should be especially alert for academic failures among his athletes, and he usually will discover scholastic weaknesses before the failures actually happen. A coach who evinces a genuine interest in the scholastic achievements of all students will usually win the admiration and cooperation of his faculty colleagues. He should keep a complete and current scholastic record on each player in his cumulative record file. Periodic checks on all players (of which they are aware) will serve to motivate them to increased efforts.

Improvement of methods—No coach ever should become wholly satisfied with his offensive and defensive patterns, for the perfect type has yet to be discovered. Most coaches settle upon a system which seems to work best for them and adjust it to their own situations. The good coach will make great use of game reports and movies of his games, to discover flaws in his system as well as strengths in another's. Conferences with outside coaches and with his own players will give him many ideas for improvements which can be tested during off-season practice or the early regular season practice sessions. A coach may have an unusual method of teaching some technique or may actually have a unique and very successful method of performing some phase of offense or defense. The winter and summer months will find these ideas being exchanged with other coaches. Anything new in a sport rarely remains the sole property of one coach for longer than half a season.

Day-by-Day

During the regular playing season, the high pressure period, the organizational ability of the coach is put to a real test. If there is a secret to coaching success, it lies in perfect organization. The good head coach puts to best use the limited time and the teaching talents of his assistants. In order to do so, he must carefully plan to make the most of each minute at his disposal. The actual practice period may range from one hour to three, depending upon the curriculum practices of his institution. It may be possible for the coach to use part of the lunch hour as a lecture period if the squad is brought together at a training table. If the pressure of academic studies is not too great, one or two hours in one evening during the week may be devoted to lectures and movie studies. If these extra hours are not available, the material must be covered during the regular afternoon practice sessions.

Day-by-day planning starts during the preseason period when the squad has been assembled to prepare for the opening game. The length of this period will vary with each school or college. Local and conference rules sometimes set the limits; the average length is three weeks. Before this period starts, a great deal of work has already been accomplished by the coaching staff in general planning for the coming season.

The results of general planning are found in the many pages of material sent out to each player of a team sport for preliminary study before he reports for practice. They usually cover the entire offensive with each play diagrammed to show the assignment of every player, as well as the various defensive formations which are part of the standard procedure for the team. The defensive formations are carefully diagrammed with thorough explanations accompanying them. Also included in the written material will be information about rule changes, helpful hints on playing the various positions, suggestions for conditioning, and general information about the schedule. These materials not only are valuable for the information they contain, but also serve to rekindle the player's interest in the sport. The coach will include in his general plan the assignments of scouts to the various games on the opponents' schedules and plans for the filming of some or all games on his schedule.

During the few weeks before the opening contest, fall sport teams may be put through two practice sessions daily, because practice usually starts before registration. For the winter and spring sports, only one daily practice can be held, because schools usually are in session when the first practice is called. During early-season practices, the time is devoted to health examinations, publicity pictures, review of fundamentals, polishing the offense, making the defense effective, checking on the ability of individual team members, and reaffirming earlier convictions regarding the personnel of the first and second teams. It is extremely important that the coach keep a check list or master plan of everything to be covered during this period and consult it daily.

During the regular season, the daily coaching staff meetings will continue. If well organized, they can be limited to a period of one and a half to two hours, but if they are allowed to become chaotic, they may drag on interminably. At the start of the week, preferably on Sunday because there are no classes to be met on that day, the staff should come together for an extra long period to draw up the weekly plan. This plan should have an aim and objective for the coming week. The aim should never vary, for it should be to win the coming game. The objectives, however, will vary from week to week. They always will be built around the needs of the team in order to win the coming game. These needs will be determined from all available information in the scouting reports and the observation of the home team in action.

The plan for each week or each contest will vary according to the above factors. In the case of football, for example, if the next opponent has shown itself to be a power team with the major portion of its attack concentrated between the tackles and with little short-passing ability, the defensive strategy would call for tightening the line and moving the linebackers close. If the same team showed itself to be vulnerable to a long-passing attack, the offensive strategy would be to concentrate on protecting the passer and flooding the deep zones with receivers. The daily workouts for the week would have to emphasize these details, and more time than usual would be devoted to them. The individual and group exercises for each day would have to contain experiences related to these phases of football. Other sports such as soccer, basketball, and even individual sports, including swimming and wrestling, also call for detailed planning. Adjustments in strategy and tactics will necessitate changes in the daily workouts, so that the team's strength may be fully utilized against the weaknesses of the opponent. A tentative plan for each day of the week should be drawn on Sunday, and coaches should agree on the amount of time to be devoted to each exercise. Each assistant coach should report on the condition of his players and offer suggestions for individual exercises to improve their techniques. A master sheet of all the items to be covered that week should be kept by the head coach; as each of them is completed, he should check it off.

As the week progresses, the daily meetings will result in revision to the original program as it was drawn up for the week. Many factors may cause the changes. Speed or slowness of learning among the players, injuries to key men, predicted weather when it is a factor, and other influences will lead to a change in the daily programs. The head coach should ask for opinions on whether or not the items on the master sheet have been completed. Care should be taken not to postpone important fundamentals too frequently, for the workouts during the latter part of the week may become too crowded. Often there will be some disagreement among the staff members regarding proper technique for some maneuver or about offensive or defensive team play. All such disagreements should be discussed during the daily staff meetings and a decision arrived at. In some cases, the staff may be equally divided, and the head coach must then decide one way or another. In all such cases, he should satisfy himself that he is making the correct move, but he should not hesitate to change if he becomes convinced that he is in error. At any rate, there must be no evidence of disagreement when the staff arrives on the practice area.

The daily meetings, if conducted on a democratic basis, will result in growth for the entire staff. Each member should be encouraged to participate in the discussions. The head coach may act as an arbitrator, or he may stimulate the thinking of his colleagues by apparent disagreement with their assertions for the purposes of determining the strength of their convictions. Many coaches operate on the latter assumption, for they believe that it causes their staff to be clear in their own thinking in order to better verbalize. Regardless of the method used in conducting the daily meetings, the purpose behind them remains the same for all, that is, to help the staff do a better job of teaching.

For the Game

The climax of the training period comes in the game itself. It is here that the coach evaluates and draws conclusions regarding his players and his teaching methods. The final preparation for the game, following the week of getting ready, starts with the morning of the day of an afternoon game. The players should eat a normal breakfast at the regular hour and follow their usual routine if at home. There is no reason for players to cut classes on the day of a home game. If some plead that it makes them nervous to attend classes on that day, the coach should discourage this attitude. If the game is played away from home, the players may desire to take a short walk after breakfast. To prevent their overdoing it, a time should be set for their return. This can be arranged at the breakfast table, and at the same time the players can be informed of the hour for lunch.

If the game is played at home, the coach may inform the players of the routine for the morning at the close of practice the night before. This means that he will see the entire squad for the first time at lunch previous to the game.

Night contests at home should not make it necessary to break the regular daily routine except for an early pregame meal in the late afternoon. The routine for night contests away from home will vary with the distance to be traveled and the mode of transportation. Plane travel allows a team to compete with very little readjustment of their daily schedule except for pregame meals, whereas a bus trip may cause players to miss classes and to spend one or two days in an unusual routine. Whether a contest is night or day, away or at home, the hours preceding the contest will be carefully planned to avoid confusion or indecision on the part of players, coaches, trainers, managers, and other personnel associated with the team. An afternoon football contest illustrates the regimen necessary for a smooth preliminary to the actual game.

A time schedule is very important on this day, and the coach should endeavor to adhere to it as closely as possible. The best method of making it is to start with the time of the game and work backward including all steps that must be taken between breakfast and the start of the game. Hence, the schedule would appear like this:

2:00 P.M.	Game
1:57 P.M.	Leave dressing room with starting team
1:55 P.M.	Squad leaves dressing room (except starting team)
1:35 P.M.	Leave field
1:10 P.M.	Leave dressing room
1:05 P.M.	Call squad together for short talk
12:30 P.M.	Start dressing
12:00 Noon	Special taping by trainers
11:00 A.M.	Lunch and short discussion of strategy
10:30 A.M.	Quarterback meeting

9:30 A.M.   In hotel (if away game)
7:30 A.M.   Breakfast

After the squad has started to dress, the time should be checked by a manager or an assistant coach who will inform the head coach two minutes before the start of each procedure listed on the time schedule.

The lunch itself should be light, but substantial. The usual type consists of roast beef or small broiled steak, potato, green vegetable, toast and beverage; however, recent studies show that a high carbohydrate meal of spaghetti or macaroni may be better. Some players are unable to eat even the lightest meal before a game; it is better to allow them to forego it rather than upset them emotionally by forcing them to eat.

Following the lunch, a short discussion of the day's play, including game strategy, can be held. There must be no attempt made to excite the players at this point. Questions should be answered quietly and puzzling situations thoroughly explained.

When the coach arrives at the site of the game, he should inspect the field with one or two of his assistants. They should look for holes, muddy or wet spots, the direction and force of the wind, and the angle of the sun. The coaches must pass all of this information to the captain and the quarterback. While the coaches inspect the field, they should check the phone connections between the player's bench and spotter's booth to make sure they are in working order.

Dressing-room organization is necessary to prevent confusion and chaos at a time when order and quiet must prevail. It is usually necessary to have rules prohibiting anyone except players, coaches, trainers, and managers from entering the dressing room. Exceptions are sometimes made for officials of the school or college, but if they are aware of the rule most of them hesitate to break it.

As the time approaches, the atmosphere of the dressing room is charged with emotion. Players indicate by their actions whether they are too tense or too relaxed. A wise coach looks for these signs and plans his pregame talk accordingly. This talk should be short and to the point, without too much emphasis on information to be remembered, for this is not a good situation for memorization of facts. He can, with a word or phrase, cause the boys to relax and untie the emotional knot which has them strung too high, or he may bring them out of their lethargy, making them willing and eager to start the contest.

The warm-up period on the field must be well organized so that there will be few, if any, idle moments for the players. A calisthenic drill which emphasizes stretching and loosening of muscles preferably may come first, followed by group work on kicking and passing. Assistant coaches will direct this work; it should be on the actions which the boys will most likely carry out in a game. Therefore, linemen will charge, block, and run interference; passers will throw, while backs and ends catch; punters will kick, while linemen and ends cover; place kickers will work on their specialty. The head coach will send the team off the field promptly at the designated time on his schedule. The watch on which the time is checked should be compared with that of the official timekeeper for the game.

When the squad has reached the dressing room, all members should be seated and remain quiet for about five minutes. The coaches may use this time to review important details with players. The warm-up period on the field will usually have put the squad in the proper frame of mind for the game; so there is no need for the coaches to stimulate them. Five minutes before time to leave the dressing room, the head coach may announce the starting lineup and designate the opening play in case the team should receive the kickoff. This opening play, which is psychologically important, should have been decided upon by the coaches and the quarterback during their morning meeting. Alternative plans also must have been made in case the situation does not allow for the execution of this play.

Some coaches send the starting team to the field one or two minutes after the main squad as a mark of distinction. For several reasons, this is not a good plan: First, the captain or captains are expected on the field a few minutes before the scheduled start of the game to meet with the officials and the opposing captain; Second, the choice of being on offense or defense is not determined until the toss of the coin, so the starting team is unknown until then; Third, squad morale is better promoted when all members arrive together to share the crowd's greeting.

The player's bench should be organized in such a manner that men are grouped according to positions. This enables the substitutes to discuss common problems as they occur on the field. It also allows the coaches to talk to a group instead of to one man and make substitutions quicker and easier. It is a good plan to have all players leaving the game report to the head coach for an exchange of information before being seated. The coaches and managers should be separated from the players in order that they may be contacted quickly and easily. One assistant coach should be on the phone from the spotter's booth, and he should write down game information as he receives it. Another assistant coach or manager should record all time-outs and substitutions as they occur.

Within the first few minutes of the game, the spotter should inform the head coach of the apparent defensive and offensive strategy of the opponents so that it can be compared with that which was anticipated. Quick changes in tactics may have to be instituted if the pregame planning proves to be faulty.

At halftime, the team should leave the field promptly and return to the dressing room. This first five minutes of the intermission should be devoted to resting and refreshing the men who have played. In the meantime, the assistant coaches may be gathering information from the players and giving advice where necessary. With all information pooled, the head coach should carefully and quickly review the high points of the first half play and develop the strategy for the second half. He probably will make extensive use of a blackboard to illustrate what he is talking about. An assistant should be keeping track of the time and inform the head coach when there is five minutes left to the intermission. At this time the squad may be sent out and the starting team for the second half, except the captains, will remain for last minute instructions. They should be allowed to remain seated until it is time for them to go to the field.

The first few minutes of the second half will reveal any changes in the opponent's strategy and all this information should be relayed to the bench by the spotter.

Written postgame reports by players, coaches and spotters will reveal much information that even the movie camera may miss. These reports should be prepared within twenty-four hours after the game. After the movies have been developed and shown and the postgame reports compiled and analyzed, a final written summary should be made by a member of the staff. This should be placed in a file with scouting reports and other information gathered about that particular team. Hence, there will be a separate file for each opponent, and the information will be found valuable for reference over a period of years.

The pregame organization for basketball is practically the same as for football, with a few minor exceptions. Playing surface conditions will not vary except for size of court. With the exception of tournament games, most contests will be held at night. The same principles of organization will hold for the period before and during the game. In fact, the running evaluation of the team's efforts may be even more sophisticated. Managers and assistant coaches can chart the number, type, and degree of success of each shot made by every player. This gives a graphic picture of the game progression. Offensive and defensive strengths and weaknesses are immediately apparent. Half-time dressing-room organization is identical with that of football. Every minute must be allocated either to rest, critique, or reorganization. All contests which allow an intermission should be planned thoroughly to make the best use of the time available to adjust pregame plans to changing conditions of the contest.

ORGANIZATION FOR LEARNING

Regardless of all other responsibilities faced by the coach, the greatest will be that of teaching his athletes to play the sport in a particular manner known as his "system." To be successful, he must be not only a teacher, he must be a *good* teacher, one who plans for learning to take place through the use of sound teaching methods.

Learning is the process of developing useful habits of behavior through the acquisition of skills and/or knowledge and the assimilation of proper attitudes.

One may also look at learning as a means of bringing about changes in an individual. The objectives of the sports program or the outcomes of sports participation may be considered the resultants of such a process of change. Teaching is concerned with aiding the process. A youngster may practice pitching a baseball under the tutelage of a coach. He says that he is "learning to pitch." After a suitable number of practice periods, he says that he is a "pitcher," i.e., he possesses certain motor learnings which enable him to pitch a baseball in the proper manner.

The task of teaching may be separated into two distinct but interdependent aspects, namely, the curriculum and the procedure or method. The former deals with the *what* of pupil stimulation, while the latter is concerned with the *how*. Any substantial change in one of these aspects will affect the other. A coach who switches from one offensive system to another will be forced to alter his teaching methods; whereas a clear change in his method will affect the nature of the material being transmitted or absorbed.

In dealing with the question of method, most authorities agree that there is no one best pattern for all teachers to follow. Success appears to be dependent more upon the skill of the user than upon the type of approach. A lecture delivered by an expert has far more educative value than a badly planned and weakly executed project type unit. Time is an important factor in the coach's work, and he must pay special attention to the organization of the learning experiences given to the young men under his tutelage, so that the best use may be made of the limited hours at his disposal. All planning should be in terms of the learner, since the purpose of any curriculum plan or practice schedule is to stimulate learning. The learning will come from what the learner reacts to and experiences. The needs of the individual player and squad will be the determining factor in selecting the material to be learned. They may be knowledges to be gained, skills to be acquired, or reactions to be automized.

The teaching and learning of the game or the problem of *how* still confronts the coach after he has decided *what* is to be learned. Burton has summarized the important characteristics and principles of the learning process, and from these may be derived several concepts especially adaptable to athletic coaching.

The objectives and outcomes which are products of the learning process should have meaning for the player, i.e., they should "make sense or else he will regard them as nonessential, unimportant or superfluous, and promptly forget them, if he does learn them."

The experiences should be many and varied. Enthusiasm dies with monotony. Practice sessions should be broken up into distinct periods with provisions for rest and "breathers." The whole atmosphere of the sports training program should be conducive to learning. This can only come from careful attention to such details as adequate facilities, good equipment, sufficient space, competent assistants, methods of instruction, number and length of scrimmages, and the number of offensive and defensive plays offered to the learners.

The mutual acceptance of a common goal or purpose between the teacher and learner, together with an avid interest in the outcomes by the learner, will facilitate the learning process. The interest in the activities may stem from an original idea of the learner or from his acceptance of the ideas of the teacher. At any rate, the enthusiasm of the player for the practice experiences will be greatly strengthened if he understands the what and why of the coach's methods. A player who devises a method of meeting a sports situation and whose suggestion is met with genuine approval by his coach will strive with utmost vigor to perfect the needed technique for carrying out his method. Motivation to learn is an outgrowth of orientating the learner in terms of objectives, goals, and outcomes which satisfy a need.

To be of maximal value, the learning experiences should be similar to the actual experiences which will confront the learner in his normal activities. The coach who devises a system of practice workouts designed to afford experiences unlikely to occur to that player will find a lack of interest in that type of practice among his players. The learning process must include experiences which are real and lifelike, not artificial. The closer the drill comes to resembling actual game conditions the more it will appeal to players. The experience should also be offered in a sequential order, taking into consideration the type of learning situation, the experience of the player, the physical prowess of the player, the degree of difficulty in the material offered, the speed at which meaning emerges, the degree of skill and understanding demanded and many other details. Whatever is offered to the learner should be characterized by some system of organization, for random and detached details are soon forgotten.

The learning process advances more effectively through a relationship between the teacher and pupil which creates mutual confidence and respect. Self-discipline and the desire to learn should be natural outgrowths of a system of teaching which guides and encourages rather than one founded on tyranny and fear. The day of the bullying, arrogant, roughneck coach has gone. Today it is desirable to have a keen, intelligent, understanding, and sympathetic teacher who is ever mindful of the importance of group morals and unification of purpose among the squad members.

To reach its optimum effectiveness, any process of learning, together with the attaining of its products, should be adjusted and modified in relation to the individual differences among the learners. The difference may be in physical structure, organic power, neuromuscular control, or in interests, attitudes, intelligence and aptitudes of the learner. The selection of a system for the teaching and learning of a sport necessarily must take into consideration the characteristics of the learners and make allowances for the differences in the speed of learning among the various squad members. The very nature of the game itself will necessitate a choice of players for the various functions based on differences in physique and temperament.

The learning process enjoys a favorable environment in a situation where the learner has constant knowledge of his progress toward clearly established goals. This means that the learner will share in evaluating his own effectiveness. The coach has a responsibility for making it clearly understood just what he is requiring of the player in every skill to be learned. His weak points must be pointed out together with movements to be worked on in order to overcome the weakness. The boy will need the benefit of good examples and adequate demonstrations in order to have some scale against which to measure his own efforts.[4]

Other sources may be used to derive similar concepts of learning, for those listed do not exhaust the available supply. These may be used as initial guides and, in this study, will serve as nuclei in the development of Chapters III to VIII inclusive.

[4]William H. Burton, *The Guidance of Learning Activities.* New York: Appleton-Century-Crofts, Educational Division, Meredith Corporation, Third Edition, 1962, pp. 316-317.

SUMMARY

The aim of education and, consequently, that of its agencies, such as schools and colleges, may be said to be the enabling of students to develop competency in meeting the problems of modern living. Each department of an educational institution should contribute in its own unique way to the realization of that aim through a program based on objectives leading toward that aim. The physical education department, of which the sports program is a part, should have an aim in harmony with the general aim of education and should have as its objective the development of certain skills, knowledges and qualities through physical activities.

A coach's philosophy will reflect his attitude toward the factors connected with the coaching of his sport. His actions, his treatment of individuals, and his approach to problems are determined by the value he places upon such factors as winning or losing, friendship of colleagues, respect of players, conservation or flashiness, offense or defense. For him, the degree of importance he attributes to a factor determines the amount of effort expended in meeting the problems of that factor.

Coaching success, like that of almost any enterprise, will be affected by personality. It is extremely important for a coach to know himself, his good points, bad points, strengths, and weaknesses. He should be able to see himself as others see him. His awareness of the personal qualities that aid or hinder his work is not enough. The will to work toward a better personality is required of those who realize that a change is necessary. A sincere change in attitudes is called for if a coach is to bring about improved personality. Otherwise he will be masquerading and his players will spot him for what he is—false.

The privileges of faculty rank for the coach bring with them responsibilities to the student, the department, and the institution, which he cannot ignore. The close personal relationship between the coach and player gives the coach excellent opportunities for personal, social, and moral guidance, but he must be ready to aid all students in solving their problems. Because the coach has such a great influence on the lives of students under his care, his own conduct is always expected to be above reproach. As a member of the faculty, a coach is expected to actively cooperate with his colleagues in the physical education department. In doing so, he should accept his share of the responsibility for formulating departmental policy as well as teaching enthusiastically in the required and intramural programs of the institution. A coach's duties should include such items as membership on regular school committees and active participation in faculty meetings. The well rounded program of professional preparation which the coach undergoes in preparation for teaching should be put to use in helping to solve the many problems facing all regularly appointed members of the teaching staff.

A good coach is usually a good organizer. How well he organizes the elements at his command will largely decide the success of his program. Among the elements which he must put to optimum use are the hours of practice, the talents of the assistant coaches, the talents of the players, the financial budget for his sport, the field equipment and other mechanical aids. The organizing process involves everything from the use of psychological principles of learning to planning the opening play of a game.

Any time not taken up with actual coaching on the field will be devoted to meeting and solving problems related to his coaching and teaching duties. Throughout the year, the coach may busy himself with the selection of assistants and scouts, the budget for his sport, the purchase and care of equipment, the completion of the schedule, the planning of trips, the planning of off-season practice, the guidance of students, and the improvement of coaching methods.

The day-by-day planning which takes place during the regular playing season puts the organizing powers of the coach to a severe test. The objectives for each day of the week should be carefully selected, and the activities of the practice sessions should be devised to attain these objectives.

The player is expected to learn a sport by going through guided experiences of playing the sport. In planning these experiences, the coach should consider several concepts of learning, such as making the experiences meaningful, offering rich and varied experiences, orienting the learner in terms of goals, offering the experiences in sequential order, observing the principle of individual differences, taking advantage of the social implications of team play, and allowing the players to share in the evaluating process.

Planning for the game involves the problem of having the players arrive at the start of the game in the best possible mental and physical condition. The normal daily routine of the players should be upset as little as possible. Plans should also be made for the securing and utilizing of information regarding the play of the team and its opponent, so that game strategy may be adjusted to situations.

Test Questions

1. What is meant by a person's philosophy?
2. Make a list of factors connected with a coaching position which will affect the coach's philosophy.
3. What do you consider to be the most important traits a coach should possess to insure success in his profession?
4. How can self-analysis affect a coach's personality?
5. List at least six traits generally considered to spell failure for an athletic coach.
6. Why is it necessary that a change in habits be preceded by a change in attitudes?
7. Why are coaches considered to be in favorable environment for student guidance?
8. Describe the proper attitude for a coach toward his departmental responsibilities.
9. Explain the statement that a coach should approach his tasks as an educator, not as a hired professional.
10. What responsibilities should a coach feel toward his assistants?
11. How would a coach respond to a responsibility to his sport?
12. What is the focal point of attention in all educational and sports planning?
13. Name some problems facing the coach in his yearly planning.
14. What is the major factor in determining the size of a coaching staff?
15. Explain how day-by-day planning is integrated with weekly planning.
16. How is the time schedule for a game day organized?
17. What is the value of postgame reports by players?
18. Define "learning."
19. Briefly summarize the concepts of learning which apply to athletic coaching.

Discussion Questions

1. Should all athletic coaches be required to have physical education training?
2. What is meant by the statement that "a coach must *command* loyalty rather than *demand* it"?
3. Is a dual responsibility of coaching and teaching in any way detrimental to the quality of either role?

4. Should governing bodies such as the N.C.A.A. set standards for all facets of athletic competition?
5. How much responsibility should a coach assume for the conduct of his athletes off the playing field? Should it be the same for both high school and college coaches?
6. What can be done to meet the demand for women coaches, now that active competition is being promoted for girls and women?
7. As the quality of coaching improves, does the need for better facilities and equipment decrease?
8. If a coach feels that his philosophy of coaching conflicts with the philosophy of education of his school, should he conform or attempt to institute change?

Suggested Readings

BOOKS

1. Beck, Robert H. *The Three R's Plus.* Minneapolis: University of Minnesota Press, 1956.
2. Bucher, Charles. *Administration of School and College Health and Physical Education Programs.* St. Louis: C. V. Mosby, 1967, Fourth Edition, pp. 37-100.
3. Cowell, Charles and Schwehn, Hilde. *Modern Principles and Methods in Secondary School Physical Education.* Boston: Allyn and Bacon, Inc., 1965, pp. 200-204.
4. Davis, Elwood C. *Philosophies Fashion Physical Education.* Dubuque: Wm. C. Brown Co., 1963.
5. Dean, Everett. *Progressive Basketball.* New Jersey: Prentice Hall, Inc., 1950, pp. 26-7.
6. Hartford, Ellis F. *Education in These United States.* New York: The Macmillan Co., 1964, pp. 463-503, 448-458.
7. Howard, Glen and Masonbrink, Edward. *Administration of Physical Education.* New York: Harper and Row, 1963, pp. 20-29.
8. Johns, E., Sutton, W., and Webster, L. *Health for Effective Living.* New York: McGraw-Hill Co., 1966, p. 44.
9. Lieberman, Myron. *Education As a Profession.* Englewood Cliffs: Prentice Hall, Inc., 1956, pp. 214-241.
10. Massey, Harold and Vinegard, Edwin E. *The Profession of Teaching.* New York: The Odyssey Press, Inc., 1961, pp. 95-103.

11. Rice, Emmet and Hutchison, John. *A Brief History of Physical Education.* New York: A. S. Barnes & Co., 1952, pp. 206-22.
12. Richey, Robert W. *Planning for Teaching.* New York: McGraw-Hill Book Co., 1963, pp. 166-197.
13. Riccio, Anthony C. and Cyphert, Frederick R. *Teaching in America.* Columbus: Charles E. Merrill, Inc., 1962, pp. 347-399.
14. Shepard, George and Jamerson, Richard. *Interscholastic Athletics.* New York: McGraw-Hill Book Co., 1953.
15. Vannier, Maryhelen and Fait, Hollis. *Teaching Physical Education in Secondary Schools.* Philadelphia: W. B. Saunders Co., 1964, pp. 53-57, 87 and 106.
16. Verderame, Salvatore. *Organization of Championship High School Basketball.* New Jersey: Prentice Hall, Inc., 1963.
17. Voltmer, Edward F. and Esslinger, Arthur A. *The Organization and Administration of Physical Education.* New York: Appleton-Century-Crofts, 1967, Fourth Edition, pp. 1-47.
18. Walker, Bob. *Organization for Successful Football Coaching.* New Jersey: Prentice Hall, Inc., 1960, pp. 1-33.
19. Webster, Randolph W. *Philosophy of Physical Education.* Dubuque: Wm. C. Brown Co., 1965, p. 209.
20. Williams, Jesse, F., Brownell, Clifford and Vernier, E. L. *The Administration of Health Education and Physical Education.* Philadelphia: W. B. Saunders Co., 1966, 6th Edition, Chapters I and II.

Suggested Readings

ARTICLES

1. Alderson, D. J. "Officials and Coaches are on the Same Team," *JOHPER,* Vol. 34-9, November 1963, p. 41.
2. Ashenfelter, John. "One Coach's Philosophy of Coaching," *JOHPER,* Vol. 36-2, February 1965, pp. 22 and 58.
3. Ashford, Volney. "Coaching Philosophy," *Coach and Athlete,* Vol. 26-2, October 1963, pp. 21-22.
4. Baley, James A. "Physical Education and Athletics Belong Together," *The Physical Educator,* Vol. 23-2, May 1966, pp. 77-78.
5. Benson, Cy. "In-Service Staff Training," *Scholastic Coach,* Vol. 36-9, May 1967.

6. Blackman, Robert L. "Pre-Season Organization," *Proceedings Fortieth Annual Meeting American Football Coaches Association*, Los Angeles, Calif., January 1963.
7. Blaettler, Richard. "Should Special Preparation and /or Certification Be Required for Coaching?" *Coach and Athlete*, Vol. 29-3, November 1966, pp. 24-25.
8. Bryant, Paul. "Football Practice Organization," *Coach and Athlete*, Vol. 30-2, September 1967, pp. 12-13 and 46.
9. Bucher, Charles. "Employing the High School Coach," *Current Administrative Problems*, Committee Report of AAHPER, Washington, D.C., 1960.
10. Cook, J. R. "What Makes a Top College Basketball Coach?" *Scholastic Coach*, Vol. 36-7, 1967, p. 17.
11. Dahlem, Glenn G. "Scouting Baseball," *Coach and Athlete*, Vol. 38-7, February 1966, pp. 36-48.
12. Donn, Henry F. "Role of Coach, Physician in Program," *American School Board Journal*, Vol. 153, August 1966, pp. 44-45.
13. Eskridge, Bill. "That Half-Hour Before Practice," *Scholastic Coach*, Vol. 36-1, September 1966, p. 108.
14. Gallon, A. J. "For More Efficient Coaching—A Weekly Time Chart," *Athletic Journal*, Vol. 46-9, April 1967, p. 34.
15. Goldfarb, Joseph M. "Motivational Psychology in Coaching," *Scholastic Coach*, Vol. 37-6, 1968, p. 54.
16. Hafner, Ray L. "More Than Victory," *JOHPER*, March 1962, p. 29.
17. Hanks, D. "Organization Begins With The Coach," *Scholastic Coach*, Vol. 26-2, October 1959, p. 66.
18. Hartman, Betty C. "Training Women to Coach," *JOHPER*, Vol. 39-1, January 1968, pp. 25 and 76.
19. Hunter, Gene. "Effective Practice Organization," *Scholastic Coach*, Vol. 32-3, November 1963, p. 32.
20. Jensen, A. "Football Coach's Year-Round Organizational Check List," *Scholastic Coach*, Vol. 35-10, June 1966, p. 28.
21. Keith, Dwight. "Success in Coaching," *Coach and Athlete*, Vol. 21-6, January 1959, p. 12.
22. Keith, J. Arthur. "How Coaches Teach," *The Physical Educator*, Vol. 24-4, 1967, p. 162.
23. Larson Leonard. "Why Sports Participation?" *JOHPER*, Vol. 35-1, January 1964, p. 36.
24. Lathan, George. "Develop Your Own Basketball Philosophy," *Scholastic Coach*, Vol. 27-2, October 1957, p. 56.
25. Lawther, John D. "The Role of the Coach in American Education," *JOHPER*, Vol. 36-5, May 1965, pp. 65-66.

26. McBee, Gene. "Pre-Season Planning for Basketball," *Coach and Athlete,* Vol. 30-3, October 1967, pp. 18, 31, and 37.
27. McKay, Joe. "Pre-Game Preparation—Physically and Psychologically," *Coach and Athlete,* Vol. 28-3, October 1966, pp. 26-27.
28. Merola, T. "Staff and Organization," *Athletic Journal,* Vol. 27-9, April 1967, p. 34.
29. Mikula, Thomas. "Winning Isn't All," *JOHPER,* Vol. 24-8, October 1953, p. 17.
30. Mills, Chuck. "Conducting the Staff Meeting," *Athletic Journal,* Vol. 42-8, May 1963, p. 22.
31. Moore, Al. "Essential Personality Traits for Coaches," *Athletic Journal,* Vol. 41-2, October 1962, p. 44.
32. Moser, Chuck. "High School Football Organization," *Scholastic Coach,* Vol. 29-7, March 1960.
33. Mudra, Darrel. "A New Look at Leadership," *JOHPER,* Vol. 35-3, March 1964, p. 32.
34. Rentz, James A. "The Responsibilities of the Coach to the Coaching Profession," *Coach and Athlete,* Vol. 38-8, March 1966, pp. 24, 30-31 and 33.
35. Rice, N. "Qualities of a Good Coach," *Bulletin of the National Association of Secondary School Principals,* Vol. 43-451, December 1954, p. 152.
36. Ryser, Otto E. "Do You Practice What You Preach?" *Scholastic Coach,* Vol. 34-4, December 1965, pp. 38-39.
37. Schafer, R. C. "Definition of a Coach," *The Clearing House,* Vol. 36-7, March 1962.
38. Sexton, Dennis. "Game-Day Psychological Devices," *Scholastic Coach,* Vol. 35-9, May 1966, pp. 74, 82-83.
39. Shirley, J. D. "Profile of an Ideal Coach," *JOHPER,* Vol. 37-11, May 1966, p. 59.
40. Van Meer, Ray. "Winning With Organization," *Athletic Journal,* Vol. 47-8, March 1968, p. 48.
41. Veller, Don. "Helpful Hints in Organizing Football," *Scholastic Coach,* Vol. 29-8, April 1960, pp. 24-26, 58-59.
42. Veller, Don. "Head Coach and Assistant Rapport," *Athletic Journal,* Vol. 47-8, April 1968, pp. 66-69 and 77.
43. Wallace, Roy. "Coaches Philosophy," *Coach and Athlete,* Vol. 26-10, May 1964, p. 18.

Chapter II
SETTING THE STAGE FOR TEACHING AND LEARNING

"Offer Rich and Varied Experiences"

THE BEST SITUATION FOR LEARNING

The coach, like all teachers, is concerned with the problem of having the learning process proceed in as orderly a fashion as possible. One of the most important factors to be considered in bringing about effective learning is the setting in which the learning is to take place. The setting or learning environment will be affected by methods, materials, and personalities. The emotional atmosphere created by the coaches can promote or destroy learning by the group. The emotional climate of the group is already favorable when athletes report for a sport; the fact that they are there of their own volition indicates some personal motive or drive. It is true that members of the group already have a general interest in the sport, but they may not have a natural interest in the various exercises necessary for learning the required skills; so it becomes imperative that the coaches set the stage for the boys' interest by their own contagious interest, inspiration, and enthusiasm for the methods and materials used in the program.

Each player should be able to feel that at least one person on the coaching staff is taking a personal interest in his health, welfare, and progress. This situation is not too difficult to create when there are coaches for the various divisions of the team, for they will have a chance to know intimately the players in their group. In the small high school, the head coach will know all his players very well. Every player should feel free to approach the head coach on the field at any time, to secure advice or assistance with any problem connected with the sport. When the emotional climate is healthy, the players will display an interest in the progress and welfare of their fellows. Encouragement and commendation from teammates will fan the fire of enthusiasm in the young player.

The learning experiences offered to the players will largely be made up of drills and exercises. For the most part, the materials will be the players themselves, but a well rounded program will also make use of much field equipment and other artificial aids. The drills and exercises should be challenging; that is, they should not be so far below the growth and ability of the learner that he becomes bored and disinterested. The experiences should be varied so as not to become tiresome. The same drill, day after day, will accomplish little in the way of increased ability except to establish a habit of performing the drill. The fundamental skills of any sport, with a little ingenuity on the part of coaches, may be taught in a variety of exercises.

A good learning situation is one in which the learner sees meaning in what he is doing. He sees a connection between the exercise and the functional use of the thing he is learning. This suggests that the learning situation itself should be functional. Why not carry on learning in the setting in which the skill or knowledge is to be used? This is the theory of learning by doing. The closer the exercise resembles actual game conditions, the more meaning it will have for the players, because the use or function of the material to be learned will be obvious to them.

The learning atmosphere should be one that encourages experimentation and exploration. Coaches often become so stereotyped in their thinking that scouting reports on their teams show identical characteristics year after year. Their opponents know what to expect from them before they play their first game of the season. With changes in personnel occurring each year, bringing the many individual differences to a squad, it would seem wise to make use of the talents and creative ability represented therein. The players and assistant coaches, if inspired and encouraged, will experiment with methods and often come out with something superior to what is already being done. The head coach should be flexible in his system and open-minded toward innovations. He need not accept each idea, but he should display an appreciation for the interest and ingenuity of those who create them so that their interest may be maintained and purposes strengthened.

The best learning situation then depends upon the atmosphere created by the coaches, players, methods, and materials. The environment is created and acted upon by the individuals within it, and it, in turn, acts upon them. If it is good, the whole group will be interested, eager to act, and continually motivated throughout the learning experience.

FACILITIES AND EQUIPMENT

Facilities are practice and playing surfaces; fixtures such as stands, charging machines, baskets and backboards, diving boards, baseball hitting cages, blocking and tackling pits, dressing and shower rooms, and training rooms. Equipment is personal gear, balls, bats, blocking armor, first aid supplies, movie cameras and projectors, bulletin boards, blackboards, photographs, drawings and mimeographed material. All these are common "tools of the trade" in coaching.

The purpose of facilities and equipment is to enrich the program. This is accomplished by affording many and more varied experiences in learning situations. For instance, blocking may be taught by having football players work against field dummies, or against the blocking machines which hold stationary dummies, or against teammates who are protected by blocking shields. A baseball pitching machine delivers 8-12 accurate pitches per minute into the strike zone, compared to the 2-3 by a human being. Therefore, a batter gets more good pitches to swing at, and more players are able to bat during a practice session. If a squad has only a small space in which to work, it becomes necessary to work with one or, at the most, two large groups. As the practice space increases, the groups will become more numerous but smaller in number, allowing for a more varied program and more individualized attention.

The personal equipment of players should be of good quality. Safety, comfort, and durability are the criteria for selection. The common belief among coaches that a team dressed well plays well has probably gained credence due to the feeling of confidence and poise that comes to players who are well equipped.

Although a coach should always strive to improve the facilities and equipment that are available, he may find it impossible to bring about immediate changes. If he is resourceful, he will adapt his methods to the situation and carry on to the best of his ability. Ingenuity and imagination, if given a free rein, will enable the staff and players to improvise and create many original devices for improving learning. Commercial products are usually good, but self-prepared facilities and equipment may, in many cases, have a closer relationship to the contemplated learning than any commercial product. A blocking dummy or a charging sled designed and built by those who are teaching and learning a particular style of blocking or charging will contain many features which emphasize the characteristics of that particular style. Webbed-top hurdles, small-diameter baskets, batting tees, and special flotation devices for swimming, all are inventions of coaches who found them especially well suited for teaching some phase of the sport as they wanted it learned.

Modern coaching techniques make extensive use of visual materials. The blackboards and bulletin boards of dressing rooms are usually filled with drawings, opponents' records, diagrams, photographs, and printed reminders. Written material on such items as scouting reports and new plays are constantly being given out during the season. The movie camera and video tape enable coaches to capture details that would otherwise be forgotten or overlooked.

A variety of filming techniques are used in sports. Swimmers are usually photographed from beneath the water surface through an observation window. Gymnasts are best filmed from the apparatus level, including all moves from the ready position through the completed dismount. Divers, baseball players, tennis players, and golfers should be filmed from overhead and ground levels and from two or more angles, to reveal technique. Team games such as basketball, soccer, and football should be filmed from a high elevation. Some basketball coaches prefer the game to be filmed from an overhead position at midcourt, but this is difficult to arrange in most gymnasia.

To film a game properly is an art that has to be learned. The coach must inform the operator of the details he wishes to have covered throughout the game. In football, for instance, the shot of each individual play should include (1) the defensive setup, (2) the offense alignment, (3) the initial movements of the offensive line and backfield, and (4) the passage of the ball until it is "dead." A cameraman who has a good knowledge of the game will sense the need for long or close-up shots during a game and vary the type of lens used in the camera. After the film has been developed, it should be carefully previewed by the coaching staff before it is shown to the squad. The highlights should be marked for special attention. Criticism of the team play when the film is being shown should be positive as well as negative. Good plays deserve commendation just as bad plays deserve condemnation. Poor play due to laziness or indifference may be sternly dealt with, but mistakes caused by lack of ability or experience must be examined tolerantly.

The playing and practice fields, lecture rooms, dressing and shower rooms, equipment rooms, training rooms and first-aid equipment are all material factors of the learning environment. They will produce an atmosphere that inspires or breeds indifference. If equipment is good, clean, and efficiently handled by managers and coaches; if the locker rooms, shower rooms, and toilets are scrupulously clean; if towels and soap are freely provided; and if the training room is well equipped and efficiently managed, then those who work in this environment will be inspired to keep it so. Too often coaches and administrators are guilty of indifference to health hazards in their athletic programs. The conditions that surround the actual exercises are all part of the approach to learning, and they must be inspiring and conducive to learning.

An excellent teacher can do a creditable job with very little equipment and inadequate facilities, but that same teacher could do a much better job in a more favorable environment for learning. The alert coach constantly is searching for newer and better ways to accomplish the task of teaching his sport and he is keenly interested in improving the setting in which learning takes place. The American Association of Health, Physical Education and Recreation, in conjunction with the Athletic Institute, periodically prepares excellent reports on facilities for all types of programs including athletics. The authors set up standards for design and construction of fields and buildings which go to make up part of the learning environment for sports.[1,2]

PRACTICE PERIODS

As has already been pointed out, the various exercises scheduled for the day are planned during the daily staff meetings, but certain items should be standardized for the sake of efficiency. Such things as the starting time for practice, the prepractice routine, and the hour for stopping should be definitely set. Players will make their own plans for getting dressed and on the playing area and adjust their personal routines in accordance with a definite prearranged time schedule. Each division of the squad should be designated a section of the practice area, and the members of that division will report there to their coach as they arrive. Players must be taught how to "loosen up" through a system of stretching exercises, so that they will not be too dependent on the formal calisthenics drill which opens the formal practice period. When the player feels that he is ready to participate, he may practice on a specialty if he has one, or he may work on some individual technique which he feels needs

[1]"College and University Facilities Guide." *AAHPER and The Athletic Institute*, 1968, 1201 16th Street N. W., Washington, D.C. 20036.

[2]"Planning Areas and Facilities for Health, Physical Education and Recreation." Ibid., 1967.

improvement. Some players are eager to learn and improve their techniques, while others are not favored with this urge. For this reason, it becomes necessary to include practice sessions on these techniques at regular intervals in the body of the regular practice session.

Dividing the session into a number of short periods on a variety of skills serves several purposes. First, it prevents monotony which would impair the team's progress in acquiring skills. If practices are known to be lively, interesting, and pleasant, the players will approach the day's tasks with eagerness and anticipation rather than with a feeling of "getting the chore done." When the various drills and exercises are derived from meaningful situations, they have an air of genuineness about them which stimulates learning and aids in forming the attitude that practice is a normal and necessary step to complete learning.

Second, broken-up practice sessions enable the learning periods to be dispersed over a long time rather than confined to a long session over a short time. The evidence for learning seems to be in favor of the short distributed period over the long, concentrated practice. Hence, if in baseball the master plan of the week calls for one hour of relaying throws, the drills will be distributed over three days, each having a twenty-minute session. There are several facts concerning spaced learning, particularly in the early stages, which all coaches will recognize as being particularly applicable to situations arising during the off-season or preseason practices.

1. The player may try a variety of techniques to get the job done.
2. One of the techniques may prove to be the most successful for him. It can be followed up in a subsequent drill by concentrating on that correct technique.
3. If too many techniques prove to be faulty, none of them will during a short drill become established as a bad habit.
4. Often the interval between practice sessions tends to erase the faulty elements of a performance, leaving only the correct responses to be recalled when the player resumes his practice.

This last statement may explain the phenomenon which seems to occur when players who appeared hopeless in spring practice return after the prolonged recess period of summer vacation and perform like veterans.

In athletics as well as in most learning, it would be more advantageous to distribute rather than to amass practice periods. Practice sessions should not proceed in an even tempo of intensity but rather in a rising degree, reaching a climax of intensity near the midpoint of the afternoon. The most important phase of the day's work, the period when the coaches stimulate the players to apply the most pressure, should come when the players have reached a stage of physiological and mental readiness in which they perform at their best. The session may be roughly divided into three periods of intensity; the first for warming up, the middle or climax period for pressure, and the final period for cooling off and lessening of tension. Each of these periods may vary in length, but the warming-up and cooling-off periods are usually about equal. An average midseason daily schedule for baseball and football is suggested as follows:

Baseball

Wednesday—Main objective is to improve the defense against runners taking an extra base on balls hit to the outfield.

3:30   Individual calisthenics
3:40   Warmup throwing and catching
3:50   All players practice starts and short sprints
3:35   Bunting drill—offense and defense
4:15   Outfielders throw to bases; infielders throw to first base
4:20   Team defense against extra base attempt
        Starters in regular positions
        Substitutes act as runners.

Coach at home plate hits to outfielders and/or between them. Runner starts from home plate after the coach hits the ball and advances as far as he dares. Coach will call for some runners to remain on base and announce the "outs." Defensive team will play according to position of men on base and "outs."

4:35   Rest period. Coach comments on drill.
5:00   Batting practice. Pitchers pitch to five or six batters each.
5:30   Infield drill. Outfielders and pitchers jog two laps and shower.
5:35   Infielders jog one lap and shower.

Football

Wednesday—Main objective is to improve the short-side attack.

Prepractice: work on specialties.

3:30   Calisthenics
3:40   Work on machines; squad divided into three groups; five minutes each on blocking, charging and tackling machines

3:55 Sprints
4:00 Rest; short talk on day's practice by coach
4:05 Dummy scrimmage; two groups, teams I and II versus two B-squad teams; stress the following short-side plays—end run, off tackle, tackle trap, inside tackle, running pass.
4:25 Unit work on short-side attack; unit divides as follows:
1. LT and split end
2. LG, C and RG
3. RT and tight end
4. Backs (two groups) (Run against dummies) Each unit to drill on its assignments for the five short side plays. GO HARD!
4:55 One spot scrimmage; two teams I and II versus B-squad teams
5:20 Wind sprints
5:25 Jogging; set own pace
5:30 Showers and dressing
6:30 Dinner

The following features are found in this type of practice schedule.

The program of activities is varied.

Conditioning work is interspersed among other items and held to a minimum.

Early drills are insightful and give meaning to the work that follows.

The most intensive work comes midway.

The most exhilarating part of practice (scrimmage) (batting) follows the intensive work.

Jogging at the end aids the tapering-off process.

Although only one rest period is designated as such, there are opportunities for relaxation between plays.

REST PERIODS

Sports are usually games of action, and the action of each individual player depends upon his physical fitness. Physical fitness—the ability of the organism to respond to demands put upon it—combines a number of factors:

1. Strength and endurance—gained by training the muscular and cardiorespiratory system.
2. Performance skills—derived from practice and dependent upon

rhythm, balance, flexibility, and neuromuscular response.
3. Will to perform—derived from the knowledge of why he is
   performing.

In other words, for the athlete to perform well, he must be
strong, well conditioned, skilled, and motivated.

Mental and physical fatigue appear to be enemies of physical
fitness and, therefore, hindrances to good learning. Power and skill
fade when the body becomes physically tired, and the inclination to
learn disappears when the training program settles down to dull,
tedious routine. Physical fatigue may be only a temporary condition
which can be overcome by the introduction of rest periods into the
program. Mental fatigue is more psychological but just as real as its
physical counterpart; and it can be overcome by offering the players
new stimuli such as is found in a rich, varied practice schedule.

Whether the human body suffers from either mental or physical
fatigue, it is capable of rejuvenating itself. The circulatory and
excretory systems combine to rid the body cells of waste products
and replenish them with energy materials. There must be, however, a
period of rest during which the body can carry out its refueling act.
Rest may be gained (1) through sleep; (2) when the body is totally
relaxed although fully awake; and (3) by changing the routine.

Sleep is included in health habits that are part of the outcomes of
sports participation. The coach should continually aid the formation
of these habits by citing the value of keeping training rules. The
ability to relax seems to be a characteristic of great athletes.
Youngsters must be taught not only the value of relaxation but also
how to relax. Coaches are sometimes guilty of inconsistency by
preaching relaxation and at the same time insisting that players
remain on their feet throughout an entire practice period. It is
possible to relax when standing or when kneeling on one knee, but
the art must be acquired through practice.

Gaining rest through a break in routine may involve more than
merely having a variety of practice experiences. Sometimes a radical
change is beneficial. Spending an hour at a fun game other than the
regular sport, a relay race, or even granting a complete holiday in
midseason, will serve to renew life when the squad exhibits signs of
lethargy.

High school coaches are faced with the problem of teaching
complex skills to adolescents who often appear to be without the
slightest semblance of coordination. Rest and relaxation are especially important, for the adolescent easily can get into the habit of
burning up his energy recklessly. Physical and emotional fatigue are

enemies that the adolescent must be taught to avoid. The athletic coach is in a position to do such a positive job of teaching here, that the youngsters will incorporate these admonitions into their habits of living. Overexertion can be avoided by frequent rest periods in the practice sessions when all activity is stopped. The unskilled performer is likely to lose a lot of energy through distractions, emotional disturbance, and uncoordinated movements, hence he becomes fatigued much quicker than the skilled, experienced performer. For this reason, for the beginners, the coach must shorten the practice periods on any one skill, and he must not be too exacting in his demands for perfection.

If it is assumed that physical fitness is a desirable quality or characteristic for the learner to bring to a learning situation in sports, then it appears that coaches should be responsible for providing opportunities for rest and relaxation in their programs.

METHODS OF INSTRUCTION

The coach's knowledge of his sport is of no consequence until he imparts it to his players. Instruction imparts knowledge, but skill must be acquired by the learner through his own practice. One acquires skills in piano playing, cabinet making, or in athletics by playing the piano, making cabinets, or playing a sport. A boy will not become a great halfback merely from listening to the coach's explanation of how to start, pivot, sidestep, and change pace. Nor will a boy become a basketball star by listening to a thorough discourse on shooting. Good instruction, however, may prevent useless and detrimental experimentation by showing the learner what to do and how to do it, thereby aiding in the acquisition of a skill. The raw recruit becomes a polished performer by practicing under the tutelage of a master teacher, his coach.

A coach is not expected to demonstrate every skill required in a sport, but he is expected to know which skills are required and be able to explain the various steps which make up the complete act. In selecting his assistants, the coach usually strives to surround himself with a staff representing a wide variety of backgrounds and experiences. This provides a rich source of teaching talent covering all phases of the game.

Teaching involves many problems, including introduction, explanation, and demonstration. Most coaches have groups of favorite experiences from which sport learning is to be assimilated by the players. These experiences are known as drills, activities, or exercises.

Methods of instruction are developed for the purpose of making the learning easier and more efficient. Most of the problems listed have been or will be discussed in this book, but the present topic will be confined to a treatment of some high points or introduction, explanation, and demonstration of activities related to athletics.

Caution: Try to anticipate the type of questions which would arise in the minds of your listeners and include the answers to them before they actually are asked.

If humor is a part of your personality, let it come out naturally at some point in the explanation. It will help the listener to remember the incident. However, do not try to be funny!

Introduction—Before allowing the squad to participate in an exercise, discuss the main purpose of the exercise. Make sure that the exercise is related to a real situation, such as part of a defensive or offensive play. This will establish the need and serve as a base for motivation.

Provide exercises that challenge. Do not have the players practicing a maneuver that is so simple that it bores them.

If artificial aids or field equipment are to be used, allow time for the inexperienced players to become familiar with them.

Provide for uninterrupted participation in the whole activity and then allow the questions to grow out of the players' experiences.

Create and sustain a positive attitude and an air of optimism. Make the players feel that they are capable of mastering any material to be learned.

Guard against showing dismay or disappointment at poor performances by the learners (there may be a time for it later.) The boys may become so amused at a coach's irritation that they lose sight of the purpose of the activity.

Make sure that each player has a chance for success. For example, if the activity calls for individuals to work against each other, match them as equally as possible in weight and ability.

Kill a drill before it dies naturally. Change the activity quickly when there is a sign of waning interest or discouragement at lack of success.

Be enthusiastic. Make the players feel that this activity is the most appropriate for meeting their needs.

Explanation—Make the explanation short, clear and concise. Repeat words or phrases only when they are needed to emphasize an important point. Get to the point as quickly as possible so that participation can start.

Know how to control the voice. Do not talk too fast, too loud, or too soft, be sure that pronounciations are correct. Be a good actor.

Be sensitive to the environment or situation for explanations. For example, long and involved explanations should not be attempted when they interrupt a spirited scrimmage. Use rest periods for explanation, but be sure the explanation is for some activity that will be undertaken immediately following the period.

Make sure that a blackboard is available. Any new drill or activity can be explained better with the aid of a blackboard.

Demonstration—Use the person who can make the most effective demonstration. It may be the head coach, assistant coach, or a player. Be sure that the demonstration is previewed in order that a correct model is offered.

Adapt demonstrations of skills or maneuvers to be used by individual team members to the player's general level of ability and understanding. Avoid extremely complex and detailed demonstrations.

Adapt the tempo of the demonstration to game speed. Make it slower when necessary for adequate observation and assimilation by players.

Do not allow the demonstration to delay player participation, but be sure it is long enough to create a clear picture of the activity.

Include in demonstrations an emphasis on socially approved conduct exemplifying the code of sportsmanship. In many of the skills and maneuvers used in athletics there are chances to cheat or just stay within the letter of the rules.

Use both words and action to call the player's attention to important details.

Adapt skills and maneuvers to varying conditions in a game. Demonstrate these adaptations and clearly explain the situation calling for them. Give adequate and understandable reasons for performing a skill a certain way.

In order that instruction and practice on an activity may have direction and meaning for the players, demonstrate the whole activity and, if possible, put it in a natural game setting so that the players may see its relation to other elements of the game.

No attempt has been made to offer these guides in any particular sequence or order of importance, and individual coaches may recognize situations in which any one or more of them may apply.

The following method is suggested for the introduction of new activities.

1. Present the activity in its entirety. Be sure, though, that the activity is a valuable and desirable part of a team's repertoire, individually and collectively. For example, present the various assignments for a defensive play in such a way that they show the contribution of each maneuver to the main purpose—to stop some particular offensive play.
2. Demonstrate the activity to show the correct movements of each player. Use coaches or experienced players who are skilled sufficiently to perform correctly.
3. Have the squad participate in the activity as soon as the demonstration is ended.

Further steps such as evaluating progress and analysis of errors may follow. Additional explanation and demonstration followed by retrials often may be necessary. No definite rule can be established for the time or place to include these items. The ability, maturity, and interest of the players, as well as the degree of difficulty in the activity, are factors influencing the number and sequence of the various steps.

TERMINOLOGY

Most coaches will agree that their players learn more from doing than they do from listening, yet it is necessary for the coach to do a great deal of talking in the teaching process. His problem, then, is one of making sure that the squad understands what his words and phrases were meant to convey.

Some psychologists suggest that verbal methods of tuition are not always beneficial, because it is difficult to describe accurately the scheme or organization of the act and as equally difficult to reproduce the act from someone's description of it. The old saying attributed to Confucius: "One picture is worth a thousand words" is never more true than in the case of teaching an athletic skill. The demonstration is vastly superior to the word picture but a combination of the two is even better. Coaches have not always bothered to verbalize their own style of performing a skill as they acquired it, and most players do not learn from listening, but from participating. There is, evidentally, some case for verbal tuition after the learner has had considerable practice, because professional athletes learn a great deal from expert coaching after they arrive in the major professional league. No matter how clear and concise the coach may be in his presentation of some athletic art, the verbal statements do not give each player a ready-made, identical picture. They merely stimulate the listeners to make their own conceptions of what is meant. If the statements refer to experiences which the players have had before, they will bring to mind a picture of the act as done before, but if the statements deal with new concepts, new meanings, and new problems, the constructive imagination of the listeners is called into play and the picture of what the coach is talking about could take many forms. Therefore, a coach should make certain that every player has the same idea or concept about the subject on which he is talking. This is dependent upon three groups of factors:

1. Clarity and simplicity of the speech in which it is presented
2. Number of parts or steps involved in the act
3. The player's learning potential—his interest, ability, desire, intelligence, and work habits.

Terminology is involved in the first of these factors. It is easy for a coach to confuse his players, especially the inexperienced, if he is not mindful of his vocabulary. The words and phrases used in explanations and in answers to questions should be short, simple, and yet complete enough to be understood. They should be meaningful in terms of the activity they describe and in keeping with the mental level of the group. A coach who tries to impress his squad by talking over their heads not only is defeating his own purpose but also is guilty of poor teaching.

There is already plenty of confusion in the terms applied to sports activities. A single football block may be given as many as three different names (pivot, reverse body, or riding block) or a single term may be used to describe three distinct types of defensive line play. For example, a line may be described as a "waiting line" when in reality it may be a looping line, an angling line, or a sliding line, all of which are separate and distinct types of defensive play. Basketball coaches must be explicit in their use of the term "screen." There are many different types of screens, so each should be given its own name and, preferably, one that describes the action; *viz.* pick screen, moving screen, inside screen, etc. Many times coaches will apparently disagree among themselves over the appropriate type of maneuver for a certain playing situation, but when they resort to demonstration, they find that they are in perfect agreement over the maneuver but are confused by its different names. If experienced coaches become confused, it stands to reason that young rookies can become completely baffled when a simple movement is given more

than one title. A coach must not take for granted that he and his
boys are of one mind when he uses terms that are common in the
slang language of three major sports:

Football	Baseball	Basketball
"Check him"	"Hold him"	Zone
Brush block	Brush back	Press
Down field block	"Dig in"	Slough off
Protect	"Guard the dish"	Pick
Cover outside	"Relay man"	Switch
Play safe	"Cut off"	Check off
Drift	"Playing for two"	Give and go
Angle	Choke up	Continuity
Squibb	Rocker step	High post
Double team	Meat hand	Screen
Swing man	Crowd it	Set shot
Corner man	Push him	Jump shot
Inside safety		

Each of these terms may be applied to altogether different types
of maneuvers, and it is the coach's job to make sure that the terms he
uses have the same meanings for the learners that they have for him.

A glossary of terms common to sports and used throughout this
text is included at the end of the book.

SCRIMMAGES vs. DRILLS

Scrimmages may be defined as that type of practice in which two
entire teams engage in all the activities of a regular game. In football,
kickoffs may be eliminated, but the other features, such as offensive
and defensive plays, making required yardage, and penalties, are
included. With the exception of substitution rules, sports such as
soccer, basketball, baseball, and hockey engage in scrimmages which
are similar to game situations. Scrimmages may be regarded as
examination periods in which the players and coaches get the
opportunity to determine how the learning is progressing.

Scrimmages have the power of making practice sessions lively,
interesting, and pleasant. The situations are real, and the material to
be learned has obvious meaning to the player. He has the opportunity
of judging for himself how well he has mastered the fundamentals
and knowledges that are required of a good player. The fact that this
evaluation is not confined to his judgment alone but is shared by the

judgment of his coaches and teammates is a source of motivation. It is obvious to anyone who has ever coached a team that, next to actual games, scrimmages are the most popular periods in the entire program.

Every coach dreams of the day when he will be able to send a complete team of experienced players on to the field. All coaches agree that the best experience is gained in playing the game; therefore practice experiences should be as close to game conditions as possible. The nearest thing to an actual game is a scrimmage. Full scale scrimmages rarely are held more than once or twice a week during the regular season, but small group (skeletal) drills done at full speed may be employed more frequently. Even these small-unit scrimmages should not be held too often, due to other factors involved, such as the promotion of physical and mental fatigues from numerous high speed workouts. Most coaches prefer to preserve the "edge" for games.

Drills are that type of activity in which parts of the whole activity of a sport are practiced. There are two varieties of drills. First, there is the drill entirely removed from the game setting. A football example could be one-on-one tackling drill in which the players are arranged in two lines facing each other and on command a player in one line tackles the man opposite him in the other line. A basketball example would be that of two lines of players passing a ball between them using various types of passes, all from a standstill position, and having little relationship with actual game situations. Similar arrangements are made for practicing fundamentals in other sports. Unfortunately, this type of drill rarely involves much enthusiasm among the players because of the artificial aspect—it is not the way the game is played! Similar arrangements are made for practicing the other fundamentals. Second, there is the type of drill where groups of players, acting as a unit, engage in practicing some phase of the sport in which part of the game element has been preserved. Skeleton drills of football are good examples of this type. A complete backfield and two ends may hold a passing drill against the secondary defense of another group. The linemen are eliminated, but enough of the game elements have been preserved to give the drill real meaning. A three-on-three basketball drill to master triangularing is another example, as is the double-play combination drill for baseball infielders. Other exercises in other sports require only three or four men, but they approximate game conditions in that they proceed at game speed and use the regular playing situations as problems. This second type of exercise may not be regarded as a true drill because the elements of monotony, irrelevance, and mechanics have been removed.

Drills of the second type mentioned here are regarded as being not merely for the purpose of fixing or perfecting a way of performing an athletic skill which the player seems to have acquired, but rather a continuation of the development process. Players are expected to grow in skill and understanding of the maneuvers that make up the drill, but this requires that the drill be more than work and sweat. They must be given a goal toward which to work, something upon which they can improve, something which has meaning in terms of game situations. It may be the perfecting of the ball-handling technique in football, the exact position in a moving pick in basketball, or the bare-handed stop and throw in fielding a bunt.

There is definite value in drills if they are conducted properly. Games are made up of so many complex skills that learning is bound to proceed at a slow pace for a vast number of players. They will profit from the guidance of the coach in learning to master the skills through drill sessions. Drill will accomplish nothing, however, if it merely is a matter of repeating the same performance over and over again without any attempt to modify or improve the act. It should be an opportunity for the learner to increase his efficiency through thoughtful analysis of his movements. The coach aids the process by helpful analysis and suggestion but, without the interest, desire, and intent to improve on the part of the player, it is sure to be time wasted. The high degree of sensorimotor coordination needed in most athletic skills requires much practice, and practice involves repetition. If it is accompanied by the personal factors mentioned above, it will be worthwhile.

Practically all athletic skills are acquired reflexes or habits resulting from many repetitions of the same performance, but no habit can become more fixed than the aims and desires of the player will permit. This is to say that drill for drill's sake is useless, but drill that is accompanied by a will to learn, a desire to improve, and an effort to gain insight into the act with a goal or purpose as a motive is a far more potent force for creating improvement than any pure drill could possibly be.

In summary, it would appear that there is a place for both scrimmages and drills in the training program. Scrimmages are undoubtedly best for whole learning, while drills are best for the learning of parts, which are wholes in themselves. A program made up of meaningful drills calls for a great deal of effort on the part of the coaches, while one made up principally of scrimmages requires less effort and is a favorite method of lazy, indifferent coaches. Excessive and premature scrimmaging, or even group drills, may be harmful to the learner if he uses a maneuver a great deal before he has mastered the correct technique. However, in order that fundamental drills will have more meaning for the players, it is desirable to introduce some team play even at the first practice. The players can see the relationship of the drills which they are practicing to the team play. The progress of a young player working on a difficult and complex maneuver may actually be retarded, for he may develop bad techniques because at this point he does not understand that they are bad. For this reason, coaches must do a lot of individual checking on their players in the early stages of learning, and there must always be some review of fundamentals throughout the season to correct careless habits that develop. Some drills, if properly planned and staged, will have all the necessary elements of a game to insure meaningful learning, and scrimmages can be used as dress rehearsals for the final presentation.

THE NUMBER OF PLAYS

One of the questions most frequently asked at coaching schools is, "How many plays should a team have?" No one answer can apply to all situations. Such factors as interest, intent to learn, intelligence, maturation, and experience affect the quantity of material that can be absorbed by a team. Some players learn easily and quickly or memorize all that is presented to them, while others are capable of far less.

The question of the number of plays involves the problem of memory which is something apart from learning. When a player learns something, it is established in a pathway of his nervous system and automatized in such a way that it can be recalled at will. Something memorized, however, can escape recall. The problem for the coach is to differentiate between the things to be *automatized* and those to be *memorized*. For instance, a lineman must learn the technique for blocking a defensive guard on a certain play, and he practices the skill until it becomes *automatic*. The guard, however, may shift his position just before the ball is snapped, and this calls for either a different type of block by the lineman or even a change in assignment. This information must be *memorized*. Some teams are credited with having many plays. In reality, they have few plays, but the players are intelligent enough to apply variations according to the situation. In a practical sense, every variation is another play, for it necessitates the coordinated effort of every team member, and each member must know his assignment.

Coaches may assume that they are simplifying matters for their players by having only a few plays with varying actions of one or two men to confuse the defense, for example, splitting off the ends, sending a man in motion, or flanking a back in football. Nevertheless, every such variation can be regarded as another play, because every defensive team will meet this changed pattern by shifting its defensive formation, and that involves a thinking process, necessitating a new type of action for the offensive player. All eleven offensive players must remember the blocking rule or the pattern for each move by the defense, even though only one or two individuals are involved in the original variation. Don Faurot, head coach at the University of Missouri, was outstandingly successful over a number of years with his Split T attack that was made up largely of four running plays and four passes set up identically either right or left. Each player learned the skills and memorized the variations against six types of defensive patterns. To operate with such a few basic plays was unusual for a major college eleven, yet the results were convincing. In modern football, the average number of different type plays used in any one game is nearly fourteen for running plays and seven for passes. Each team undoubtedly has more than those shown, and the shifting defenses of the opponents would bring the number of variations requiring memorization by each player to a high total.

Most basketball coaches, especially the high school coaches, prefer to simplify their offensive patterns. Modern play, however, dictates at least two separate offensive patterns, *i.e.,* the plays when the opponents press, and the plays when they do not press. Some coaches feel that a continuity offense with all ten players moving requires a minimum of memorization through clearly defined responsibilities for each player. The actual scoring plays come off situations as they occur in the continuity pattern. Still other coaches feel that their offensive system is quite simple when, in addition to the fast break, they included "give and go," "drop off," "fast hand-offs," and "screens." The number of defenses employed in modern basketball also varies. Almost all teams have at least one method of pressing and one or more methods against the deliberate offenses. Some coaches find it possible to employ multiple defenses, but others think it is neither fair to the boys nor beneficial to the team to burden them with too much to think about.

At what point does the total number of plays transverse the line between clarity and confusion? There are several practical factors as answers to this question, namely: intelligence of players, number and caliber of assistant coaches, teaching ability of the coaches, experience of players, size of squad, strength and place on schedule of opponents, and the type of offense used. Time is all important to the coach, and he never feels that he has enough of it. It takes time to teach fundamentals, set up defenses, and mold a well-organized attack. The time must be apportioned for all of these necessary phases so that none of them suffers from too little. The amount of help received from assistants can only be assumed to affect the number of plays that can be effectively handled by a team. No figures are available as proof. If the coach is an efficient teacher he should be able to accomplish the individual coaching in a shorter period and devote more time to plays. The size of the squad is a factor to be associated with the number of assistants. A certain amount of work must be accomplished, and a large squad necessitates having several assistants to speed the work along so that there will be more time available for plays. Experienced players do not need as much work on fundamentals as inexperienced ones, and they can devote more time to plays. Easy opponents on the schedule make it possible to spend days on new plays, for the team's normal potential will be enough to bring victory. The type and number of formations affect the number of plays. Some formations, such as the football T, and the basketball free-lance, readily lend themselves to variations, while others are limited in scope. In order to make it difficult to defend against a formation, a coach should have enough plays from each formation to keep the defense guessing.

If the stage is to be set for effective learning, it must not be overbalanced with any one phase of the game, for it will only promote confusion, dismay, and lack of confidence. Accurate records of the number and type of plays called during a season or the shots taken off certain basketball maneuvers will give a coach something tangible upon which to base his choices for the next year. The advice of his assistants and players and the results of his off-season practice are other factors for helping him decide.

SUMMARY

The program that the coach sets up for the purpose of teaching his sport should be planned in such a way that the learning situations will be conducive to the acquisition of the various knowledges and skills by the players.

The creation of a situation good for learning will involve attention to such factors as equipment and facilities to enrich the context, as well as practice periods and rest periods which affect the zest of a player approaching the job of learning. Care must be taken to introduce, explain, and demonstrate skills in a manner which will leave no doubt as to what is expected of the boy and make him eager to try his own skill at the job. In talking to his players, the coach should use meaningful words and phrases in terms of the activity they describe.

Drills have a place in sports learning. They help in perfecting some pattern of action learned but, in order to accomplish as much as possible for the learner, the drills should be staged in a manner which, like scrimmages, approximates game conditions. The number of plays is important for effective learning. Too many of them produce confusion and too few may detract from the interest of the players. Every phase of the program should be rich with opportunities for learning and play some important part in the creation.of an atmosphere that motivates the player to participate.

Test Questions

1. What factors affect the setting or learning environment?
2. How can a head coach create an atmosphere of creativity in his coaching situation?
3. How can facilities and equipment enrich the program of teaching and learning in sports?
4. What effect does locker room environment have on the acquisition of health habits?
5. Should practice on specialties be confined to the periods before and after the regular session?
6. List four advantages of short spaced periods of practice over long massed practices.
7. Why is it that some young players appear to acquire greater skill over the months when they are not actively engaged in practice?
8. What are the three periods of intensity found in a well-organized practice?
9. When should the most important phase of the day's practice come?
10. Explain this statement: "For the athlete to perform well, he must be strong, well conditioned, skilled and motivated."
11. How does the human body profit from rest?
12. Does rest involve complete relaxation such as lying down?
13. Why are adolescent athletes in need of more rest than adult players?

14. List at least three concepts of proper teaching/coaching found in each of the three areas: introduction, explanation, and demonstration.
15. What determines the number of times new material must be reexplained and redemonstrated and retried?
16. Why should a new maneuver be presented in its entirety the first time?
17. How can careless terminology interfere with the teaching/learning of sports?
18. What is the principal value in scrimmaging?
19. Select a sport and give an example of: (1) a meaningless drill, and (2) a meaningful drill.
20. What attitudes must the player bring to the drill to assure that improvement will take place?
21. Differentiate between something *learned* and something *memorized.*
22. List some factors affecting the number of plays a team should receive.

Discussion Questions

1. Should all daily drills be challenging?
2. How do you explain the fact that many fine teams are produced in schools having a minimum of facilities and equipment?
3. An ingenious coach may design and produce many homemade mechanical aids. Does it set a bad precedent for future budgeting? Should this affect his philosophy?
4. If an experienced team is returning, should a coach spend time on fundamentals or should he assume the boys know the fundamentals and proceed immediately into the more complex parts of the game?
5. Should the terminology a coach uses be an attempt toward conformity to what is being used by the profession or an attempt to identify aspects of the game or its skills with meaningful labels?
6. Must rest periods be times of complete physical, mental and emotional relaxation?

Suggested Readings

BOOKS

1. Atkinson, John W. "The Mainsprings of Achievement-Oriented Activity," in *Learning and the Educational Process* (J. D. Krumhaltz, editor). Chicago: Rand McNally & Co., 1965, pp. 25-66.
2. Biggs, M. L., and Hunt, M. P. *Psychological Foundations of Education.* New York: Harper and Row, 1962, pp. 435-454.
3. Bunn, John W. *The Basketball Coach's Guide to Success.* Englewood Cliffs: Prentice Hall, Inc., 1961, p. 85.
4. Cole, Luella. *Psychology of Adolescence.* New York: Rinehart and Co., 1948, p. 79.
5. Cronbach, Lee J. *Educational Psychology.* New York: Harcourt, Brace and Co., 1954, pp. 212-220; 300-309.
6. Crow, Lester D., and Crow, Alice. *Educational Psychology.* New York: American Book Co., 1958, pp. 141-168.
7. Davis, Elwood C., and Lawther, John D. *Successful Teaching in Physical Education.* Englewood Cliffs: Prentice Hall, Inc., 1948, pp. 498-503.
8. DiClemente, W. *Soccer Illustrated.* New York: The Ronald Press Co., 1955, p. 184.
9. Driver, Helen I. *Tennis for Teachers.* Wisconsin: Helen I. Driver Associates, 1956, p. 162.
10. Gates, Arthur I., et al. *Educational Psychology.* New York: The Macmillan Co., 1948, p. 380.
11. Griffith, Coleman. *The Psychology of Coaching.* New York: Charles Scribner and Sons, 1932, pp. 32-35, 46.
12. Harris, Theodore L., and Schwann, Wilson. *The Learning Process.* New York: Oxford University Press, 1961, pp. 5-28, 176-177.
13. Hartmann, George. *Educational Psychology.* New York: American Book Co., 1941, pp. 321-324.
14. Kingsley, Howard. *The Nature and Conditions of Learning.* Englewood Cliffs: Prentice Hall, Inc., 1946, p. 224.
15. Klausmeier, Herbert J. *Learning and Human Abilities— Educational Psychology.* New York: Harper and Bros., 1961, pp. 27-33.
16. Kozman, Hilda, Cassidy, Ruth, and Jackson, Chester O. *Methods in Physical Education.* Philadelphia: W. B. Saunders & Co., 1948, pp. 31-32.

17. McCracken, Branch. *Indiana Basketball.* Englewood Cliffs: Prentice Hall, Inc., 1955, pp. 1-5.
18. Miller, Arthur, and Massey, Dorothy. *A Dynamic Concept of Physical Education for Secondary Schools.* Englewood Cliffs: Prentice Hall, Inc., 1963, pp. 100-111.
19. Mursell, James L. *Successful Teaching.* New York: McGraw Hill Co., 1946, p. 86.
20. Thomas, R. M., and Swartout, S. G. *Integrated Teaching Materials.* New York: Longmans Green and Co., Inc., 1960.
21. Townsend, Edward A., and Burke, Paul J. *Learning for Teachers.* New York: The Macmillan Co., 1962, pp. 45-53.
22. Waters, E. C., Hawk, P. E., Squires, John Y. *Soccer.* U.S. Naval Institute, Maryland, 1961, pp. 131-134.

Suggested Readings

ARTICLES

1. Anello, Michael. "Effective Teaching: Synthesis and Originality," *Improving College and University Teaching,* Vol. XVI, No. 3, Summer 1968, pp. 174-175.
2. Baley, James. "Principles for Learning Tumbling," *JOHPER,* Vol. 39-8, October 1968, pp. 30-33.
3. Brown, William E. "Four- A-Day," *Scholastic Coach,* Vol. 36-10, June 1967, pp. 30 and 47.
4. D.G.W.S. "Athletic Scholarships for Women," *JOHPER,* Vol. 33-4, April 1962, p. 18.
5. Druse, Ron. "Some Tips for Successful Coaches," *Coaching Clinic.* November 1967, pp. 21-22.
6. Eason, Elmer. "Critique of Training and Education," *Education,* Vol. 87-5, January 1967, pp. 309-311.
7. Edwards, Donald and Adams, Gary. "Spice Up Your Practice," *Athletic Journal,* Vol. XLVI-6, February 1966, p. 70.
8. Gardner, Sprig. "Organization for Wrestling," *Athletic Journal,* Vol. XLII-4, December 1962, p. 35.
9. Harmon, John, and Oxendine, Joseph. "Effect of Different Lengths of Practice Periods on the Learning of a Motor Skill," *Research Quarterly,* 32:34, March 1961.
10. Harootunian, Berj. "Intelligence and the Ability to Learn," *The Journal of Educational Research,* Vol. 59-5, January 1966, pp. 211-213.

11. Hatch, William H. "Basic Drills for Baseball Practice," *Athletic Journal,* Vol. XLII-6, February 1962, p. 8.
12. Ireland, George. "Simplicity Does It," *Scholastic Coach,* Vol. 33-2, October 1963, p. 3.
13. Jones, John G. "Motor Learning Without Demonstration of Physical Practice Under Two Conditions of Mental Practice," *Research Quarterly,* Vol. 36-3, October 1965, pp. 270-276.
14. Kaczmarek, John C. "Equipment Care—Cardinal Obligation," *American School Board Journal,* Vol. 153, August 1966, p. 29.
15. Keith, J. Arthur. "How Coaches Teach," *The Physical Educator,* Vol. 24-4, December 1967, p. 162.
16. McCatty, Cressy A. "Underwater Photography," *JOHPER,* Vol. 38-8, October 1967, p. 84.
17. Meyer, Kenneth L. "How Many Plays?" *Athletic Journal,* Vol. 39-2, October 1948, p. 131.
18. Mills, Chuck, and Corey, Walt. "Drills for Line-backers," *Athletic Journal,* Vol. XLIX-1, September 1968, pp. 20-24, 116.
19. Murphy, Chet. "Principles of Learning with Implications of Teaching Tennis," *JOHPER,* Vol. 33-2, February 1962, pp. 26-28.
20. Paterson, Cecil. "Motivation in Practice," *Coach and Athlete,* Vol. XXVI-11, 1965, p. 18.
21. Raskin, D., Boice, C., Rubel, E., Clark, D. "Transfer Tests of the Frequency Theory of Verbal Demonstration Learning," *The Journal of Experimental Psychology,* Vol. 76-4, April 1968, pp. 521-529.
22. Reynolds, James, and Glaser, Robert. "Effects of Repetition and Spaced Review upon Retention of a Complex Learning Task," *Journal of Educational Psychology,* Vol. 55-5, October 1964, p. 52.
23. Robinson, Frank. "Coaching With Video Tape," *Scholastic Coach,* Vol. 35-5, January 1966, pp. 36 and 56-57.
24. Schmid, Melvin, McKeon, John, Moore, Alan. "Drills for Defensive Soccer," *Athletic Journal,* Vol. XLII-2, October 1961, p. 62.
25. Schulte, John M. "Training and Education," *Education,* Vol. 87-5, January 1967, pp. 309-311.
26. Silverberg, Stanley. "Team Organization and Discipline," *Scholastic Coach,* Vol. 32-2, November 1962, pp. 44-47.
27. Tansey, Jim. "A Complete Junior High Offense," *Athletic Journal,* Vol. XLV-3, November 1964, p. 68.
28. Verducci, Frank. "Mirror Offense in Basketball," *Athletic Journal,* Vol. XLVII-3, November 1966, pp. 36, 68-69.

Chapter III
THE WHAT AND WHY OF PRACTICE

"There is a good reason for everything we do."

THE UTILITY OF THE SKILL OR KNOWLEDGE

Everyone has had the experience of working at some task in which he felt strange and inadequate. Lack of experience and knowledge, improper introduction, and poor orientation to a task usually will leave a person floundering helplessly in an attempt to make some meaning out of the various elements or parts of the whole problem. Athletes are required to learn many facts and skills in the course of a season. So that the learning may proceed in as orderly a fashion as possible, the coach should attempt to orient the learner in terms of goal or purpose. To put it plainly, tell them *what* to do, show them *how* to do it, and explain *why* they are to do it.

Authorities in the field of educational psychology are in accord on the beneficial effect of mobilizing the learner's efforts by creating a goal or primary objective toward which he strives. More is involved than merely aiming the player's efforts toward the acquisition of some skill. Teaching and coaching are, at the very least, a problem of giving the learning process a pattern and order, organizing learning as a search for insight, and presenting experiences which will bring out goals and determination.

The coach who centers the early season practice periods around a few important tasks finds that his team reacts with vigor toward the completion of those tasks. A basketball coach might select a skill such as changing direction. First he will explain it as a maneuver designed to allow the offensive man to go past his guard by influencing the guard to momentarily put his weight on the wrong leg. Secondly, he will explain the proper footwork, stressing the first or fake step as well as the shoulder and head fakes which accompany the footwork, all of which must be done at controlled speed. Thirdly, he will point out the advantage possessed by the player who masters such a skill, for he will be open more often.

A football practice period devoted to the learning of blocking will have more meaning for the players if their efforts are confined to learning one type of block, the principle element or movement in the

67

block, the place of the block in the larger picture of the team's offensive pattern. For example, the pivot block is a complex physical act, having its most significant use in football where an offensive player applies the block to a defensive man whose position is on the side away from the play. In other words, the offesnive man already has his body between the defensive man and the ball carrier; and a fast pivot enables him to drive his hip into the defensive man's middle, thus effectively screening him from the ball carrier. The very "nub" of the act is the keeping of his body close to that of the defensive man and at right angles to the direction in which he is trying to go. The player's task is to master the pivot block, but he must first be made to understand the "nub" of the skill, what this skill will accomplish for him and why he needs it. The plays and situations in which the act is used must be explained to him.

In teaching the double play at second base, the second baseman must learn that the rocker step allows him to make an easy throw to first base, but it will leave him vulnerable to the baserunner who will attempt to knock him off his feet before he can get the throw away. Crossing the bag will call for a more difficult throw across his body, but it usually will take him clear of the baserunner. The player must understand that both methods should be mastered because the time available to make the play will determine the one to be used.

The success of a player's performance can be measured by the player as well as by the coach if it is made in reference to the primary objective upon which there is genuine common agreement. Both the coach and the player must have the same clear picture of a correct performance which becomes the primary objective. The player makes adjustments in each of his practice trials in the light of his progress toward the objective. A knowledge of the detailed character of a truly good performance is a requisite for the coach or for the person managing his own learning. Various methods such as models, demonstrations, explanations, pictures, and diagrams may be used to provide this common knowledge of the desired performance. The efforts of the player will be directed by the coach first to the correct stance or body position for starting, and second, to the characteristic features of the act which will make it easy to detect faulty or correct technique. As the player masters the act, he finds it possible to concentrate on fewer and fewer details, until the complete act can be done without his being aware of the conscious reactions. At this point, it has become habit or acquired reflex, and the player has become skilled. The same procedure is carried out in the teaching and learning of all the other so-called fundamentals of the game.

Although players usually have a desire to learn and to improve their efficiency, the coach will always be confronted with the task of getting them to work at it if he has failed to present the practice tasks in such a way that the players can see the reason or need for such practice. Motivation is self-generated when the player sees the worth of the act or how it will make him a better player. The ability to perform a skill may mean the difference between playing or sitting on the bench. In the eyes of the boy, to play in the scheduled game has real value. No matter what the value may be, however, the boy is motivated to learn when the specific task is presented clearly and with emphasis on its precise contribution to the all-round competence of the player in particular and the team in general. Therefore what the athlete learns is meaningful to him when it is used to make him a better performer, that is, if it results in the attainment of his goal. A modern coach realizes, however, that self-motivation continues only as long as the player feels that he has not yet completely mastered the skill; so he may laud the player's efforts and praise his progress, but he will persist in demanding further evidence of continued improvement.

ESSENTIALS vs. INCIDENTALS

Practice time should not be wasted on accessory and nonessential procedures. Some coaches continue to dwell on irrelevant phases of their game which disappeared years ago, others are guilty of indiscriminate introduction of "pet" drills or practice methods which were part of their own playing experience or picked up at some coaching clinic. Clinics and coaching schools are worthwhile institutions, and any coach will find the time in attendance well spent if he can come away with just one good idea. However, he must be critical and cautious about applying everything "new under the sun" to his particular system.

A critical analysis of the skills required of the player for each position should be made by the coach, and here he must be cautious about demanding too much of the boy. Fortunate is the coach with a tackle who can master one method of breaking a block or a halfback whose sole stock in trade is a baffling change of pace. A baseball pitcher with a blazing fast ball is "money in the bank" to his coach. Many boys easily master several skills while other players struggle vainly to acquire the knack of just one. Technical books on sports are filled with various and sundry methods of performing the many maneuvers known as fundamentals. Most of them are variations of one or two basic moves, so the initial emphasis should be on the acquisition of the basic skill. For example, most coaches are aware of three or four methods of breaking a block on the defensive lineman; yet practically all the methods are based on fast initial charge by the lineman. It would be far better for the coach to have the boy concentrate on developing a fast charge than to have him practice numerous fancy skills. Because between 55 and 60 percent of all long-shot attempts are missed, basketball coaches feel justified in spending much time practicing rebounding. For defensive rebounding, proper checking-out techniques will receive a great deal of attention, but one fundamental stands out as most essential, that of forcing the opponent out of his straight path to the basket. Other techniques must be practiced but, unless the defensive man can position himself properly in relation to his opponent, he will have no advantage in gaining the rebound.

To carry out a critical analysis of his sport, a coach should make a chart of each offensive and defensive play in his system and cross check the skill or technique required by each player in that play. Another factor that must be considered is the frequency of use. If a certain play is used extensively, the skills required for that play are more essential for the individual players than skills required for a play or defense that is used infrequently. Most coaches will be surprised at the number of times an identical skill will be called for in many different plays. The implication is obvious. This is the skill most essential for that player to master. Care must be taken, especially in squad drills, that players are not wasting precious practice time in maneuvers they will rarely use in actual game competition. For this reason, a coaching staff should devise their own drills calling for performance skills that will be required of the players most frequently in games. Some other common "time wasters" follow:

1. Prolonged practice periods falling on ball or picking up fumbles;
2. Running signals at half-speed;
3. Wind-sprints done without using the regular starting signals;
4. Batting practice against three-quarter speed pitching;
5. Basket shooting from all points in the offensive area by all players.

Any coach questioning these statements might examine the pictures of his games for the past few years to determine, for example, the number of occasions upon which a player used a fancy intricate maneuver in preference to a simple one, or the number of occasions upon which a basketball player did not take the majority of his shots from one small section of the floor. Of course, in order to be accurately scientific, the coach should determine the comparative percentage of success for each type of play or shot and decide for himself which is best. Simple but effective methods should always be chosen over intricate, unreliable ones.

In the actual teaching of a skill, much time and effort can be wasted if the coach fails to point out the important as well as the unimportant features of the act. From mere observation of a model or demonstration, the learner may gain a false impression of the essentials to an efficient performance. Beauty and grace are admirable qualities in kicking a football or pitching a baseball, but the boy who resembles a falling haystack while he punts sixty-five yards or "throws aspirins" in the strike zone is still getting the job done. The important essential in punting is to bring about a meeting of the ball and the instep at the proper angle. If the learner has progressed this far, he has learned to kick, regardless of his form. In pitching a baseball, the essential in the act is to develop a whiplike motion which will result in the ball being released at the end or snap of the wrist and not aimed as in throwing a dart. How many coaches would have allowed Dick Fosbury to practice high jumping in the reverse manner which eventually enabled him to win an Olympic gold medal? Sound aerodynamically, but so lacking in grace and normal action, it would be vetoed by most coaches, yet Fosbury's unorthodox application of force lifted his body 7' 4 1/4"! Fortunately, most of the physical skills of athletes are based on essential movements that are not only fluent and attractive to the eye but that also aid in the concentration of effort at the vital point. To this end, coaches are justified in insisting on good form where it is correlated with actual mastery in terms of results.

THE EFFECT OF CONSEQUENCES ON LEARNING

One of the earliest concepts of learning about which there has been considerable speculation and difference of opinion is the Law of Effect.[1] Thorndike, a pioneer in experimenting with this concept, found that a satisfying aftereffect acts directly on a connection to make it stronger; however, weakening influences of an annoying aftereffect are not so clearly indicated by experimental data. He

[1]Edward L. Thorndike, *Human Learning*. New York: D. Appleton–Century Co., 1931, p. 62.

concluded that annoyance does not have the direct and uniform effect in weakening a connection that satisfaction has in strengthening one.

It is probably true that the annoying consequences of unsatisfactory responses are displaced or nullified by the responses that follow satisfying results. This can be seen in the case of a boy learning to forward pass. With emphasis on bringing the ball forward, close to the head, stepping in the direction of the throw and following through with the weight on the forward foot, the learner will find that he is successful in throwing the ball correctly.

The satisfaction which comes from success following the correct procedure overshadows the failures which result when the ball is carelessly thrown; hence the boy is motivated to attempt to throw in the correct manner. The golfer who does not concentrate on his shot and dubs it is disgusted with himself and vows never to repeat that performance. A basketball player who makes the mistake of crossing his feet on defense and suffers the humiliation of seeing his opponent drive past him will be alert thereafter to avoid repeating the same mistake. He will make an effort to move by slide stepping in boxer fashion. When this style enables him to keep proper position on his opponent, he will tend to try even harder to perfect the technique. As far as psychologists are concerned, it seems safe to assume that there is a great deal of agreement among them on the concept that responses during the learning process are modified by their consequences or antecedents.

It has been found that the word "right" or some other congratulatory expression for a correct response is more effective than "wrong" or another indicator of failure for an incorrect response. For coaching purposes, it would appear then that the emphasis should be more on the positive than the negative. In the case of most players, this will probably hold true, for they react readily to praise; it is the exception rather than the rule to find a boy who is motivated only under duress. The use of any incentive will be time wasted, however, if the boy has no desire to learn or improve his performance; this might be the case if the boy has no goal or objective toward which he is supposed to be advancing.

Merely being told that he is on or off the right track will not stimulate him to learn if he has no desire to be correct. There must be a motive. In order to insure repeated attempts at learning by the player, the coach and player must have an agreed-upon goal or objective. Objectives and the experiences which lead to them must be so planned that proper responses will lead to lasting satisfaction, while incorrect or faulty responses will result in temporary unpleasantness. The use of artificial rewards or punishments is not recommended. If coaches can sufficiently motivate the desired responses with praise or congratulatory remarks, the undesirable ones should disappear because of their incompatibility with the learner's objective; but the objective must be well defined and understood (emotionally as well as intellectually) by both coach and learner.

For example, a track coach and an athlete may agree upon a 48-second quarter mile as an objective while the best time, to date, has been 50 seconds. The reduction of two seconds by a regular schedule of time trials over that period will indicate the progress toward the goal. No matter how grueling the practice schedule may be, if the recorded times indicate to the athlete that he is moving toward the 48-second quarter, he will work ungrudgingly. Contrariwise, if the workouts result in no improvement in time, the athlete's ardor for practice will cool. Frequently, he will lose what he already has accomplished because of a lack of enthusiasm for the program. There always is a reason for the setback. The job of the coach and athlete is to discover what it is that is causing the failure of the boy to improve. They may discover the fault to be one of the following: diet, lack of rest, lack of effort, time of day for workouts, home troubles, money troubles, girl troubles, or poor running technique. Once the fault has been discovered and a remedy established, subsequent time trials will again indicate progress, and the athlete's enthusiasm will return.

Good coaches recognize the importance of having the player establish a suitable goal, for the goal set and the goal striving will spur the boy to successful achievement and the elimination of errors and ineffective responses. If, for example, the goal of the player is improvement of performance, he is usually dissatisfied with his initial trial and becomes irked at his errors. Because of his desire for excellence, he keeps striving for a smoother performance; and, when improvement does come, it is satisfying because it is in accord with his motives. The field psychologists would also add to this theory that the responses are motivated by their obvious incompleteness, for the ideal response—absolute perfection—will never be realized, especially if the player is ambitious.

If the principle of the effect of consequences is to be accepted, a person must interpret consequences to refer fundamentally to the relation of means and end. The important meaning of the effect of a response is a matter of whether it furthers or retards progress toward a goal. Learning has gone on under the most adverse conditions where even the correct movement by a player has resulted in some unpleasant aftereffects; yet, if anything, the correct response was strengthened. A soccer player learning to "head" the ball will be jarred by the correct contact but may escape the impact if he "crawfishes" backward and traps the ball with his chest, but he will butt into the ball time and time again even though he knows it will result in additional bruises. The reason for his incessant behavior in the face of unpleasant reactions is the feeling of progression toward his larger desired goal. This is enough to outweigh the associated discomfiture of the necessary act.

THE ACQUISITION OF MOTOR SKILLS

Although coaches resent the implication that many of our sports are games of physical prowess, the fact remains that success depends greatly on the player's ability to command a high degree of neuromuscular control over his body. Intelligence is also a desirable and important factor in the learning of the modern games with their many varieties of offense and defense. There is no team position today for the strong but dull-witted youth. The happiest combination of qualities is that which blends speed, courage, skill, and intelligence with a desire to learn and improve performance in the special techniques required to play the game properly. Other factors being equal, the team with the more highly skilled players usually will win. It would seem, then, that the greater portion of the training periods should be devoted to the acquisition of vital motor skills in the light of some larger controlling whole.

For a skill to be important, to have value and meaning for the learner, it must have some relation to a functional situation; that is, the learner must see how and why it can be used to make him more efficient. Unless a quarterback can be made to understand how faking will pull the defense out of position, he will not be motivated to work on the perfection of the intricate footwork and hand feints required for complete faking. When a 50-meter swimmer believes that a better turn at the end of the pool will take 2/10 of a second off his time, he will put out a tremendous effort. If a defensive coach wishes to teach a crashing charge to an end, he must first make it clear that the maneuver is part of the team's defensive pattern and has as its main purpose the placing of the defensive end beyond the offensive line in such a position that the ball carrier will be forced to change his normal path. A pitcher practicing the pick-off play at first base may show little enthusiasm for the drill because rarely is the runner put out at first base, but his attitude will change if the whole act of stealing second base is included in the drill. He can see how his proper moves hold the runner close, giving the catcher a good chance to throw the runner out. Meaningful learning starts with the assurance and proof that the desired skill has ultimate practical value.

Athletic techniques are most frequently referred to as motor skills, but in reality they are either sensory motor skills or perceptual motor skills. The difference between them is as follows:

Sensory motor skills are those we have developed through actions since birth, many of them being quite natural. Example: standing, walking, running, tieing a shoelace, etc. Usually they become acquired reflexes or habits.

Perceptual motor skills. These are other types of motor skills which may start as an ordinary sensory motor skill but become subject to change in accordance with the incoming perceptual pattern. In other words, an athlete may start his move in a certain way but his execution will vary in accordance with what he perceives. Usually he perceives through his senses of sight and touch.

Perceptual motor skills are actually motor functions which are so highly developed that they can be adjusted to meet situations as they appear to the individual. The skills required in athletics are of the perceptual type, for games are of movement and changing patterns. Different situations in a game call for a variance in the execution of the act. The batter who starts his swing shortly after the ball has left the pitcher's hand may change the level of his arms and the angle of his wrists one or two times before the ball finally arrives at the plate, because of what he "perceives" in the flight of the ball toward the plate. A blocker whose job it is to keep a defensive end out of the play may have to use several modifications of the shoulder block, depending upon the degree to which the end has advanced off the line of scrimmage. The boy attempting a jump shot in basketball may release the ball later or earlier than he originally intended and may even change the arc of the shot while he is in midair because of the position of the defensive man playing him. Individuals will perform the same act in as many different ways as there are players. It would be foolhardy for a coach to demand a stereotyped performance from all members of the squad in the light of individual differences. Emphasis should center on the result rather than on the process of execution.

The important steps in learning a skill are as follows:

1. The learner must acquire a clear picture of what he is about to learn.
2. The learner will embark on a course of trial and retrial analyzing his progress and changing the movement as he sees it

necessary. Changes also will be made as suggested by other observers (coaches and fellow players) until the correct pattern is reached.

3. The learner will practice the correct pattern to develop a smooth, easy, consistent performance.

The player first must arrive at a mental conception or image of the thing to be done along with an urge to do it. This necessitates a good selling job on the part of the coach, in which he presents the problem of acquiring the skill to the boy in such a way that he will be strongly motivated to learn it. Both arrive at a common agreement regarding the goal to be reached, the degree of competency to be acquired, and the methods to be employed in reaching the goal.

To avoid the confusion of blind trial and error methods, the player must supplement his own analysis of his progress with the expert tutelage of his coach. Here is where the coach must be careful not to emphasize the "steps" toward proficiency to the exclusion of emphasis on the ultimate end to be acheived. Good form is desirable, but form is a variable quality and overrigid insistence on a certain type not suited to a learner's physique or "style" may cause discouragement and loss of confidence by the player.

The player may be said to have learned the desired act when he has successfully mastered the principles involved in the skill and has established in his mind the fundamental relationships of the skill to the different situations arising in a game. The practice periods which follow will aid in the retaining of the skill. They will not add to the learning, but they should be directed toward reaching a higher level of performance. This is the only real justification for the long drill periods that coaches inflict on their squads. To insure their willingness and cooperation in those dreary exercises, the players should be encouraged to set a high level of aspiration for themselves when they undertake to acquire the motor skills.

As a rule, the learning will not proceed as a smooth line of progression. There will be plateaus or periods of leveling off commonly termed "slumps" in sports. These are bound to occur and coaches may be faced with the problem of rearousal of the will when the player's advancements seem to be stalled. At this point, it is wrong to wait for the athlete to "snap out of it." It would be better for the coach and player to make a careful study of the practice methods and style of performance. This may reveal certain inadequacies which, when rectified, will bring about renewed progress. Many modern coaches solve this problem by taking movies of their practice sessions and making a detailed study of the action of the players.

WHOLE vs. PART METHOD

One of the interesting problems of modern pedagogy is that of the relative values of the part and whole methods of presenting material to be learned. The implications are as important for the learning of motor skills as for the learning of academic material. The coach faced with the task of teaching a fascinating but complex game necessarily must make decisions concerning the techniques to be used in offering the experiences leading to competency.

The whole method is that system by which the *entire act* or a natural unit is presented, using the various principles of explanation and demonstration, followed by actual participation in the complete act by the student. Frequent pauses are usually made to offer suggestions and corrections as the need for them occurs. The part method, on the other hand, starts with a complete analysis of the fundamentals of the activity for the purpose of creating a sequence of skills, beginning with the simple and advancing to the more complex. These are presented to the students as individual experiences and, after mastering them to a certain degree, they are welded together as integral parts of the whole activity.

In basketball, for instance, the part method technique would start first with all the fundamentals of a part such as the crossover shot, moving on to skeleton scrimmages involving a few men, and gradually working up to full game conditions where the crossover shot is used. The whole method does not consist of as simple a procedure as blowing up the ball and allowing the boys to go to it. It involves actual game conditions of full scrimmage, preceded by the coach's explanation of what is expected to be accomplished, the "crux" or "nub" of the act, and errors to be avoided. Frequent stops to point out mistakes are made, followed by suggestions or demonstrations of correct procedure.

It may be difficult to find justification for claims of superiority of either method, but it may be that faulty technique has prevented the accomplishment of outstanding results for either of them. Two common errors found in the application of the whole method are the use of a large unit composed of unrelated materials or parts, and the presentation of a whole unit which is too difficult for the existing capacities of the learners. The whole must be whole in the sense of unity. It must have parts which are interrelated in order to have meaning. An element of an act is meaningless when separated from the whole, and learning the parts separate from the whole act does not guarantee the learning of the whole. The real value of the whole method is found in enabling the players to see the interrelationships of the various elements or parts of an act in their functional setting.

For an example, take one of the complex wholes from a football system—that of pass defense. It involves many skills such as cross-step running, keeping an advantageous position on the receiver while watching the passer, the ability to intercept the ball, fast starting and stopping, changing of direction, and many other intricate moves. The coach must first start with a clear explanation of the total pass defense including the principal objective of his type of defense, whether it is zone, man-for-man coverage, or a combination. He then demonstrates the types of passes most likely to be thrown in each player's territory and the techniques used to protect against them. A passing scrimmage follows with constructive criticism offered whenever it is appropriate. Any of the above skills taken as a separate unit, entirely removed from the functional setting of a pass scrimmage, and without a connection to the whole pattern, loses its meaning. A drill on cross-stepping, for instance, means nothing to a player unless he can see how the skill is to be applied to the *larger picture* of pass defense. In other words, keep the bigger total constantly in mind.

Actually, the individual physical skills of athletics such as basket shooting, running, blocking, tackling, kicking, batting, throwing, catching, hurdling, and others may be taught better by a combination of part and whole methods. In the most complex movements are submovements which are really component parts of the whole act. These should be practiced as separate entities for the purpose of improving the general efficiency of the complete act. This is also a timesaving device, for it seems wasteful to spend the same amount of time practicing the more easily learned parts of the complex act as is spent on the harder ones, and that is what a player does when he goes through the complete act. Two outstanding exceptions may be gymnastics and diving, where flexibility, strength, and momentum are combined to complete a movement and it is virtually impossible to perform a half or any other fraction of the act. Coaches should not lose sight of the value of going through the entire performance as often as possible for the purpose of consolidating the movements. This is why the learning of fundamentals must be supplemented by frequent scrimmages or actual games. It is important to observe principles when using the combination of the two methods: (1) the learner should have the total pattern of the act pictured in mind as clearly as possible; and (2) the parts should be real with natural dividing points and not artificial segments of the game.

TRIAL AND ERROR

Two concepts of learning—trial-and-error and insight—are usually classed as being opposed to each other. In strict terms, this is probably true; however, insight may be a natural outgrowth of trial and error conducted on a well oriented plan.

Blind trial and error is the exception rather than the rule, for it occurs only when the selected task is far beyond the comprehension of the learner. Instruction should not only help to orient the goal but should also include some ways and means of reaching it; otherwise the motivated learner has no recourse other than wild experimenting. The coach should expect the boy to make mistakes on the field and should not condemn or publicly ridicule him for his errors. He still may be making progress through his mistakes. Certainly the opportunity for making them in the earlier stages of learning should not be denied him, but the mistakes must never be minimized, nor should the mistakes be passed over without an analysis on the part of the teacher and learner. Not to analyze the mistakes is a waste of time and energy, and encourages poor habits.

A more appropriate term than trial and error might be attempt and adjustment. The player usually has a mental picture of the act and some idea of how to attain it. The purpose of good coaching is to start the learner on the right path toward success by limiting the learner's attempts to the moves that have proven to be correct for other athletes. The field psychologists and connectionists are not too far apart in their analysis of the acceptance or elimination of certain moves based on whether or not they bring the learner close to his goal. The learner is making progress when he is able to distinguish and discard inappropriate movements in their conception, that is, as they occur in his mind, without going to the trouble of actually trying them. At the same time, he will select those responses which seem to have possibilities for enabling him to complete his task successfully. A boy learning to place-kick has as his aim the sending of the ball through the uprights. There are many elements to this act and each of them can be varied in different ways. Even if the boy has never kicked before and if he does not have the expert tutelage of a coach, the very nature of the act will lead him to start with a forward swing of his leg. In each successive trial, refinements in the boy's technique will be based on what he learned from previous kicks; however, good coaching prevents much of the initial fumbling and ineffectual search for the correct movement.

Experience is a factor in so-called trial and error learning. The greener the player, the more likely he is to resort to trial and error.

The veteran player when confronted with a problem will search his memory for relevant previous experiences to select the most appropriate action, and the greater his store of experience the more chance he has of coming up with the correct move. For this reason, the coach should use every opportunity to get his inexperienced players into games. Game situations offer many learning situations and add to the player's poise and confidence. The factors of experience and training also have a great effect on preceptual learning. This is illustrated in the case of an inexperienced basketball player guarding a player with the ball in position to shoot. If the offensive man makes a good fake at shooting, he will usually pull the inexperienced player off his feet to block the shot making him helpless to stop the drive for the basket which is sure to follow. The experienced player will perceive in the many mannerisms of the offensive man prior to the fake that, in reality, it is a fake. He will refuse to be pulled off balance and thereby remain in position to prevent the drive for the basket following the fake.

Situations arising in modern sports games must be approached like other educational problems, and the same rules apply. However, there is more external pressure on the athlete than on the boy in the classroom. If the solution calls for a complicated pattern of response or a difficult reforming of previous experiences, trial-and-error behavior often ensues. A defensive player who has been taught how to proceed against several types of offense, and who finds himself confronted with a new type that is merely a variation of one of the standard offenses, usually will be able to adjust himself, experience granted, and make an appropriate response. If, however, he is suddenly faced with something new and different in which he can see no similarity to previous situations, he can only guess as to the correct move on his part. For this reason, coaches should attempt to form principles of defense giving general guides of position and action rather than excessively specific and narrow rules.

INSIGHT

It has been pointed out how trial and error may occur when a wide gap exists between the task and the ability of the learner. Blind trial and error should be avoided if possible and insight substituted for aimless practice or repetition.

Insight may be the sudden (or gradual) understanding of relations between elements of a problem which leads directly to the solving of the problem. It is the light that dawns when a person has pondered over a baffling puzzle and suddenly recognizes the interrelationship of the elements of the puzzle, causing the expression, "Oh, now I see what it is!" Thereafter the solution is merely a matter of reorganizing the elements of the puzzle into a meaningful pattern. Insightful teaching is aimed at an increased understanding of a problem or skill and at the "why" of it. One of the valuable effects of this type of teaching is the development of intelligent self-criticism and self-guidance by the learner. The player not only knows how well his learning is proceeding, but the reasons for his successes and failures. He then makes adjustments in his performance to bring it closer to the image of the perfect performance which he has in mind. Practice on a skill should not be in the form of aimless drill but should be conducted in a constantly changing and improved form, motivated by the goal previously agreed upon by the learner and teacher. This is essentially in agreement with Gestalt psychology, which asserts that insight takes the place of practice or repetition as the key word in the configurationist picture of learning.

These words do not imply that all practice and drill are to be eliminated as useless time wasters, but rather that those periods should not be undertaken until the learner has the "what" and "why" of the act clearly in mind and accepts the need to master a situation by smoothing out rough spots that remain.

Some coaches have been criticized for their lack of good teaching methods on grounds that they do not bother to explain fully the "what" and "why" of an act but insist on the exact imitation of a model. Insightful learning which aims at a complete understanding of all the elements and relationships of an act enables the boy to think for himself and to make personal adaptations according to his concept of the ideal way to perform the act. For example, learning to break up the double play at second base is a situation calling for complete understanding of the "what" by the baserunner. His objective is to delay the throw to first base by the infielder who has tagged second base. He may practice several methods of sliding to interfere with the infielder's relay, because the choice of any particular style will be dictated by the position of the infielder and the direction of his movement as the runner reaches the vicinity of the base. He knows what must be done and does it in the best way he can for the given situation. This is certainly in keeping with the idea of developing the whole boy, and it aids in developing a smart player. Here again, it becomes necessary to point out that the result is more important than the method.

The sudden gaining of insight may be dramatically seen in the illustration of a football player learning to back up the defensive line.

The coach explains the duties of the linebacker, his various positions, and the methods of coming up fast or dropping back for pass defense. Because the boy's principal task is that of coming up and meeting plays at the line of scrimmage, the coach dwells for some length on the keys or cues which should evoke a response from the linebacker. These cues are the various moves of the offensive lineman as they carry out their assignments. The linebacker playing in front of them can watch for the key blocks in the line and determine where the play is most likely to hit. It may take days, weeks, or even years for some boys to learn the art of linebacking, but a coach can tell almost immediately when a boy gets the hang of it. The boy will sense the direction of the play almost at its inception and move to meet it. The secret lies in the ability to sense the direction from "reading" the power blocks which the offensive line is applying at a certain point without concentrating his gaze on the line. His practice thereafter will only serve to smooth out his performance.

Insight may be gradual as well as sudden. The slow transition from hopeless confusion to complete understanding can be just as meaningful as the sudden perception of the whole secret to a problem. Intelligence is a factor in insight, for the intelligent person is more apt to see relationships between the elements of an act or problem than a dull person, especially when the relationships are vague. A coach should constantly bear in mind that if his system calls for the execution of difficult tasks, trial and error may be the only resource for many of his squad, and learning will consequently be delayed. His boys may develop the skills without complete understanding of the "what" and "why," and this means that they will many times be at a loss to know just where the skills apply. Knowledges, too, may be learned in parrotlike fashion, such as using a particular type of defense against certain offenses. The score, the time left to play, and other factors can alter a situation, and if the boys do not have complete understanding of what they learned about defense, they will not be able to adjust it to meet the new situation. Following the insight theory of teaching and learning, a coach would aim constantly at the production of insights, for without them there is no understanding, and without understanding there is no true learning.

SUMMARY

The efforts of players to learn should not be dissipated in fruitless and formless exercises but should be mobilized into lines of endeavor which point to the attainment of some goal or purpose. The player will be motivated to learn some skill or knowledge when he is made aware of the contribution of that skill or knowledge toward making him a better performer and improving the team's chances of winning. Time should not be wasted on incidentals, and the learner's efforts should be concentrated on the parts of an act which are essential to a fine performance. In order for the player to be continually motivated, the goal or purpose which he has in mind must be so desirable that he will be satisfied with nothing less than the accomplishment of that goal.

The perceptual motor skills of sports should be taught in such a manner that they have meaning for the player, that is, so that the player can see their relationship to a functional situation. A combination of the whole and the part methods of teaching seems to be the more efficient manner of coaching. Many phases of the game need to be broken down into component parts and practiced separately, but the players should never lose sight of the place of that part in the larger total setting. Players are not to be criticized for errors which occur as a result of their experimentation when that method happens to be their only recourse in learning. Lack of knowledge or of experience will cause players to resort to trial-and-error behavior; so the job of coaching involves a problem of getting players to understand the "what" and "why" of their acts. Insightful learning aims at complete understanding of all the elements and relationships of the acts, so that the players may make personal adaptations as they see the appropriateness of such action.

Test Questions

1. State, in simple terms, the meaning of orienting the learner in terms of goals.
2. What is meant by the "nub" of an athletic technique?
3. What causes motivation to be self-generated when learning athletic skills?
4. How does a coach decide which are the most essential skills for his athletes?
5. What are the implications for practice in the difference between essentials and incidentals?
6. Name a few "time wasters" with which you are familiar.
7. The satisfaction that comes from success in performing an athletic skill causes the player to repeat it as quickly as possible. What psychological law is thus illustrated?

8. How could the use of an incentive be wasted on an athlete?
9. List a combination of qualities found in practically all good athletes.
10. What determines the value of a skill in the mind of the athlete?
11. Explain the difference between a motor skill and a perceptual motor skill.
12. What are the usual steps followed in learning an athletic skill?
13. When the athlete goes into a "slump" with no improvement apparent, what might a coach do to assist him in "snapping out of it"?
14. Explain the meaning of the "whole" method of teaching. Illustrate, using a sports situation.
15. Is the "part" system of teaching applicable to coaching? Explain.
16. When using a combination of the above two methods, what important principles should be observed?
17. How does coaching eliminate blind trial and error?
18. State a more appropriate term than trial and error in coaching.
19. What is meant by insight? How does it function in sports situations?
20. What is the relationship between "reading" an opponent's movements and insight?

Discussion Questions

1. Does the number of senses involved in a perceptual motor skill have bearing upon the complexity of the skill to be learned?
2. Are not all athletic skills perceptual motor skills to some degree?
3. What is the most important essential in: (1) the 50-yard dash; (2) kicking in football; (3) shooting a basketball; (4) hitting a baseball; (5) making the double play at second base?
4. If a boy has professional potential as a catcher but can be a toprated pitcher for his present competition, should the coach use him as a pitcher?
5. How best can you get your team into top physical condition and make the task enjoyable?
6. Would you agree that a simple explanation of the law of consequences is that if something works, do it again?
7. What are some determining qualities in an athlete that would make a coach decide to use either the whole or part method?

Suggested Readings

BOOKS

1. Adams, W. C. *Foundations of Physical Activity.* Champaigne: Stipes Publishing Co., 1968, pp. 58-74.
2. Broer, Marian. *The Efficiency of Human Movement.* Philadelphia: W. B. Saunders Co., 1960, pp. 222-326.
3. Burns, T. *Fumbling Techniques Illustrated.* New York: The Ronald Press Co., 1957.
4. Burton, William H. *The Guidance of Major Specialized Learning Activities Within the Total Learning Activity.* Cambridge: Harvard University Press, 1944, p. 86.
5. Bunn, John. *Scientific Principles of Coaching.* Englewood Cliffs: Prentice Hall, Inc., 1965, pp. 105-259.
6. Cowell, C. C., and Schwenn Hilda. *Modern Principles and Methods in Secondary School Physical Education.* Boston: Allyn and Bacon, 1964, pp. 173-215, 146-147.
7. Cratty, B. J. *Movement Behavior and Motor Learning.* Philadelphia: Lea and Febinger, 1967, pp. 59-60, 303.
8. Edwards, Don. *Baseball Coach's Complete Handbook.* West Nyack: Parker Publishing Co., 1966.
9. Fitts, P. M. "Perceptual Motor Skill Learning," *Categories of Human Learning.* New York: John Wiley & Sons, Inc., 1965, pp. 177-197.
10. Johnson, S., Updyke, W., Stolberg, D., and Shalfer, W. *A Problem Solving Approach to Health and Fitness.* New York: Holt, Rinehart and Winston, 1966, Chapters 10, 11, and 12.
11. Johnson, G. B. "Motor Learning," *Science and Medicine of Exercise and Sports.* New York: Harper and Bros., 1960, pp. 614-615.
12. Juba, Bill. *Swimming as Taught by Experts.* New York: Arco Publishing Co., Inc., 1961.
13. Julian, Alvin Jr. *Bread and Butter Basketball.* Englewood Cliffs: Prentice Hall, Inc., 1960.
14. Kingsley, Howard. *The Nature and Conditions of Learning.* New York: Prentice Hall, Inc., 1946, p. 86.
15. Moore, Jim, and Micoleaux, T. *Football Techniques Illustrated.* New York: The Ronald Press, Inc., 1962.
16. Skinner, B. F. *Cumulative Record.* New York: Appleton-Century-Crofts, Inc., 1961, pp. 42-48.

17. Slusher, H., and Lockhart, A. *Anthology of Contemporary Readings.* Dubuque: Wm. C. Brown Co., 1966, pp. 296-308.
18. Smith, K. V., and Smith, W. M. *Perception and Motion.* Philadelphia: W. B. Saunders Co., 1962, pp. 1-15.
19. Woodruff, Asahel D. *The Psychology of Teaching.* New York: Longman, Green & Co., Inc., 1948, p. 79.
20. Wright, Wilhemina. *Muscle Function.* New York: Hafner Publishing Co., 1962, pp. 3-26.

Suggested Readings

ARTICLES

1. Alderman, R. B. "Influence of Local Fatigue on Speed and Accuracy in Motor Learning," *Research Quarterly,* Vol. 36-2, May 1965, pp. 135-140.
2. Bevan, William. "Perceptual Learning: An Overview," *Journal of General Psychology,* 1961, pp. 69-99.
3. Broughton, Bob, and Nelson, Dale O. "Verbal Conditioning in Selected Skills." *Scholastic Coach,* Vol. 36-3, November 1967, p. 38.
4. Bryant, Paul. "Defensive Preparation for a Game," *Coach and Athlete,* Vol. XXXI, No. 2, September 1968, pp. 14, 24.
5. Dyer, Pete. "Coaching the High School Kicking Game," *Scholastic Coach,* Vol. 32-8, April 1963, p. 24.
6. Hoitsma, Harry. "Coach's Dilemma." *JOHPER,* Vol. 32-10, December 1961, p. 25.
7. James, Newton E. "Personal Preferences for Method as a Factor in Learning," *Journal of Educational Psychology,* Vol. 53-1, February 1962, pp. 43-47.
8. King, William H., and Irwin, Leslie W. "A Time and Motion Study of Competitive Backstroke Swimming Turns," *Research Quarterly,* Vol. 28, March 1957, p. 257.
9. Litsky, Frank. "Marques Haynes—King of the Court Clowns," *Boy's Life,* February 1968, pp. 28, 51.
10. Lockhart, A. "Conditions of Effective Motor Learning," *JOHPER,* Vol. 38:3, February 1967, p. 26.
11. Maughan, Ralph D. "Discus Throwing Techniques," *Scholastic Coach,* Vol. 34-4, November 1963, p. 23.
12. McKain, Hal. "Scientific Tennis Training," *Athletic Journal,* Vol. XLVI-6, February 1966, pp. 56-57.

13. Meadows, Paul C. "Are We Really Coaching Fundamentals?" *JOHPER*, Vol. 34-4, March 1963, pp. 34-35.
14. Nelson, Dale O. "Improve Performance by Utilizing Fundamental Principles of Movement," *Athletic Journal,* Vol. XXXIX-3, November 1958, p. 26.
15. Pierson, William R. "Note Concerning the Focus of Attention in the Sprint Start," *The Physical Educator,* Vol. XX, October 1963, p. 119.
16. Posner, M. I. "Components of a Skilled Performance," *Science,* Vol. 152, No. 3730, June 24, 1966, pp. 1712-1718.
17. Ryan, E. D. "What Does Psychology Have to Offer Coaches and Trainers?" *Proceedings National College Physical Education Association for Men,* January 1965, p. 37-38.
18. Scharf, R. J., and King, N. H. "Time and Motion Analysis of Competitive Freestyle Swimming Turns," *Research Quarterly,* Vol. 35-1, March 1964, pp. 37-44.
19. Sigerseth, P. O., Grenafer, V. F. "Effect of Foot Spacing on Velocity in Sprints," *Research Quarterly,* Vol. 33, December 1962, p. 599.
20. Surburg, Paul. "Audio, Visual, and Audio-Visual Instruction With Mental Practice in Developing the Forehand Tennis Drive," *Research Quarterly,* Vol. 39-3, October 1968, pp. 728-734.
21. Singer, Robert N. "Understanding the Learning Process," *Athletic Journal,* Vol. 45-3, November 1964, pp. 52-53.
22. Vardell, R. A., Davis, R., and Clagston, H. A. "The Function of Mental Practice in the Acquisition of Motor Skills," *The Journal of General Psychology,* Vol. 29, 1943, pp. 243-250.
23. Veller, Don. "Compendium of Common Sense Principles in Modern Coaching," *Scholastic Coach,* Vol. 28-2, October 1968, pp. 68-74.

Chapter IV
CONTINUITY

"First Things First"

PLANNING FOR CONTINUOUS IMPROVEMENT

A task facing all educators, including coaches, is that of arranging the content of their courses in some sequential order so that the learner has a favorable chance to proceed toward the goals set up for that activity and to provide for the maintenance of the learnings. Since all plans for learning and the improvement of learning must start with the learner himself, a good principle to guide one's teaching or coaching is to start with the learner where he is and take him where you want him to go. To do this properly, a coach must gather a great deal of background material on the individual members of his squad. If he knows their mental level, physiological as well as chronological ages, amount of experience, degree of interest in the sport and amount of skill, he can better plan the experiences which will unfold for them during the practice sessions.

Continuous improvement by a player is thought of as being a process by which the learner acquires more and more mastery of the complex motor activities that make up our sports, the fundamental skills. The first attempts at these fundamentals by the learner are usually awkward, slow, halting, and totally lacking in grace because they are voluntary and the player is experimenting with the responses from each trial. Expert performance is not a mere copy of the same movement done with greater speed but is an entirely new activity pattern. The expert performance involves the functioning and combining of the simple movements, each done with *speed and finesse.* The player is now more selective in his choice of muscle groups to act, some to contract, others to relax. As he repeats the performance over and over again, it smooths out and becomes reflexive rather than voluntary. Thus, in sports activities, proper drill on the more simple movements and wise grading of the exercises from the simple to the complex (providing the "goal set" is present) will lead to the mastery of a complex fundamental involving a series of perfected simple movements. For example, the fundamental of fielding a baseball involves a number of body postures and movements which may be taught by starting with a pickup of a stationary ball. The infielder merely takes one step, scoops the ball into his glove and straightens up. The important features such as leaning forward from the hips, bending the knees, centering the body over the ball and having the left foot forward (for right-handed throwers) can be mastered in the original drill. Fielding becomes more complex as more and more action is added. The athlete will take several steps and field the ball on the bounce being sure that he catches it either just after it hits the ground or at its highest point of bounce. The same simple movements and postures are involved no matter how fast the ball is coming or at what angle it is approaching. The expert fielder still goes through the simple maneuvers, but he does each of them well and with more speed. In teaching the fundamentals of a sport, a teacher (coach) will observe certain principles which should contribute to the development of a better performer:

1. Have a complete knowledge of the correct and incorrect features of the fundamental you are teaching.
2. Select the proper sequence for the presentation of the skills to move from the more simple to the complex.
3. Fit the rate of gradation to the more complex to the learning capacity of the athlete.
4. Stress the essential features of the skill, not the incidentals.
5. Adjust the correctable faults before they become automatized.

This treatment of simple and complex skills is not meant to convey the idea that all coaching is a progression from parts to wholes; for much of the teaching on the practice field starts with experiences in the whole situation, such as a scrimmage to show the relationship of the various parts (fundamentals) to the whole (game). In the illustration of learning to field a baseball, the coach may start the boys on an infield drill of picking up a ball and throwing it to first base in order to show the relationship of the various simple movements to the complex act of playing the infield. The complete complex acts of running, fielding, throwing, and so on, are themselves only units of the game; and when they are being learned and practiced the learner must see them in relation to the whole game in order to have meaning for him.

All units of practice should be in sequential order so that they may reinforce one another and, in so doing, help to make the learner's progress continuous. Some coaches are guilty of haphazard planning of practice schedules, and this results in what is termed "cold-storage" coaching. The drills have no bearing on one another or on the objective for the day. Suppose that the basketball group-work practice schedule for a day includes screening practice, especially between the center and the guards. When the squad is called together there is no emphasis on the deliberate offense or on the plays where the center and guards screen off. The players have gained something from the drill, but the value will be lost unless the learnings are to be put to use in the total situation of a real or dummy scrimmage. Sports fundamentals, like the academic tool subjects, should not be taught in isolation and stored for later use; they should be made to function at the time they are needed. A player can better appreciate the need for the long hours of practicing an offensive maneuver when he gets into a scrimmage or game and sees how it functions to help his team score.

Each practice session or lesson unit should have some goal or objective toward which the learning is directed in order to be effective. The goal may be general in nature, such as the pass attack. This may be regarded as a whole. The various parts of a football pass attack (running, feinting, throwing, catching, blocking) are smaller wholes within themselves. They will lose their value unless they can be seen in relation to the larger wholes, such as pass attack, running attack, punting, punt returns, and so on. They should be explained to the players in terms of their contribution to the entire game of football. They must be offered in a well planned, coherent organization so that the average boy can see their place.

GROWTH

As educators, coaches are concerned with giving practice units (drills and exercises) a form of continuity which will result in the promotion of growth among their players. The term growth refers to mental growth as apart from physical. The separation is purely arbitrary for the two operate simultaneously within the organism; but for the purpose of this discussion, the term growth will refer to the mental item—in reality, to the increase in intellectual capacity. Mental growth can be regarded as everincreasing power to learn, to discern and cope successfully with progressively more difficult intellectual problems. For normal growth, there are some facts that can be relied upon:

1. People develop intellectually at a rate directly proportional to their initial capacity—that is, the bright ones remain bright and the dull ones remain dull.

2. In mental development as in physical, there are extreme individual differences.

3. The rate of increase is rapid in the early years, slows down considerably after the teens, and then declines slowly.

There is reason to believe that some individuals develop abilities in the late college years, and some people feel that the most productive period in life is the middle years. The reason for this apparent contradiction may be that at nineteen, when his mental capacity is at its highest, the youth has not had the experience to use it profitably. The physical, mental, and social traits of most people appear to change in early life. Information, interests, and attitudes change as a result of new experiences, and what seems important to youngsters seems trivial in the eyes of an older boy. This involves a problem of motivation, as many coaches discover when military veterans return to college and resume their athletic pursuits.

Growth is not inevitable. Many factors affect its evolvement. If an athlete lacks mental and emotional potential, he may miss opportunities for growth. The opportunity must be present. An athlete who sees no utility in the skill or knowledge he is to learn, or who feels sure that his efforts will neither be recognized or appreciated by the coaches will lack spirit for the enterprise.

If the coach has been careless about setting the stage for proper learning, if his drills are a series of dull and uninspiring repetitions, if he disregards the levels of achievement already reached by his athletes, and if he ignores the importance of individual differences, he will be hampering his own cause.

A coach, as a teacher, has no desire to defeat his own purpose, yet he may do just that if he disregards other important factors in mental growth, among which is the matter of "pacing" or fitting the task to the individual. In other words, the easy tasks are designated for the weak or uninspired, and the difficult ones for the strong or intelligent. Situations should be difficult enough to challenge the learner but not so difficult that they dismay, discourage, and finally antagonize the learner because of the hopelessness of the situation.

This is to say that the athlete learning a new act will not be enthusiastic about the practice if he feels that the situation is hopeless. If, for example, he does not have the height to master a certain defensive technique in basketball, or as a baseball player he sees an intricate system of signals as mass confusion, he will develop a resistance against the learning situation itself.

This concept must be strictly observed with young, inexperienced players. Care must be taken not to put them into a game or even practice situations which are too complex, too frightening, or beyond their physical strength.

There are several characteristics of growth which have interesting implications for coaching. Growth is continuous, is dependent on aims, develops from basic needs toward higher interests, progresses from the simple toward the abstract and from the crude to the discriminating, and is a process of change. A program of sports learning, in order to be continuous, should have each drill or unit of practice complete in itself but related to other units in such a way that each would contribute to the completion of a larger whole or the attainment of the goal. The units should not be practiced and then stored away for some future use. The skills and knowledges expected to be acquired through the drills and practice sessions must be within the learner's ability. He should be able to see the function and utility of these acquisitions and, in doing so, should acquire the attitude of wanting to succeed. Football drills on faking, pivoting, buttonhooking and cutting have utility only for pass receivers. Because all players are not called upon to perform them in games, these drills for an entire squad are meaningless. Some players are physically unable to perform the acts; others have not had enough experience to comprehend the necessary steps to each of them. For these players, the drills have no meaning and hence no appeal.

Long range planning is fine in any program, but a coach would be wise to concentrate his teaching program on the experiences which have immediate meaning for the players. Coaches have been known to use valuable practice time lecturing on the social and moral values of participation in sports. While the implication is not denied, the situation is too far removed to have much significance to the boy in his present surroundings. He is more interested in learning how to stop the offense of the team he will meet in the next game.

Each skill, each bit of knowledge about the game, is a small, complete unit in itself, but is has a place in the larger picture—the game. The value of the knowledges and skills is greatly enhanced if the player is able to generalize about them in such a way that they have greater utilization for him. Skill in drag bunting is valuable , but if the baseball player has no knowledge of when to use it and when not to use it the value is limited. If, however, he is cognizant of the limitations as well as the advantages of the act, he will be more skillful in its use.

In teaching involved maneuvers such as the quarterback spin and ball handling from the T formation, a coach will find that most of his players are very awkward in their first attempts but gradually smooth out their performance as practice continues. The coach's job here is to get the boys to focus on the key to or nub of the correct act, such as balance with weight over the spinning foot. As insight develops, they will drop more and more of the awkward, irrelevant moves and substitute smooth, polished action. The nub of the act is of first importance. If this is submerged in a hail of directions and orders for each little phase of the act, the boys will be hopelessly confused, and their progress will be retarded.

As the player grows in understanding, he improves in efficiency. The knowledges and insights which arrive as the player goes about the task of learning a phase of the game enable him to see the folly of extraneous effort. As a result, he drops the unessentials to the act, perfects the simple parts of it and combines them into an effective operation. The coach's teaching, then, should be in the direction of encouraging complete understanding of the "what" and "why" of an act as well as the "how."

Growth in mental power is potential in every squad. It awaits effectual provocation through enthusiastic coaching; it involves organizing the program to stimulate the boys to greater efforts to learn the game.

EMERGENCE OF MEANING

In order for the entire learning program of a game to have the quality of continuity, the various phases of the game must contribute to the emergence of meaning. Each drill, each lecture, each explanation must aid in unlocking the door to complete understanding of what is required and suggest to the learner the shortest and most efficient route to a successful performance.

By emergence of meaning is meant the awareness that the material to be learned has a definite form or pattern and the various elements have a certain relationship to each other and to other materials. Material that is utterly lacking in form or pattern is extremely difficult to learn and probably never is fully learned. Most students of psychology have undergone the experiment of trying to memorize a list of nonsense syllables as opposed to a list of related words. The former took much more time than the later because the syllables were meaningless.

The system of numbering football plays is a good illustration of either meaningful or meaningless material. Arbitrary or random selection of numbers to denote plays will result in a hodgepodge of numerals, each having a separate meaning but entirely unrelated to one another. A definite form or pattern should start with numbers for the backfield men and numbers for each offensive hole. For example, starting with the right side of the offensive line, the

numbers should be even running from 8 to 0. From the center to the
left, the numbers should be odd or 1 to 9. (See Figure 1.) The
offensive backs could be numbered from one to four. The snap

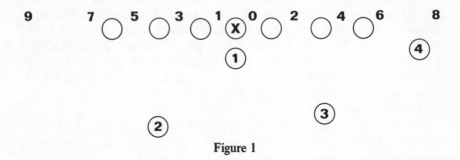

Figure 1

number can be prefixed to the play number, so that the complete
play call would be a 3-digit number. Thus, a play numbered 234
would indicate a buck over the guard with the ball to be snapped on
the second audible after the team is set. (See Figure 2.)

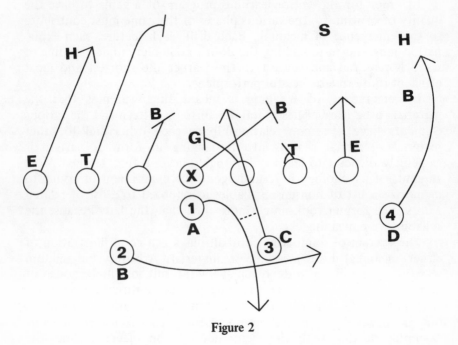

Figure 2

Lettering or phrasing can be added to indicate a certain type of play. For instance, the number 245-I could indicate an inside trap on the defensive tackle with 1 giving the ball to 4 on a crisscross. In this case, the letter "I" indicates an inside trap. (See Figure 3.)

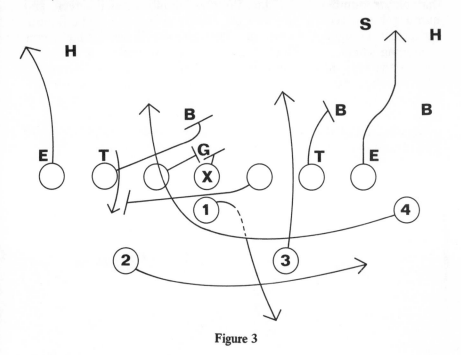

Figure 3

Multiple defenses in modern football often make it necessary for a quarterback to change the play originally called in the huddle when his team gets set at the line of scrimmage. These commonly are termed "automatics." In order to give some meaning to the call, the following system is offered.

Let us assume that the play called in the huddle was #234 but the quarterback, after setting his team at the line of scrimmage, wishes to change to play #21, an end run. The quarterback would call #221, the "key" number being the snap signal 2. Thus, any play number called at the line of scrimmage, prefaced by the same snap number called in the huddle, becomes an automatic call. Any first digit other than the one called in the huddle makes the number a "dummy" and the original play will be the one run. For example, number #321, #464, or #132 would be "dummies." The snap number is the key or "nub" to the plan and has meaning for the team but is meaningless to the opponents who do not know what was called in the huddle.

Some basketball offensive patterns are numbered similar to football plays, except that there is no snap signal. Each of the five positions is numbered. The man playing that position has that number. A call of 321 by the offensive captain or play maker means that player number 3 will start the play, number 2 will screen, and number 1 will receive the ball for a shot if possible.[1] The famous basketball Triangular Continuity Offense was a series of patterns producing screens and blocks which set up a player for a shot. The key to the system was the maxim "(1) pass, (2) cut for basket, (3) take your receiver's place" (if he did not get a return pass from his receiver). When the player learned the maxim and executed each move, the entire meaning of continuity emerged. After acquiring an understanding of the what and why of triangularing, the player could drill until movements became automized. (See Figure 4.)

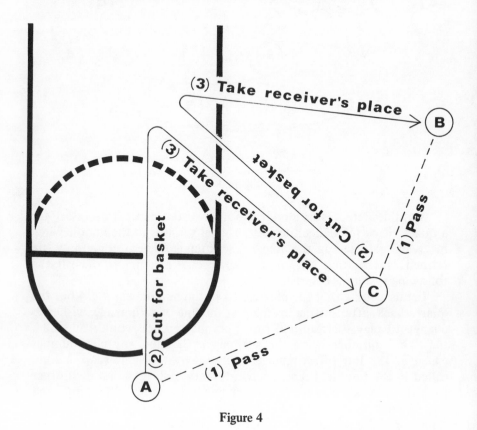

Figure 4

[1]Hogeland, Zeke. "Instant Offense: Attacking by the Numbers," *Scholastic Coach*, November 1963, Vol. 33, No. 3, pp. 22-24.

A passed to C and cut for the basket. He did not receive a return pass. When C passed to B and cut for the basket, A took his (C's) place, thereby setting up a screen for C. If C did not get the ball he takes B's place, setting up a screen for B. B may pass to A, who is now out in C's original spot, and cut for the basket. The other players will get involved whenever they receive a pass.

In baseball, control signals between catcher and pitcher can be made meaningful by using four points on the catcher as target locations. For example, the knees as low targets and the shoulders as high targets. Digit signals 1, 2, 3 and 4 designate the four target areas and remain constant regardless of whether the batter is right or left-handed. #1 digit calls for a low outside pitch, #2 digit for a low inside pitch, 3 digits for high outside and 4 digits for high inside. Such numbering provides meaningful association for the players in that #1 and #2 are the lowest numbers for the low pitches, while #3 and #4 are the highest numbers for high pitches. Also, #1 and #3 are *odd* numbers for *outside* pitches. The letter "O" is the beginning letter for both words, giving another association. (See Figure 5.)

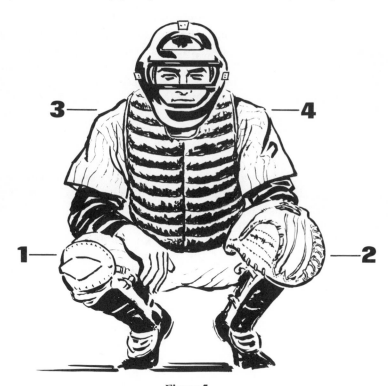

Figure 5

It has been said that the emergence of meaning in a learning situation goes through the following stages:
1. The learner recognizes that the material to be learned has a hazy, incomplete form or pattern.
2. He acquires a general idea of how to proceed.
3. He eliminates all moves except those that lead toward success.
4. All the details of the problem finally fall into place, presenting the learner with a complete, distinct picture of the material and its use.

This cycle probably indicates why, in giving directions, a teacher should first explain the general nature of the material at the level of the learner's insight. As an example, a basketball coach in explaining a new zone defense would tell first whether the defense is designed principally to pressure outside or close-in shooters, and then whether it requires a one-, two-, or three-man front line and is to be played as a straight zone or a combination. From that point the various details would have to be taken up with the individual players, explaining each man's responsibility and the best method of caring for it. This is a natural method of learning, beginning with an undifferentiated whole and proceeding toward the mastery of detail. Learning is facilitated by the use of meaningful material. The meaningfulness of learning material is dependent upon the following basic conditions:
1. The player's experience in his present position or similar positions and his general knowledge of the game.
2. The player's talent for relating a new situation to one in his past. If a new situation has enough factors similar to those already familiar to the player, he should adjust to the new problem.
3. The logical formation of the skills or knowledges to be learned. The athlete must be able to recognize how each part of the new material fits into the larger whole of an offensive or defensive pattern.
4. The functionality of the skill or knowledge to be learned. If the player can see that the new material has value for him, that is, that it could make him a better player, he will be motivated to learn it.

In summarizing these points in application to a sport situation, it seems safe to conclude that the coach should fit his system to the abilities of his players, offer the learning experiences in sequential order, organize the material to be learned in a recognizable pattern, and make the experiences as similar as possible to game situations.

TRANSFER OF LEARNING

One of the purposes of a logical organization or continuity of learning experiences is to make the experience more meaningful to the learner. That is, they will have for him a meaning which goes beyond the immediate situation. Certain fundamental principles will become obvious, and he will form generalizations which he can transfer to a new situation containing elements similar to those of the first. A well coached player, it would seem, is one who can effectively bring to a new situation the training he received in another. This is made possible through his ability to attach wider meanings to those practice experiences than the immediate factors involved. As he learns to tackle a walking player, he also learns to tackle running, twisting, dodging players. An outfielder learning to throw to a cut-off man for a play at home plate is also learning to throw to any base.

This is not to say that transfer of skill is general, for there is conclusive proof that transfer is highly specific and occurs only when the practiced movements are identical. In other words, there are few basic motor skills which can be transferred from one game to another. It does not necessarily follow that a good basketball player will be a good baseball player. Probably there is some transfer of skill between motor activities, but only when they require the same body manipulations, although the learners might not recognize the similarity between the two acts. For example, the same muscle groups act almost identically in throwing a javelin as throwing a baseball from the outfield. Similarity is also found in throwing a forward pass in football and a catcher's throw to second base. Transfer will occur, however, when the learner recognizes the similarity between the elements of a new situation and those of a former situation in which he learned certain reactions. To bring this condition about successfully involves good teaching.

Coaches have been known to wail: "We went over that situation time and time again, but in the game the kids forget." The chances are that the boys did not forget—they never really knew what they were supposed to know. They did not learn, did not comprehend, did not generalize. If they had done so, there would have been a transfer of that learning from the practice situation to the game. Transfer depends on the amount of meaning that has gone into the learning—the amount of understanding the athlete really has about the thing he is supposed to be learning.

For instance, a basketball coach may have assigned his only big rebounder to defend against the "post" man in the opponent's attack because he wants him to be in position to play the backboard. In the course of the game, the opponent may move away from the post position to the backcourt while a teammate shifts to the post. If the big rebounder did not fully understand the purpose of the defense, he might follow his man to the backcourt, thereby removing himself from the rebound area. If he understands his prime responsibility, he would call for a switch in defensive assignments with a teammate who is now guarding the new post man so that he would be in position to get the rebounds. In the latter case, the boy comprehended the real purpose of the team's defensive alignment, and he knew that a change in the offensive pattern called for a change in the defense. Recognition of the elements of a new situation are necessary if learning is to be transferred to the new situation.

Because the transfer of learning from one situation to another calls for the recognition of the interrelatedness of elements, it seems safe to say that transfer is really a test of insight. When the essential principle involved is recognized in both situations, the correct response can be expected. The ability to comprehend the theory behind an experience, to generalize the problem and its solution, makes it possible to adjust to a new experience in which the learner recognizes components identical with those of the original experience. A good example of this type of learning can be seen in the play of a defensive end who has been taught to play against double teaming by driving forcefully into the inside man of the double team. In the practice sessions he may have worked against a double team formed by a slot back and fullback. In a game, the double team may be formed by a back and running guard. The inside man in this situation is the guard, but the principle of hitting the inside man holds because it is a double-team situation. The end in this case will drive into the guard when he recognizes the identical elements and applies the principle.

If the coaching is mechanical instead of insightful, the boys may appear to be well trained when they go through routine performances; but if the players are suddenly faced with an unexpected situation which may be unlike the training situation only in one or two respects, they will fail to adjust to it because of their lack of real understanding—their failure to see the meaning of the training.

Another illustration of this point may be seen in the coaching of a defensive line to slant charge and to protect territory. The theory behind the slanting line against certain formations is to slant the defensive players across the heads of the offensive players in order to prevent them from going down field against the secondary defense. In the straight charge to protect territory, the important principle is to keep the defensive men together as a close unit in order to protect the territory in front of them. A slanting line which was coached to understand the theory behind the slant would play the offensive man, no matter how they shifted their positions or split their spacing. Each offensive man would line up in such a position that he could slant across the head of his opponent and thus prevent him from going down field. In the case of the territorial charge, meaningful coaching would prevent this line from shifting or widening out with opponents who split off, because the underlying principle is that of protecting their territory regardless of the position of the offense.

Good teaching which encourages generalizing will call for the relating of practice drills or experiences in such a way that what is established in the mind of the player in that experience will contribute to his advantage in future experiences.

Transfer cannot be regarded as absolute. We call attention to its uncertainty in two respects: (1) there may not be enough identical factors between the old and new situation to instigate a recall and transfer; or (2) recall may occur because of the similarity of some factors, but utter dissimilarity in a few key factors may make the transfer of the old response a grave error.

For example, a baseball team may have learned to expect a bunt with men on first and second base with none out. They will hold the runner close at second base to make it more difficult for him to advance to third on the sacrifice. However, late in the game with the batting team behind by a few runs, it is reasonable to expect the batting team to save its "outs" and be hitting away. Recognizing this, the defensive team will play loose. On the other hand, with a pitcher or a notoriously weak hitter at bat, the chances are that the hitter will elect to sacrifice in order to escape the double play. The situation of men on base and none out is identical, but the elements of score, inning, and personnel make the situation different. It appears then that training should also include the ability to differentiate; that is, to see the basic differences between situations so that persons do not react alike to all situations that appear alike.

One factor or element of difference may be very important. Meaningful learning will have to include experiences which not only allow the learner to form generalizations applicable to new situations but also train the learner to distinguish the basic elements in each situation so as to determine whether or not the generalization will apply.

CRAMMING

A method of coaching which may serve to neutralize the quality of continuity in the teaching program is that of cramming. This statement is not to be construed as an indictment against all forms of cramming, for there may be much good derived from one type and much harm from another. Cramming falls into two types: (1) the sudden introduction of something entirely new and concentrating all the time and energy into the learning of it, and (2) a skeletal review of all the learning that has gone before.

The first type is exemplified in the practice of giving a team on the eve of a game an entirely new series of plays or a new defensive formation. The entire practice period is devoted to mastering the details of the new material, and little time is left for anything else. This type of cramming has the advantage of being new and will probably remain in the memories of the athletes at least overnight.

However, the disadvantages far outweigh this point. For instance, there is a great expenditure of physical and mental energies that might well have been used to reinforce the learning of plays and techniques used during the regular season. Moreover, there is no assurance that the new material has been firmly fixed in the minds of the players. It is certain that the short period of time does not allow for automatization. The players will be left with feelings of doubt concerning the reliability of the new "stuff" under game conditions. The sudden introduction of new material just before a game also disregards the factors of time, repetition, and distribution of practice which are regarded as being advantageous to learning.

One of the most serious consequences which may befall a team as a result of cramming of this sort is a loss of morale. The players may gain the impression that the coach is pinning his hopes for victory on the effectiveness of the new material. If it should then fail in the game, the players could easily reason that all is lost because, if the coach had confidence in the old material learned earlier in the season, he would not have ignored it at the last moment.

The second type of cramming, that of repeating in summarized form all of the learning previously covered, may be regarded as an aid to learning. An example of this type of cramming is seen when the coach devotes part of the final workout prior to the game to a review of the important points about the opponents and a drill on the important phases of his own system. This may call for rapidly running through plays and defensive patterns as well as questioning the players on their knowledge of the scouting reports.

A definite plan for the season is a good teaching instrument. It can be refined to include weekly and daily workouts so that the coach can, at any time, determine how much work has been accomplished, how much remains to be done, and how much time has been spent on any particular part of the game. This knowledge is a help in deciding which phases of the system to stress during the cramming session. This type of planning encourages the use of good continuity in the drills and other experiences with consideration for making them realistic, distributing the work periods, repeating just often enough, and seeing that the players understand the underlying principle behind the learned movements. These are the foundations upon which the good coach's system is built and, if it is solid, the coach may safely call for a cramming session in which the old regular plays are revived, half-forgotten moves are relearned, the game strategy is organized anew, and new excitement is felt by the squad. A disadvantage of this type of cramming is that it requires rigid adherence to the prearranged teaching plan.

Students often resort voluntarily to this second type of cramming in preparing for academic tests. Various reasons are given for their actions. To some students, cramming makes them feel secure—they know they have reviewed the field. To realize that they have made an extra effort by cramming may ease their conscience, whether they have learned anything or not. Applying these observations to the athletic situation, it seems safe to conclude that this form of cramming affords a tension release and at the same time intensifies the importance of the coming event. The coaching staff might easily be included in the group who feel the ease of their conscience, knowing that an extra effort has been made to ready the team. The intensification of the importance of the game should never, of course, be carried to the point where it rebuilds tensions which would hinder performance.

Some authors regard another forced draft style of teaching as cramming—the practice of offering large masses of material to the learner, much of which requires great powers of concentration as well as numerous skills on the part of the learners. The team may find it impossible to master all of the plays (offensive and defensive) because of the limited time allowed. As a result, it looks like a team inexperienced in carrying out assignments. Because the players do not have sufficient time to understand thoroughly the principles involved or the theory behind each play or formation, they confuse the elements of one situation with those of another. For example, they may get their offensive assignments confused or cover the wrong person or territory on defense. These are cases of negative transfer caused by one job of learning interfering with another.

Had less material been presented in a sequential order, aiming at continuous improvement, striving for mental growth, making sure that the experiences were meaningful to the players, and encouraging the formation of generalizations and differentiations, the job of learning would have been simplified instead of being made more complex.

OVERCOACHING AND STALENESS

Modern sports have brought upon the coaches and players many pressures, all of them centering about the desire for winning teams. In his desire to do the best possible job, the coach may often overlook the important factor of limits. There are limits to the amount of work the players can stand, the amount of knowledge they can assimilate, and the length of time they can be emotionally stirred. There are also limits to the degree of stereotypeness that can be expected in the performance of each player. The coach's enthusiasm for his task might actually result in an acute case of over-coaching.

There are several types of overcoaching, but three cases may be recognized as definite symptoms. In the first case, a coach may think that his way of performing a skill (if not his own, some adopted method) is the one and only correct method of performing that skill. His reasons for so thinking may have no scientific foundation, and they might actually be based on his preference for uniformity. Such an attitude overlooks the concept of individual differences and results in frustrations caused by his effort to force conformance upon players whose habits and skills are unsuited to that particular type of action. On the team level, this kind of overcoaching may be seen in forcing men to play a type of offense to which they are wholly unsuited, physically and psychologically. A football team made up of slow, powerful, methodical individuals is best suited to a power offense; a team composed of alert and imaginative players is at its best with a multiple wide-open offense. The same may be said for basketball where the offense should suit the temperaments of the players. It would be foolhardy to expect tall, heavy, methodical, average-speed boys to play a fast-breaking, free-lance type of game.

In the second case, a coach may have the habit of continually pouring out information to his team. It is bad strategy for a teacher to tell all he knows in the first few meetings of the class, for it leaves him without ammunition when the students start challenging his knowledge. It would seem wiser to have something in reserve to satisfy the curiosity of the more precocious students.

Another good reason for limiting the amount of information to be remembered is that the players may not have sufficient time to consolidate all they know. Instead of exercising the skills they have attained to date, they will be thinking about what they are "supposed to do in this case." Overcoaching of this sort makes a player lose self-confidence and ease of action. He will think too much about "what" and "why" when he is supposed to do something. At this point, some waggish coach will admonish a troubled player to "stop thinking, you're weakening the team." Obviously, the players must receive a respite from further instruction and given a chance to learn what has already been presented until they react reflexively instead of rationalizing each move.

In the third case, a coach may keep his players at their maximum or psychological limits of learning and performance for an extended period. The practical limit is that point reached in practice which is below the maximum or best efforts of the learner. The potential of physiological is the limit reached when the person is highly motivated and expands all his energy in acquiring the knowledges and skills he is supposed to master. During games and even during some phases of practice, the players should be expected to perform at their maximum, but if forced to maintain a learning level equal to their potential for many weeks, they will go stale.

Staleness may be defined as a condition in which an individual not only seems to be learning at a slow rate but also appears to have lost much of the ability already acquired. Physical staleness may be due to overwork, and the coach can get a clue from observing the weight charts or checking the appetites of his players. Loss of weight and lack of desire for food are indications of staleness. Others are irritability, depression, and loss of skill. The tremendous amount of social pressure to succeed in athletics may often cause a player to fret and worry over his performance to the point where he is exhausted before he starts to compete. It seems safe to assume that a team constantly overworked and pressured is certain to become mentally and physically fatigued.

In reality, our sports are games and, as such, are supposed to be founded on an element of play. When a game ceases to be play and takes on the element of work, it loses the quality which attracted the boys to it. Whenever a physical activity is regarded by a person as fun or recreation, it is capable of capturing his interest and stimulating him to long and arduous efforts. Whether the efforts are work or play depends upon his reasons for participating. One important factor, that his participation is voluntary, has a great effect on his attitude.

A boy may expend a tremendous amount of energy in the drills and exercises of preseason practice. To him, it is fun—real play— because it is something he wants to do. There is no external compulsion connected with it; he does it because he likes it, and because his mental attitude decrees that it is play it produces less fatigue than does work. Even pros like it. The same boy, going through the identical routine late in the season may have to be driven. His performance shows signs of deteriorating. The reason is that the sport has become drudgery in his mind. He no longer gets a physical and mental "lift" from practice. It becomes increasingly difficult to get him keyed up for games. When this point is reached, it would be well for the coach to examine his program and see if he has not been keeping his boys at the physiological limit for too long a period.

A weekly schedule for the playing season of team sports which should aid in preventing staleness might follow these lines as main objectives:

Monday	Scrimmage for the players who did not participate in the last game. Give regulars a light workout including a review of material in which they appeared ragged.
Tuesday	Introduce new plays (if any). Long dummy scrimmage.
Wednesday	Scrimmage. Use new plays with old. Work some against opponent's style of attack and defense.
Thursday	Short skeleton scrimmages. Work principally against yesterday's weaknesses. Dummy scrimmage own stuff with full group.
Friday	Short, snappy workout. Review week's work and fix in mind the material to be used Saturday.

Some coaches, believing that it aids in readying a team, eliminate either Monday or Friday workouts when the season is far advanced. Although it is a matter of opinion, it seems safe to assert that the psychologically ready team is usually physiologically ready, for they will not come to the game with the right mental attitude if they are overworked, bored, and fatigued. When a team displays the symptoms of staleness, the coach should ease up on his practice schedule, change the routine if it has become monotonous, eliminate superfluous plays, check on the eating and sleeping habits of players and, in general, allow the boys to "play" the game instead of working at it.

This is not to say that coaches are guilty of overworking their athletes. Recent studies show that the physiological limits can be extended much beyond what was formerly considered the ultimate. Our great modern champions in all sports are now doing as much in warm-up as former champions did in an entire practice period.

FORM AND ACCURACY vs. SPEED

Any person who has ever attempted to learn a skill knows that his rate of learning is not a smooth, steady form of progression but is rather an irregular process, sometimes fast, sometimes slow, and at times arrested to the point where skill is actually lost. The skills which make up modern sports are very complex in nature and, as in all complex movements, the learner is almost bound to strike plateaus or slumps in which his progress comes to a halt. Coaches are insistent upon good form in the performance of the various acts required of their players, and yet they strive for increased speed in the execution of those acts. The boy who is learning the act usually arrives at his own decision to concentrate on either speed or form. When a learner regards a task as being complex, he is likely to concentrate for a time on one phase of the act which might be form, accuracy or speed. Such concentration of effort might be very advantageous in the long run, but for the time being it will result in a period of no all-round improvement.

As has been pointed out previously in this book, learning a complex motor skill is not merely a matter of speeding up the performance of a simple act. It calls for learning new responses and new organizations, dropping some inappropriate gestures and substituting more relative ones. In the early stages of learning, form and accuracy may be stressed for some skills, but as the learning proceeds into its later stages emphasis should be placed on *refinement* and *precision.* Precision is characterized by greater smoothness, economy, stability, rhythm, *speed,* and exactness.

The overemphasis of any one phase of a skill or act may result in a loss of all-round effectiveness. This may happen when a baseball coach dwells for long periods on the cross-step by the runner in stealing a base. When the players concentrate on the cross-step alone, they are very likely to become hesitant and awkward in making the second and third steps which are also very important in maintaining the rhythm of the whole act.

Acts of skill are often regarded as not being as adaptable to rhythmical organizations as verbal materials, but coaches are well aware that certain athletic skills are aided by the adoption of a rhythmical pattern of movement. Such acts as the golf swing, swimming strokes, football pass and punt may be broken up into units which can be perceived together in serial order, each one blending and flowing into the next.

The purpose of emphasizing form in athletic skills is to improve the total act. Anyone who has coached a boy to throw a forward pass knows that when the boy masters the correct form of throwing, his accuracy improves greatly. It makes the difference between being a good forward passer or being a mere thrower. Balance and "follow through" are the most important elements of the act, and very few boys seem to have the natural ability to have their bodies under control while they are throwing the ball. Most passers would probably show great improvement if they were made to start with the correct stance, step in the direction of the throw, bring the ball forward close to the head so as not to pull the body off balance, and follow through putting the weight on the forward foot. There are many other factors to good forward passing, such as gripping the ball, faking, staying within the protective pocket, tilting the nose of the ball, and so on, but these are additional items to the basic act. The correct form has to do with the control of the body so as to make the movement one of smooth progression.

Coaches might consider that in the question of accuracy versus speed the effort should be applied according to the requirements of efficiency. This means that if the purpose of an offensive skill is to get position on the defensive man, the emphasis should be on speed, whereas, in such acts as hitting a tennis ball, place kicking, basket shooting, and the like, the emphasis should be on accuracy. Every fundamental of a sport can be examined for its most important aspect. This would determine the direction of the emphasis when learning the fundamental.

The direction of emphasis might not always result in improvement in one direction to the exclusion of all others. Some experiments indicated that learners emphasizing speed in a skill developed accuracy even to a greater extent than those who made accuracy the primary aim. Both groups acquired the same amount of speed of execution, but the form of the accuracy group was smoother. It may be that certain types of skills are learned more easily when performed fast rather than slowly and methodically. There are some skills, such as pole vaulting, that lay emphasis on both speed and perfection of movement. Another example is the skill required to play Chopin piano music; one must not only learn the pattern of movement represented in the piece but also acquire the ability to execute the pattern at great speed. The art of basketball dribbling approximates this skill somewhat, for the success of the player depends on his ability to twist, turn change direction, change hands, and to do all of these things at high speed.

Another consideration, basic to the development of skill is the proper rate of speed which may not be the maximum but is an optimum pace for a particular activity. The rate at which some football movements are performed is of utmost importance. A good punter, for instance, gets his kick away under two seconds (usually between 1.6 and 2 seconds). When learning to punt, a boy may take longer than two seconds while he establishes the proper form and when he attempts to speed up his kick he will usually lose a great deal of effectiveness. The answer for this problem is not to relearn the old slow pace but to acquire a new pace habit. During punting drills, the boy may acquire a pace habit which is much slower than the optimal because he becomes lazy, or indifferent, or he actually may be unaware that he is slowing down. During a game, he is afraid of having his kick blocked so he speeds up the performance which is a change in the pace habit, and the results may be just as disastrous as though he were forced to change his kicking form. Other examples are batting practice against straight, slow pitching and basketball shooting at slow, deliberate speed. Swimming offers an excellent example of how the wrong pace can do real harm when sprinters are put through the same long distance workouts as distance swimmers to build up stamina. The slow pace is done with a deeper body angle than in sprinting. In addition, the high bow wave which builds up in sprinting is virtually absent in the slower distance swims. The factors of the slow, over-distance workout are so unlike those of the sprint that not only will a different pace habit develop but faulty technique may also creep in.

The implication for coaching in these examples is that many practice drills and experiences should be conducted at game speed that approximates game conditions in order that optimal pace habits may be acquired.

In conclusion, it seems safe to say that in the learning of athletic skills which require form, accuracy, and speed, the coach should strive for form and accuracy in the early stages of learning, but not at a slow speed. As the learner progresses, the coach should insist on the boy increasing his speed to the rate at which he will perform in games. Subsequent practice sessions should include drills done at maximum speed to increase the optimum pace.

SUMMARY

The drills or experiences which the coach offers his players as a method of learning should be arranged in an order of progress which will promote continuous improvement. The various skills and knowledges should not be learned in isolation and stored for future use; rather they should be learned as integral parts of some larger whole in which the use of that part is seen to function. In order to contribute to the process of mental growth, the learnings which the players are expected to absorb should be difficult enough to challenge their abilities but not beyond their capacities to accomplish. The material to be learned should have a definite form or pattern that is easily recognized and related to other phases of the game already learned.

Coaching should strive for the production of insights. If a player understands the essential principle of an act, he can generalize and transfer his learning from an original situation to one in which the elements are essentially the same as the original. Cramming—fixing in mind the learnings which have taken place earlier but which may have been half forgotten—aids the process of continuity. Other types of cramming are to be avoided, as they may cause new learnings to interfere with old and result in confusion within the mind of the player.

Because of the danger of going stale, the team should not be kept at a high pitch emotionally for long periods, and the practice periods should not be allowed to become stereotyped and monotonous. When a sport loses its element of fun and becomes drudgery, it is time for the coach to call a halt and examine his program for faults. In dealing with the question of form versus accuracy in coaching skills, a coach should analyze each fundamental to decide its most important aspect for efficient performance and place the emphasis where it is needed. Form may be emphasized in the early stages of learning for most athletic skills, but the player should ultimately strive for good form at game speed.

Test Questions

1. Define continuous improvement in athletic skills.
2. Explain how the smooth performance of the skilled athlete became reflexive rather than voluntary.
3. What principles should the coach follow in teaching the fundamentals of sports skills to athletes?

4. Explain growth in athletes in terms of intellectual capacity.
5. What factors may prohibit growth?
6. How does the concept of pacing affect the learning process, especially in young players?
7. Why should the material learned in a practice have a quality of immediacy?
8. What effect does form or pattern have on the learning process? Explain.
9. List the stages in the emergence of meaning which the learner experiences in new situations.
10. The meaningfulness of material to be learned by athletes depends on four basic conditions. Explain how they operate to facilitate learning.
11. Why does it not necessarily follow that a good basketball player will be a good baseball player?
12. In order for transfer to occur, what must the learner see in the new situation?
13. What is the effect of insight on transfer?
14. Explain how the ability to generalize and to differentiate affect transfer.
15. How might cramming affect morale? Would it ever result in a feeling of security?
16. Explain how cramming could result in negative transfer.
17. How could a failure to observe the concept of individual differences result in overcoaching?
18. How does attitude affect the physiological limit of athletes, especially in practice?
19. List some common symptoms of staleness exhibited by athletes.
20. In the early stages of learning athletic skills, should form, accuracy, or speed be stressed?
21. What is the purpose of emphasizing form in athletic skills?
22. In the question of accuracy versus speed, what will determine the direction of effort?
23. Why is pace so important in the process of learning athletic skills?

Discussion Questions

1. At what period in a season is a team most apt to go stale?
2. Should essentials be taught first, or should the coach strive for the performance which will show the best improvement regardless of proper sequence?
3. Is ease in the emergence of meaning affected more by an athlete's intelligence or his perceptual ability?
4. Is it important to justify immediately the reason for practicing a certain technique and how it fits into a game situation?
5. You are coaching at the junior high school level and have a boy who blocks many shots. You realize that later in his development he will not be able to do this. Would you change the boy's style of play at the present time?
6. Why is a good plan occasionally to practice some athletic skills such as basket shooting and punting at a pace faster than game speed?
7. Should a player be given as much information as possible about the material to be learned on the theory that the more he receives the more he will learn?

Suggested Readings

BOOKS

1. Barret, M., Biles, F., Harvey, V., et al. *Foundations for Movement.* Dubuque: Wm. C. Brown Co., 1968, Chapter 7.
2. Crow, L. D., and Crow, A. C. *Educational Psychology.* New York: American Book Co., 1958, pp. 63-81, 141-168.
3. Davis, Elwood C. and Wallis, E. T. *Toward Better Teaching in Physical Education.* Englewood Cliffs: Prentice Hall, Inc., 1962, p. 115.
4. Karpovitch, Peter V. *Physiology of Muscular Activity.* Philadelphia: W. B. Saunders Co., 1965, pp. 199-205.
5. Kretch, David, and Crutchfield, Richard S. *Elements of Psychology,* New York: Alfred A. Knopf, 1961.
6. Larson, L. A., and Yocum, R. D. *Measurement and Evaluation in Health, Physical Education and Recreation Education.* St. Louis: C. V. Mosby Co., 1951, pp. 161-2.

7. Ley, Katherine, and Miller, Donna-Mae. *Individual and Team Sports for Women.* Englewood Cliffs: Prentice Hall, Inc., 1962, p. 4.
8. Moorehouse, Laurence E., and Miller, Augustus T. *Physiology of Exercise.* St. Louis: C. V. Mosby Co., 1953.
9. Ramsey, Jack. *Pressure Basketball.* Englewood Cliffs: Prentice Hall, Inc., 1965, pp. 188-189.
10. Reidman, Sarah. *The Physiology of Work and Play.* New York: Holt, Rinehart and Winston, 1950, pp. 102-143.
11. Ricci, Benjamin. *Physiological Bases of Human Performance.* Philadelphia: Lea and Febinger, 1967, pp. 30-34.
12. Townsend, Edward A., and Burke, Paul. *Learning for Teachers.* New York: The Macmillan Co., 1962, pp. 115-134.
13. Travers, Robert M. *Essentials of Learning.* New York: The Macmillan Co., 1964.

Suggested Readings

ARTICLES

1. Adler, Jack D. "Make Golf Simple for the Beginner," *JOHPER,* Vol. 26-4, April 1957, p. 54.
2. Briggs, George, and Naylor, James. "Relative Efficiency of General Training Methods as a Function of Transfer Task Complexity," *Journal of Experimental Psychology,* Vol. 64, 1962, pp. 505-512.
3. Cureton, Thomas K. "Progressive Training and Avoidance of Staleness," *Health and Fitness in the Modern World,* Athletic Institute, 1961.
4. Grieve, Andrew W. "Are You Coaching or Overcoaching?" *Athletic Journal,* XLVII-3, November 1966, pp. 42-43, 55.
5. Griffin, T. "Control Continuity for the Small Team," *Scholastic Coach,* Vol. 37, November 1967, pp. 20-21.
6. Hendrix, John W. "Sequence Drills for Intercollegiate Tennis Team Practice," *JOHPER,* Vol. 27-5, May-June 1956, p. 44.
7. Henry, Franklin M. "Coordination and Motor Learning," *59th Annual Proceedings, College Physical Education Association,* 1956, p. 68.
8. Jones, Ben D. "Developing Speed and Accuracy in Passing," *Athletic Journal,* Vol. XLI, September 1960, p. 18.

9. Krumdick, Victor F., and Lumian, Norman C. "Motivating the Athlete," *Scholastic Coach*, Vol. 33-2, October 1963, pp. 50-51, 65-67.

10. Louise, Sister Florence M. "Mental Growth and Development at the College Level," *Journal of Educational Psychology*, Vol. 38, February 1947, pp. 65-82.

11. Oxendine, Joseph B. "Effect of Progressively Changing Practice Schedules on the Learning of a Motor Skill," *Research Quarterly*, Vol. 36-3, 1965, pp. 307-315.

12. Peck. Robert R. "How to Capitalize on Split Second Scoring Opportunities," *JOHPER*, Vol. 31-8, November 1960, p. 44.

13. Reeves, Fred J. "The Basketball Coach at Work," *Coach and Athlete*, November 1967, pp. 16-17, 32.

14. Sills, Frank, and Trantman, Donald. "Peripheral Vision and Accuracy in Shooting a Basketball," *Proceedings Annual Meeting of National College Physical Education Association for Men*, December 1965, pp. 112-114.

15. Singer, Robert V. "Understanding the Learning Process," *Athletic Journal*, Vol. XLV-3, November 1964, pp. 52-53, 59.

16. Salley, W. H. "The Effects of Verbal Instruction of Speed and Accuracy Upon the Learning of a Motor Skill," *Research Quarterly*, Vol. 15, May 1952, pp. 231-240.

17. Szymanski, Frank. "A Clinical Analysis of the Jump Shot," *Scholastic Coach*, Vol. 37-2, October 1967, p. 8.

18. Trow, William C. "The Problem of Transfer," *Educational Digest*, Vol. 24, February 1959.

19. Toner, John. "Defensive Code and Signal System," *Athletic Journal*, Vol. 31-1, September 1961, p. 26.

20. Wolf, Wolfgang. "A Contribution to the Question of Over-training," *Health and Fitness in the Modern World*, Athletic Institute and the American College of Sports Medicine, 1961, p. 291-301.

21. Young, Dick. "Control Pitching Signal System," *Scholastic Coach*, February 1961, p. 26.

Chapter V
COACHING THE PLAYER

"Observe the Principles of Individual Differences"

INDIVIDUAL DIFFERENCES IN PHYSIQUE, APTITUDE, INTERESTS AND MENTALITY

For team games, the principal efforts of the coach and his staff should be directed toward the promotion of a group cooperative enterprise. Nevertheless, the team is made up of individuals, and to attempt to submerge each personality in favor of a mass treatment of the squad is to overlook the important concept of individual differences.

The fact that individuals vary widely among themselves has been known for many years, but among educators no group has been more sensitive to the enormity of these differences than athletic coaches. In the coaching situation, we should observe two groups of educationally significant differences. One group may be classified as objective or measurable, the other as qualitative or subjective.

I. Objectives or measurable qualities are those lending themselves to modern methods of precise appraisal.

    (a) Intelligence

    (b) Physical Attributes—height, weight, speed and explosive power

    (c) Age

    (d) Experience

II. Qualitative or subjective qualities are those which are difficult to measure precisely, but coaches become adept at using observations, interviews, conferences, questionnaires, and other tools to better understand players.

    (a) Working Habits

    (b) Parental Influence

    (c) Social and Cultural Background

    (d) Avocational Interest

    (e) Aptitude for the Sport

    (f) Mental Health

    (g) Emotional Stability

The student who reports for a sport brings with him all these personal characteristics that aid or handicap him in the process of learning to be a good performer. The coaches must understand as much as possible about the individual, make allowances for strong and weak points, and adjust the training program so that the learning may proceed in terms of the individual's objective and qualitative differences.

Racial differences in aptitude for sports appear to be unimportant. All things being equal, the same amount of devotion to practice and play will result in equal skill development regardless of ethnic or racial backgrounds. Differences in experience are readily recognized as important by all coaches, for inexperienced players are not capable of absorbing the same amount or same type of sports learning that the veterans can handle.

Differences in home environment will affect the progress of the learner in sports. A boy whose home life is associated with work, hardship, and sacrifice is more likely to enter into the practice activities with less reluctance than is the boy who is accustomed to ease and luxury. Boys who come from depressed mining areas or crowded, industrial, and metropolitan areas appear to be more competitive-minded than those who live in suburban, residential areas.

Psychologists attribute the above phenomena to the following factors:

1. Aggressive behavior results mostly from frustrating experiences that are more apt to be found in poor neighborhoods.
2. Youngsters from poor neighborhoods have seen the success of aggressive, exploitative actions of people, and have adopted it.

However, these differences in behavior disappear as the individuals adjust to the group and as competitive attitudes are directed into group action. Large universities drawing athletes from all areas of the United States, some from cities, others from rural areas, find the more sophisticated city boys make more progress during the freshman year. The sophomore year and following ones erase the distinguishing characteristics of the groups.

The coach's background of training in physical education will teach him the folly of expecting the same level of performance from boys of the same age. He knows that variations in height, weight, strength, and speed are found in all groups. Because interscholastic and intercollegiate sports appeal to boys who are above average in motor skills, there is a good chance that those boys would rank above average in all-round physical development; but within the squad will be found enough differences in organic vigor to warrant special consideration for many players. Some boys tire quickly while others appear to have unlimited stamina. Variations in speed will be very wide among squad members, and the coach usually selects men for various positions according to the amount of speed displayed. In football, backs and ends have the greatest speed, guards next, centers and tackles the least. In soccer and hockey, the forward lines are the fastest. In modern basketball, it is difficult to classify any position as slow, but usually the forwards will be among the speedier. Even within positions variance may be great because speed is only one quality; ability, interest, and aptitude for the position may make it wise to select a boy for a certain position regardless of his speed. In a practical sense, many factors will determine the fitness for a position.

A boy's interest in a sport may be almost taken for granted if he remains out for the sport. At the age when most boys are engaging in either high school or college athletics, they have narrowed their play activities to one or two sports, with the majority engaging in one. They probably have found a special interest or aptitude for that sport; yet if a person watches a hockey, football, or lacrosse squad in practice, he will observe very apparent differences in enthusiasm for the activities. Some players seem to enjoy the physical contact no matter how tired they become, while others very quickly lose their zest for rough going. Passing appeals to some boys, while others prefer running. Wide open, fancy offense is liked by most players, but there are those who enjoy the bruising, hard-blocking, power offense. On any squad there will be the youngsters who enter into every minute of practice with boundless enthusiasm, while other members show animation only for actual contact.

A boy who shows a special aptitude for some phase of a sport usually is interested in improving that skill in that specialty. For example, a basketball player who has the knack of hitting the lay-up shot is willing to work at his faking and driving in order to rid himself of a defender and get free for the shot. The two skills are different, but they are inseparable in the making of a good scorer. The player easily understands this, and his interest in all-round improvement is a motivating force.

In this age of specialists in football, there has emerged an opportunity for the coaches to practice individualization. That is, they need no longer ignore the tackler who cannot block, the kicker who cannot run, or the forward passer who is weak on defense. Today the coach can allow and encourage the development of these specialties which are expressions of particular talents. Practice on many of these skills can usually be carried on independent of the group activities, giving the youngster a chance to determine his own best methods of procedure and to follow them out. The coach should always be available for helpful suggestions which he can give in the most casual and informal manner. The fact that the player knows that his worth is recognized and appreciated is often enough stimulant to keep him working.

Present in most squads will be individuals who differ in temperament, emotional response, and fighting spirit. These must be dealt with as they are observed, so that the learning can proceed best for each individual. The conditions of some classrooms may present only intellectual heterogeneity; but the average playing field will expose in the same group of students mental extremes as well as a tremendous variety of differences in height, weight, organic power, experience, environment and nutrition—all of which enter into the difficulties of properly coaching an athletic team.

INDIVIDUALITY OF PERFORMANCE

A squad drilled in the performance of some particular act of its sport, to the point where each member executes the act almost identically, may be a well drilled squad but not necessarily a well coached one. To insist on similarity of performance from each player is to ignore the concept of individual differences. One player may display a variety of methods in performing the same act over and over again. It has been established that human beings show a great deal of flexibility and plasticity in simple situations and much more in complex ones where transfer from past training figures largely. The procedure used in going around a barrier may be followed many times but never with exactly the same movements, and as activities increase in complexity the possibilities of variability of performance increases rapidly.

Infielders making the stop, twist, and throw for a double play will perform the act in a variety of ways. The position from which the ball is fielded each time necessitates slight changes in approach, balance, and arc of throw. A football lineman may be called upon to pull out as a running interferer to block a linebacker. He may go through the act from start to finish a dozen times or more and show a great variety of movement. His constancy consists of starting from an initial position and progressing to the ultimate goal (the linebacker) through a certain sequence of directions, but the actual movements follow no identical pattern. Even in a signal drill this is so, and in dummy scrimmage it becomes more apparent that his movements change. In actual scrimmage or game conditions the situation becomes more complex because of moving men, therefore the pattern of response on the part of a player must also become extremely varied.

Because of the inevitable necessity of compensation, it would seem wise to allow the learner to practice under varying conditions so that he becomes used to making adjustments. As long as the player is able to recognize the various elements of a situation and act accordingly, he is making some progress. For instance, the running interferer who finds that the linebacker did not stay behind the line of scrimmage but waited in the hole must quickly change the type of block he had intended using. The object or goal of his pulling out is to get rid of that linebacker, and this he must do in the most effective manner. As long as his mind is set clearly on the goal of keeping the linebacker off the ball carrier, regardless of how the linebacker moves, the blocker will adapt a body move of his own to accomplish the goal.

Players vary in their degree of muscular coordination. Skeletal muscles causing the body to move are laid down in antagonistic pairs which are designed to function harmoniously. That is to say, there must be fine timing between the contracting and relaxing groups. No two athletes will use the same muscular groups in an identical manner in performing a sport skill. There will be differences in the number of muscle bundles involved, in the amount of power applied, and in the timing between contraction and relaxing of the antagonistic groups. Good control of all the factors results in a high degree of muscular coordination. Anyone observing professional athletes can detect wide variations in form during the performance of identical acts, yet the majority of them are considered skilled performers. They get the job done.

Different factors enter into the learner's choice of form. Some boys will imitate the coach's form as he demonstrates: other may imitate some star performer—the school hero or another idol. In this respect, they may imitate his mannerisms rather than the fundamentals of the movement, and the coach must then explain the difference between the unimportant flourishes and the essentials. The player's purpose will greatly affect his choice of form. A lazy boy who "wants to get by" will select a form which requires the least effort on his part, regardless of its effectiveness. In shoulder blocking, for instance, he will do a great deal of leaning and pushing instead of driving and lifting. His upper arm will hang loosely at a small angle from his shoulder because to hold the arm up for a wide blocking surface requires energy and effort. A boy who strives for grace and beauty will work hard in smoothing his performance to the point where it indicates mastery. It may actually require more energy and endurance to hold his form throughout a contest than to hold a form with less grace, but for him the acquisition of smooth, sinuous continuity of movement in his play is worth the extra effort. A player who is concerned only with the end result may pay less attention to form and more attention to effective movements. His form may vary greatly in each successive try with only the barest of fundamentals remaining. Those movements necessary for the completion of the job are the ones which are retained and assimilated; the others will vary as the situation changes. An injured or otherwise handicapped player will adjust his form for ease, comfort, and economy of motion, just as major league baseball pitchers change their style of delivery when they become older. For example, fast-ball hurlers sometimes make suitable variations in their pitching form which are less strenuous than the overhand speedball delivery.

When a boy's choice of form or style does not fit his conformation, speed, or strength, the coach should suggest and even insist that the player try something more appropriate. There is no point in allowing a boy to practice something which for him will never be effective. The ultimate lack of success in using that style may result in discouragement and finally in a lack of interest in the game.

Individual differences are so pronounced in motor acts that no single style or form can be recommended for all players. A person's style becomes part of his individuality. Every distinctive motor skill has a characteristic structure, and the essence of learning it lies in the vivid picture of the correct technique in the mind of the young player and his ability to reproduce that picture by his own body movements. The fact that these body movements are not identical among all learners creates the difference known as style.

MOTIVATING THE PLAYER—MOTIVES AND INCENTIVES

On the basis of intrinsic interest, sports are in a more advantageous position than most academic subjects in the matter of motivating in order to maintain interest. The fact that the boy participates voluntarily is an indication that he has already been motivated to some extent. The nature of the motivating force may be difficult for the coach to discover. As a matter of fact the boys may be either unable or unwilling to state their personal reasons for reporting, but they are there nevertheless—a group of indviduals, all apparently expressing a desire to learn. Anyone who has coached knows that the desire is not constant; neither is it perpetual. It will fluctuate from day to day with a change in practice activities, and it may die altogether. Some form of stimulation is needed in order that the learning process may be vigorous and continuous.

To motivate is to induce an action or to provide the inducement to act and, possibly, to act in a particular manner. We might say that motives are tendencies to use skills and knowledges in attaining a goal; abilities referring to patterns of behavior which have been developed.

Some psychologists differentiate between motives and incentives. A motive is a predisposition within the boy himself which drives him toward some goal. An incentive is usually thought of as being something outside the boy's body, in that it is provided by someone or something other than the boy himself. Ryan offers the following as a partial list of motives and incentives which affect learning.[1]

Factors Relating to the Release and Direction of Activity (Motives)	Factors Relating to the Incentive Situation
1. Wants and Needs	1. Rewards and Punishments
2. Traits	(a) Material rewards
3. Attitudes	(b) Praise and blame
4. Interests	(c) Punishment
5. Habits and Skills	2. Group Recognition
6. Purposes	3. Knowledge of Progress
7. Affective and Emotional Conditions	

These motives and incentives obviously are interdependent and must be considered in relation to each other. For example, a reward must be compatible with an individual's attitudes and traits in order for it to reinforce a learning activity. A boy who is extremely selfish may not strive hard to win a championship cup for the team, but he will go "all out" to win if the winning team members are to receive individual medals.

Motives—A coach can take advantage of the youngster's need for activity in order to stimulate the learning of some sports techniques; but, aside from physiological needs, there are those which come about as a result of the individual's experience. A wise coach will

[1]Ryan, David C. "Motivation in Learning," *Psychology of Learning*. National Society for the Study of Education. Forty-first Yearbook, Part II, University of Chicago Press, 1942, Chapter 8, pp. 308-09.

openly or subtly point out the relation between being a regular varsity player and the mastery of certain skills. The implication is that the goal is attainable to those who are willing to work hard to acquire the skills.

Acquiring knowledge or learning a skill is facilitated if related to the individual's personality traits Learning an activity which is not in accord with a person's existing traits is not going to be successful from the standpoint of efficiency. Crashing end play on defense will appeal to the boy who is inclined to be rough, but it is detested by the timid, cautious type of player. A type of play which violates the spirit of the rules or which is unquestionably "dirty" will not appeal to the average boy. A method that is tricky, cleverly designed, and spectacularly executed will appeal to almost all boys, but especially to those who are inclined to be dramatic.

Traits are similar to attitudes with the exception that attitudes are always acquired. Attitudes may be expressed as opinions, beliefs, or sentimental feelings. Bad attitudes for learning, especially for athletics, are indifference, cynicism, fear, insecurity, antagonism toward the coach and teammates, discouragement, and lack of self-confidence. Favorable attitudes are interest in achievement, self-confidence, security, goodwill, and cooperation. The coach should be alert to discover signs of a poor attitude and take immediate steps to cure it. The player's attitude will greatly influence the amount of effort he will put forth in practice and in games.

Interests may be either traits or attitudes but, at any rate, they are learned responses which definitely facilitate attention. It is to be expected that if a person is really interested in an activity the learning is bound to be more efficient and better retained, for interest is the keystone in the arch of learning. Learnings are likely to be of interest to a player if he has had previous experience and previous success with them. Activities that are pleasant and that challenge his level of intelligence and ability are also likely to be interesting.

Habits and skills serve as motives to learning when they are of the type which can be used in new learnings. The association of habits and skills learned in former situations with new situations should be pointed out by the coach.

Purpose has to do with the learner's focus on the goal to be attained. When it can be clearly understood and seen as desirable by the learner, it serves as a vital motivating force. A boy who knows that the acquisition of a certain skill is going to raise him above the classification of "scrub" needs no other stimulant to cause him to practice diligently on that skill.

Incentives—Material rewards may be regarded as definite incentives toward learning. Though such gifts as gold charms, watches, sweaters, and the like undoubtedly stimulate effort on the part of some individuals, it is doubtful if these alone are responsible for the enormous amounts of time and effort that are expended by the average athlete. It is more likely that the intrinsic values of the sport are more potent motivating forces.

Promises of postseason games involving extended trips serve to stimulate interest in winning performances and may or may not be regarded as worthy incentives.

Praise and blame are symbolic forms of incentives. Verbal commendation is usually satisfying and appeals to the desire for approval. Blame or reproof means disapproval and is annoying. Coaches should not expect that praise and blame always produce the desired result, for in some cases they not only lose their effect but actually produce the opposite effect. Praise may react wrongly on some boys, especially gifted performers. It may feed their egos to the point where they become unbearable to the coach and their fellow players. Praise should be given sparingly and judiciously. Punishments are sometimes meted out by coaches for failures in carrying out assignments. The punishment may be physical or mental. Some coaches make players run a number of laps (a stunt which usually has no connection with the material being practiced); other coaches give players a sarcastic, ridiculing tongue-lashing. No player should be shamed or humiliated in the presence of his teammates. A quiet, private conversation will serve to explain the coach's displeasure with the player's performance. It is better to make use of a boy's interests and ambitions to stimulate learning.

The effect of group recognition is a strong incentive to action in sports as well as other activities. There is no doubt that players feel the esteem in which the average student body holds those who compete on the interschool basis. Publicity programs have aided and abetted this situation, and the coach may never have to point it out to his players as a means of inciting effort. To gain the esteem of his fellow players is a motivating force, and the boy who feels that his team is looking to him for an unusual performance may try much harder to fulfill their expectations. Competition among players for starting berths is a well known device for stimulating effort, and most coaches look for the day when they will be forced to make a guess as to which players to start. Rivalry and competition appear to have a facilitating effect on learning.

When the learner has the knowledge and ability to check his progress toward his chosen goal, self-evaluation may act as a motivating force. The fact that he can see his successes and failures from day to day will keep a boy at a task of learning some athletic skill.

Motivation and meaning are related in that the learner will not be motivated by a method of acquiring skills or knowledges that for him has no meaning. He is not going to be interested or satisfied if he sees no value in the thing to be learned. A player cannot be expected to be persistent in his endeavors to learn if the learning has no relationship to his goal. If the material to be learned is beyond his ability or too simple to interest him, he will become bored and even resentful. Motivation, then, must begin with organized, meaningful material, taking into consideration the athlete's human qualities of mind and spirit.

EMOTIONS

Sports are activities founded largely on emotional expression. In it are exercises for the deep-rooted passions that control behavior in anger, fear, hate, desire, affection, joy, courage, sorrow; or the emotional experiences in everyday conduct which have to do with cooperative effort, loyalty, sacrifice, risk, sportsmanship, rivalry, and self-assertion.[2] The degree to which control of behavior is learned through sports experiences will depend upon the knowledge of the coach and his willingness to foster the process.

That a coach will have an understanding of the changes which take place in the bodies of his players when they become emotionally upset is not too much to expect. Coaches spend much time on teaching proper physical stance so as to make the player more efficient in his initial movements. To be upset emotionally is to lose one's mental stance which is just as bad as being poorly postured physically.

The general result of a rise in emotions is the mobilization of energy and endurance by the body. There are several distinguishing features in the bodily response to an intense emotional state. In connection with intense anger and fear there are changes mediated through one of the sympathetic divisions of the autonomic nervous system and influenced by secretions from the adrenal glands. Among the changes are the following:

Blood pressure rises, blood vessels are constricted and the heart beats faster. The bronchioles are dilated, digestion is

[2]Herbert G. Crisler, "Educational Implications of Intercollegiate Football." *Research Quarterly*, Vol. 1:35, March 1933.

slowed, the flow of saliva and gastric juices is reduced. Glucose, ordinarily stored in the liver is released into the blood which carries it to the tissues of the body, notably the skeletal muscles. The increase of blood sugar allows the muscles to contract to the point where they sometimes quiver from sheer tension. An increased number of white blood corpuscles are also found in the blood stream as a safeguard against a possible infection.

Through these and other changes in varying degrees, the body mobilizes energy and endurance to meet emergencies. It has been found that football players, when observed for physiological changes, do not appear to experience as much emotional buildup during the days and hours preceding a contest as do wrestlers, and boxers are even more emotionally taut. All groups, however, show an appreciable rise just prior to the start of a contest. Anyone who has been closely associated with contact sports is bound to recall' many displays of emotion not only prior to games but in practice activities as well.

The bodily components of high emotional excitement may be an aid or a hindrance in the efficient execution of the game skills. Certainly a degree of anger can cause a boy to throw off the effects of inertia and bestir himself to meet some opponent or perform tasks a little out of the ordinary, but hindering effects can also result when he gets "too high." There will be an evident display of mental inefficiency when the individual is acting wildly, and much energy will be consumed without contributing to any constructive use. The history of sports is replete with incidents of overstimulation causing players to commit basic errors, especially in the early stages of a contest. This uncontrollable condition can afflict an entire team when a pregame session of buildup becomes too highly charged with emotion.

Tests have shown that high emotional states caused by anger increase an individual's physical efficiency, his ability to run fast and hit hard. Because these acts are valuable assets in contact sports, it can be assumed that emotional rises can be beneficial to the player when not carried to extremes.

From a functional standpoint, emotion may be considered as a condition of heightened feeling which may be pleasant or unpleasant according to whether the interest involved is gratified or thwarted. When inexperienced players are introduced to many of the skills of sports, some frustration and emotional distress are likely to occur because of the particularly difficult nature of the acts. If desire to be a good performer is great within the athlete, success will stimulate him to continue with great vigor. Failure or frustration may cause him to withdraw, or he may drive forward with increased but angry effort. Efficiency in performance fails in either case, and wise direction is needed from the coach.

The variances in behavior are due to individual differences and must be treated individually by the coach. Veteran coaches know that there is a very delicate balance between the good and bad effects of emotion. Under milder emotion and less critical situations, learning may proceed rapidly or not at all. The problem, then, is virtually one of creating a degree of tension which will facilitate learning and yet avoid the extreme degree of tension and excitement that disorganizes the actions of the individual.

What coaches should be looking for is that optimum level of impulse or incentive which leads the individual to efficient learning. Below that level there is no learning because of unconcern or indifference, while above that level the emotional disturbance accompanying the impulse or incentives is so great that it interferes with smooth, progressive learning. A good coach is aware of this relation. He is alert to lags in the learning process which may be due to emotional causes. He considers the individual differences among his players, stimulating those who lack animation and quieting those who are nervous and excitable.

Because sports offer so many opportunities for the direct expression of emotions through motor activities, it behooves a coach to be alert to his opportunity and duty to make each experience educative. Emotional reaction in some boys will be violent to the point where they disregard rules, sportsmanship, and even their assignments on a play. Such a player must be immediately removed from the game or practice and not allowed to reenter until he has regained control of his passions. If this done without fail for each occurrence, the principle of such a disciplinary measure will be learned by all members of the squad.

FEAR

Fear has about the same emotional effect on the body as anger, and its expression may range from paralyzing terror to worry and mild apprehensions. Every coach has seen the effects of fear on some players, especially beginners. There is an emotional blocking which inhibits action. The sinking feeling in the stomach and the shaky knees are symptoms. This is caused by "interference"—the emotional blocking of responses, superimposed by fear, stage fright, or the sight of large and powerful opponents. Fear is one of the most powerful of the emotions and may be associated with a natural urge to avoid or withdraw from situations that are painful, unpleasant or frightening. Some situations, especially those in a contact sport, seem to carry the threat of bodily injury, and that is provocative of fear responses. The player may also imagine himself in a perplexing situation and thereby produce worries and anxieties. Adolescent boys are likely to become worried over the possibility of being considered "yellow." All these emotional reactions have the same unwholesome effect on a person's efficiency and conduct. There are no true mixed feelings. A person responds to one stimulus or another but never simultaneously. For instance, a young rookie may be happy over the fact that he is in the game but at the same time be extremely fearful of a failure to make good which shows in his play. It seems that fear is the stronger of two emotions and gains the subject's attention. The other emotion of happiness will be blotted out. When fear is the dominant emotional state, the individual may docilely accept the implications of inferiority. There is something unwholesome in this acceptance of defeat which, to a coach, can be either infuriating, nauseating, or both.

There is no need for such an attitude on the part of a coach. He should understand that fears are the result of conditioning and, as such, are subject to modification if handled properly. One of the important areas of guidance is that of helping students overcome fears. For many boys, there is a fear reaction in learning to block, tackle, box, wrestle, tumble, or participate in any form of bodily contact. The overcoming of these fears is very important to the development of personality. The satisfaction and confidence which result when such fears are conquered is surprising.

Knowing that the thought of vigorous bodily contact creates a state of fear within some boys, the coach should direct much of his effort to the control and elimination of fear. If a boy is made to realize that fear is a tension system which arises because he does not know how to meet a situation, half the battle for its control is won. When the boy clearly perceives the situation and realizes that his fear is handicapping him, he is ready to be taught new behavior, usually aggressive action. Often the examination of the situation leads directly to correct action or else shows that fear is unnecessary. The very fact that the player recognizes the element of danger in a situation shows that he is not stupid or reckless. He is capable of searching for the best method of performing, and by concentrating on that he may eliminate his fear.

Among the best known methods of controlling fear is that of getting into action fast. Unnecessary delays before the start of a contest or the beginning of a rough drill should be avoided. There is a psychological basis for the universal belief among football players that the man making the first tackle will play a great game. The success of his initial effort is enough to relieve the tension and other disagreeable feelings. Acting the part of the aggressor is another method. Anger is an antidote for fear, and if a man can approach a situation with a feeling of indignation without a loss of efficiency through overstimulation, the ill effects of fear will disappear. There is a delicate balance here, but an intelligent coach can control the stimulation. Being philosophical about the situation often helps a person to get rid of his fears. When the player can be made to realize that his opponent has about the same perspective of the approaching game as he has and therefore must be suffering the same fears, he probably will relax and may even assume an aggressive attitude to further aid his own cause.

Another method often practiced by players to rid themselves of fear is to shift their concentration from their own troubles to those of a teammate. It is amazing how solicitous of the welfare of a neighbor a football or lacrosse player can get when game time approaches. He will aid a teammate in adjusting his pads or seeing that his jersey fits just right or in numerous other little considerations. He may also shift his thoughts to his own preparations and give undue attention to a minute detail such as tying a shoelace or adjusting a thigh guard. Another method of controlling fear is to concentrate on some phase of the pregame program with which the players are familiar and do it vigorously. Signal drills with little ball handling are good for football teams, but care must be taken not to let the drills get too complicated; emotions are enemies of habit, and fumbles will be numerous if much ball handling is included. This would be disastrous for morale.

A coach can combat the fears of his men by encouraging a friendly spirit of comradeship among the players. They can be told that everyone realizes that they are all somewhat afraid. The feeling of tension is nothing of which to be ashamed, because it is a normal reaction. The knowledge that the player next to him is also a bit uneasy can be reassuring to a youngster. Time is an important factor just before a game, and when the coach sends his men out of the dressing room there should be little time left for delays before they get into action. Long, drawn-out demonstrations or pregame spectacles should be avoided after the team has reached the field.

Fear will handicap the development of a youngster into a good athlete by causing him to draw back or retreat from contact or any difficult assignment, and so it may be classed as an undesirable habit.

The coach may take it upon himself to break the boy of this habit by any one of several methods. The object of any habit-breaking procedure is to bring forth a new desirable type of behavior in place of the undesirable behavior in the same type of situations which formerly elicited only the undesirable type. To put it bluntly, the coach is trying to make his boy tough and courageous in the same situations in which he has been "crawfishing."

There are several methods of breaking undesirable behavior habits resulting from fear, and all of them probably have been tried by coaches. The *endurance* method is one in which the individual is led to develop a slowly increasing toleration for the stimuli which produces the undesirable reaction. In this method the player is started off by an introduction to tasks that will arouse only a samll degree of fear. Gradually there will be an increase of this stimulation (the roughness of the drill or the toughness of the opposition) to the point where he is going at full speed without exciting the undesired response. This may seem too slow and tedious, or it may exasperate the old "rock-and-sock" coaches, but it must be remembered that the boy is experiencing a battle within himself during the process. Patience, perseverance, and self-control are demanded of the boy. This method is also good for increasing skill, so it can probably be regarded as best from the standpoint of permanent adjustment.

Sublimation adjustment is a second method, and in it the individual consciously attempts to invent, produce, and establish a new reaction capable of inhibiting the undesirable habit. Congratulatory remarks from the coach whenever the player shows even the slightest inclination to overcome his fear will aid the process. Praise from his teammates for any type of aggressive play is a powerful stimulant. The good feeling that comes to a player as a result is much more desirable than the momentary relief from shying away from trouble, so the habit of driving in hard becomes the dominant one.

The *saturation* method has probably been tried many times by coaches when they become exasperated with a boy because of his timidity. This method is one in which the individual repeatedly subjects himself to the stimulus which produces the undesired response, in the hope that it will be simply exhausted by repetition. A boy is supposed to become so tired of cringing and ducking in the face of contact during a long repetitious tackling drill that he becomes numb to the effect and so eventually develops a normal reaction to the situation. Subsequent trials at the same situation are supposed to prove increasingly easy. This is somewhat akin to the idea of repeatedly diving from a high platform, even though frightened, until eventually the fright wears off. The method may appeal to some coaches, but it is not easy for the victim himself.

Another method of habit breaking is the *scene shifting* method. It is founded on the belief that certain elements in the present surroundings are inducing a particular type of behavior and that a change in environment which eliminates those stimuli will bring about the desired changes. Changing the entire game environment altogether is rather difficult, but many coaches will recall instances of players performing with more ease when they were shifted from one position to another. It may be that elements of the situation in the first position produced fear and anxiety in the player, ruining his effectiveness; whereas in the new position he felt secure and relaxed.

Habits may be eliminated by other methods; perhaps some are less painful than others, but no easy method exists.

No boy really has a "yellow streak" if he continues out for a contact sport. The fact that he is there, day after day, fully realizing that he has to face combative experiences, proves that he possesses a certain degree of moral fibre. He may be subject to feelings of fear and anxiety and actually shy away during contact work, but if he continues to try he is making strides toward combating his fear. Fear is a normal experience when individuals are faced with the unknown. They worry, fret, and become generally apprehensive of what lies in store for them. Knowledge and skill help to control fear. When a youngster knows that he has the knowledge and ability to at least match that of his opponent, confidence is likely to take the place of fear. A coach should always bear in mind that fear is a natural outgrowth of the normal urge to avoid physical discomfort, and that conduct emanating from it has been learned by the boy. It is up to the coach to bring about a process of reeducation which will result in the boy learning new, desirable responses.

TEMPERAMENT

Temperament usually refers to an individual's personality, but anything that indicates character, indicates personality. A person's type of personality is derived from a general pattern that characterizes his total behavior. An individual's personality includes both his attitudes and his traits. Attitudes are a person's point of view toward a thing. They generally refer to a disposition to react favorably or unfavorably toward some object of reference. Traits refer to a person's unique manner of behaving or responding, such as his manner of speaking, manner of listening, or manner of receiving praise or condemnation. Traits are more personal than attitudes. Allport writes:

> Temperament refers to the characteristic phenomena of an individual's emotional nature, including his susceptibility to emotional stimulation, his customary strength and speed of response, the quality of his prevailing mood, and all the peculiarities of fluctuation and intensity in mood; these phenomena being regarded as dependent upon constitutional makeup, and therefore largely hereditary in origin.[3]

Like intelligence and physique, temperament might be said to designate a certain class of raw material from which an individual's personality is fashioned. The term temperament is conveniently employed when speaking of dispositions that are almost never changed throughout a lifetime. When a person's disposition seems firmly fixed and unchangeable, it is likely to be spoken of as temperament. Certain dispositions are regarded as good or desirable, while others are thought of as poor or undesirable. A person having a good disposition may have a number of qualities such as optimism, cheerfulness, friendliness, sociability, emotional stability, tolerance, abundance of energy, helpfulness and modesty. A poor disposition is credited to those who are haughty, lazy, dishonest, selfish, egotistic, overbearing, melodramatic, timid and unreliable. (See Personality Traits of Coaches—Chapter I.)

Some authorities agree that people can be distinguished by degree of emotionality. At least nine types are generally distinguished, and coaches will recognize many of them as being represented on almost any squad. There will be the merry, the spirited, the explosive, the annoying, the indifferent, the genial, the depressed, the nervous, the moody, the reactionary, and the hypercritical. Of course, there are the everyday adaptable normals, and it may be difficult to assign some players to a definite category in the list. For all practical purposes, it is possible to find one descriptive term which fits each of them best. Effective teaching and coaching requires the recognition of the individual as a person, not only a recognition of his special talents and weaknesses but also an understanding of his behavioral traits. Recognition of these factors is as much a part of an educational diagnosis as is the understanding of the person's height, weight, intelligence, and aptitudes. Skillful handling of the individual players involves a knowledge of their temperaments and an intelligent directing of their activities so as to enhance the admirable

[3]Gordon Allport, *Personality*. New York: Henry Holt and Co., 1937, p. 54.

features of their temperaments while discouraging the unharmonious features.

The merry type of player is one who has plenty of enthusiasm but seems to be short on common sense. He is likely to be regarded as "hair-brained" by his fellow players and the coaches. As a rule, such boys become team comedians or the recipients of many jibes and jokes. The coaches must be alert to see that these jokes are not carried to such an extent that the boy is forced to quit. The enthusiasm of the boy for his work can serve as a good example for the rest of the squad, and it should be rewarded by the boy's chance to play when circumstances warrant it.

The spirited type of player can be motivated easily and, when his inner tensions explode into physical activity, he is capable of extraordinary feats. Care must be taken not to overstimulate this type, for they can easily become so jittery that their efficiency is greatly impaired. Sometimes it is best not to start an excitable boy but to send him into the game when it is a few minutes old or after the opening tempo has subsided.

Explosive types are those people who fly into sudden rages, who "lose their heads" or have temper tantrums. This sort of player is likely to be a central figure in all disputes involving rough play and other personal fouls. Disciplinary action for such conduct must be quick and positive, leaving no doubt in the mind of the boy that his lack of control over his temper leads only to a job as a bench-warmer.

Probably the best known of the temperamental types is the annoying. Unfortunately this type seems to be often associated with abundant talent in the way of sports and other activities. During the learning process, they will invent all sorts of excuses for themselves, but the coach must insist on their going through the regular routine with the other players. Because much of their "griping" is habit and lacks a solid foundation or cause, it can often be ignored and, in most cases, will soon be forgotten by the player himself. Such players may be annoying to the other members of the squad unless the coach finds the opportunity to explain to the squad that the player's behavior, though odd, is meaningless and trivial. The lack of a responsive audience may cause him to cease his fussing and fuming, especially if the coach points out to him that he will receive sympathy only when it is deserved.

Indifferent types are those who seem utterly incapable of emotion. It is very difficult, if not impossible, to get this type of player to change his tempo of playing. When he is blessed with a talent for some sport, the phlegmatic boy will be a steady, cool player, but if he lacks certain skills it will be very difficult to bring about much improvement in his play. Inertia seems to be too difficult for him to overcome, and it is unwise to plan upon this type taking over a varsity position as a result of his improvement.

Genial, friendly players can be treated as normal types. They are pleasant to have on the squad; and, if they are good players in addition, the practice field is a happy place. Depressed, unhappy people are not found often on an athletic team because the natural exuberance of youth, as displayed by the players, is incongruous with their feelings.

The nervous type of player is very common on the athletic field. Such a boy is very tense and nervous, especially in his early stages of learning. The coach should take every opportunity to calm the youngster and be more lavish with praise than censure. As players mature, they lose some degree of their anxiety, but never all of it, and they must be constantly watched when contests become intense. Such a player may "freeze" in the face of conflict and will have to be removed until he regains his composure. During the learning process he should be given frequent rest periods, for the excess tension within his body increases fatigue.

Moody individuals are those whose temperaments seem to chance constantly. They will be friendly, happy, and enthusiastic one day and gloomy, phlegmatic, or irritable the next. There are reasons for such changes, and if the change is working havoc with the player's efficiency, the coach should make an effort to discover the cause. Personal problems are usually at fault; if the coach can be of assistance in solving them, he should offer to do so. Players whose temperaments are so pliable can be motivated rather easily, but keeping their morale at a high level will be a problem.

Another type that might be added to the list is the selfish or excessively individualistic person. He is the one who constantly plays to the spectators rather than for the good of the team. The urge to dominate or to win admiration overcomes his urge to belong to the group. This habit is also a product of bad training and, as such, calls for drastic measures by the coach. Regardless of the boy's individual ability, he should be punished for this lack of team spirit by being benched until he understands that there will be no glory for him until he is willing to share the cooperative glory of the team. Attempts to reason with this type of individual usually are fruitless, and direct action seems to be the only alternative.

The reactionary type of athlete is one who constantly refers back to learnings received from parents, friends, or former coaches. Insulating himself against further learning, he rejects almost everything being taught by his present coach in favor of knowledge, technique, and strategy acquired in the past. His nostalgic references to the way "we used to do it under Mr. ..." annoys teammates and coaches alike. It is not unusual for him to seek out former tutors for advice, sympathy, and reassurance that his conduct is justified.

The hypercritical athlete will not accept coaching without questioning the value of it. He is highly opinionated, deaf to advice, and censorius. It is difficult to convince him that a skill or knowledge is worth the hard work necessary to master it. Frequently he voices a lack of confidence in the ability of his teammates to play a particular offense or defense, a trait which does nothing for his popularity.

The hypercritical, reactionary, selfish, and annoying types may be referred to as problem athletes. Their behavior is outside the bounds of normalcy even for adolescents, and when found in adult athletes, it indicates somewhat maladjusted personalities. It must be remembered that their difficulties center around faulty attitudes that must be corrected before proper habits of behavior can be instilled.

Most authorities agree that temperament can be changed little, if at all, by education, but the individual can be better taught to understand himself—to become aware of the significance of his moods and to increase his powers of self-discipline in the situation met in everyday life. The personality of each player should be studied until it is so plain to the coach that he can readily adjust his own attitudes toward each boy to bring about a quick readjustment of the boy's temperament. The coach must get the boy "back into line" when the player allows his temperament to set him apart from the intents, purposes, and goals of the team.

The coach must also watch out for his own temperament, which may be moody. He must not allow something outside his sport to affect his behavior on the field or in the gymnasium. The players should not be made to suffer because of the coach's quarrel with his wife or a fellow motorist in a traffic line.

An individual peculiarity often misinterpreted by coaches and athletes is the "threshold for pain." It refers to a person's ability to endure pain without interrupting activities in which the person is engaging. It is not a psychosomatic disorder, for it has a definite physiological basis. People are made aware of the world about them through the action of their senses of touch, taste, sight, smell, and hearing. The degree of sensitivity in each of them varies with individuals. In the case of a low threshold for pain, the sense of touch is extremely acute. The sensory nerve endings of touch are imbedded in practically every tissue of the body. Whenever they are subjected to high pressure, such as that from a blow, they receive the message or stimulus clearly and strongly and deliver it to the brain where it is interpreted as severe pain. The same blow received by the average person might register mildly in the brain and, in the case of a dull sensory apparatus, the message hardly would be noticeable. Athletes of the latter type are said to be "able to take it."

The acutely sensitive athlete really feels the extreme pain to the point where he is unable to perform his assignment. It is better to remove him from the game until the feeling of pain subsides, and normally that is a matter of only a few minutes. Usually the boy will be anxious to return to the game, a fact that puzzles many people. Coaches and players who do not understand the workings of the sensory apparatus often accuse the hypersensitive boy of being "yellow" or of not being "able to take it." In reality, the boy possesses an abundance of courage just to be able to face the possibility of being hit and suffering intensely. A lesser man would drop the contact sport in favor of some milder activity.

The coach has a responsibility for explaining the above phenomenon to the squad so that the players may have a proper understanding of a peculiar individual difference.

COMPETITIVE SPIRIT

When competing, most individuals have a desire to win or at least to make a creditable showing. This desire may not be strong enough to make a boy a fierce competitor. For this, an individual must have a liking for personal combat, the kind of activity that calls for speed, strength, skill, and fortitude.

One quality of character displayed by many young men playing sports which never fails to amaze and evoke admiration among coaches is that which can best be described as a "craving for crisis." Some boys seem to glory in situations that tax their energies, ingenuities, courage, stamina, and resistance to pain. Other boys may not actually dislike the rough element of contact, but they do not get as much of the keen, unadulterated joy out of tough going as do the real competitors. The boys who possess this extra spirit are those the coach prefers to have in the game when the breaks are going against them and the opponents are enjoying a good day. It is not so much a matter of being able to rise to the occasion as it is a habit of always giving forth with the extra effort. Other players may not actually quit when the situation seems hopeless, but their play will not be marked by top effort; whereas the real competitor gives out with all his energies regardless of the situation.

It is a mistake to credit this quality to either heredity or environment alone, for it is affected somewhat by both. Inheritance has very little to do with courage or competitive spirit, other than the fact that a person born with defective endocrine system will not be stimulated to act positively in the matter of courage or ambition. Any quality of spirit, as recognized in sports, can be explained in terms of physical condition and training. A boy with a good body that is functioning normally—that is, when his digestion, circulation, senses, respiration, and the like are in good condition—is potentially ready to operate. This does not mean that a boy must have a powerful, well-developed body in order to be a good competitor, for the fiercest, most energetic players on the squad will often be scrawny, spindle-legged individuals. Competitive spirit seems to be more of a glandular function than muscular. The tendency to react at a high rate of speed and vigor comes from training, and that, in turn, may come from experiences on the playing field, in the home, or in the neighborhood environment.

Competitiveness meets all the criteria for learned behavior. Goals appear to change as persons mature, and these changes are usually paralleled by a maturity in competitive techniques. That is, there is a shift from early childhood habits of grabbing another's toys to a more refined manner of competing for positions of honor or recognized status. In the present society, there is a struggle for material gain, for power, and for prestige, but because of differences in environment there are, apparently, variations in this element of competition. Some college coaches prefer to have players who have a background of hard work in mining areas or crowded industrial centers. The difficulty of the job, the poor living conditions, and the limitations of social opportunities are thought to develop in them an aggressive attitude, perhaps fostered by a desire to improve their lot. However, this type of behavior does not result solely from economic situations, but from a complex including many non-economic factors.

A competitive spirit is sometimes regarded as a natural part of an "athletic instinct," but there is no such thing as "athletic instinct." Some boys appear to possess the knack of performing well in complicated fundamentals of football such as tackling, blocking, pivoting, changing pace, forward passing, and other techniques. Possession of these talents is probably the result of a transfer of skill from some boyhood game that included many of the same rough elements which make up those skills. The long hours of playing a rough boyhood game may cause the boy to develop habits of driving hard and recklessly. Habits are acts which can be done without thinking, but rough, aggressive habits of behavior which become second nature do not become instincts.

Competitive spirit can be a habit of persistence. Players can be taught to set goals for themselves and to carry on toward these goals regardless of the type of opposition facing them, and these habits may become so firmly established in the training that they cannot get away from them. If habits of competition are to be learned, the learner must have a chance of succeeding if the motivation is to continue. Some sports techniques call for aggressive behavior. Examples might be the driving lay-up in basketball, a take-down in wrestling, or a hard charge in football. When learning aggressive behavior against an opponent, the boy should be matched against another of somewhat equal size and ability. If he is easily overpowered by a superior adversary, he will not develop the desired habit but might even acquire a defeatist attitude. He should frequently experience the satisfaction of success in order that the habit of correct performance (hard driving) be established. On the other hand, the opposition should not be too weak or the boy may develop the habit of an easy, careless movement because it met with frequent success.

There are two cautions to be observed in regard to aggressive behavior in team sports. First, an aggressive youth may assume that the principle objective of a game is literally to destroy an opponent.

Competitive self-assertion is a powerful motive, but it can be wasted if left to flourish as an individual's private struggle against a rival. Young adults may compete just as vigorously, if not more so, as members of a team than they do alone. It is the coach's task to turn this strenuousness into channels where it can be marshalled as a group enterprise with reference to some threat or some goal that concerns them collectively. This means educating the fierce competitor not to concentrate his energies in a private struggle with his opponent but to use them for the goal of the team.

Second, the high emotional state of some aggressive competitors causes them to forget the game plan under which they should be operating, with each man concentrating on his job for each play. A boy who runs aimlessly about the field, throwing his body at any opponent who appears in his vision would do better if he concentrated on the play in question and carried out his personal assignment to completion.

As in all learning situations, there will be some degrees of success in acquiring the habit of being a strong competitor. Some individuals will develop further than others and those who learn best will find the greater satisfaction in "carrying the fight" to the other fellow.

SUMMARY

Although the coach's efforts are directed toward the building of a team in which group cooperation is carried out to a high degree, the coach should recognize that the team is made up of individuals who bring to the learning situations many personal qualitative and measurable differences. The measurable differences may be physical such as height, weight, and speed, or mental, such as intelligence. Among qualitative differences are such things as special interests, aptitudes, and methods of working. Both types of individual differences cause players to vary in their style of performance, for no two persons will carry out an assignment in exactly the same manner.

Motivation to learn and improve will result from various sources, but the best type of motivation is that which stirs the learner through its compatibility with his own goal or purpose. When activities are meaningful to the player—that is, when he sees that they are the means by which he may improve his performance—he is more likely to enter into them with enthusiasm. A rise in emotions during competitive sports activity is to be expected, but the degree of rise will vary with individuals. A coach should strive for the optimum level of incentive for each player, so that all may be stimulated without being disconcerted.

Fear is a natural form of emotion which inhibits learning and so should be fought against at every opportunity. There are several methods of breaking fear habits; experience, knowledge, and skill are recognized as factors which build up confidence and reduce fear in individuals. Variations in temperament will be found in every squad, and some variations may be extreme. Where a type of temperament acts as a handicap to a player, the coach should strive to make the individual understand his own disposition and take steps to readjust it, if possible. A coach should realize that there are differences in the power of the sensory nerve apparatus among his athletes. Hypersensitivity will cause a "low threshold for pain," meaning that the boy's hurts will be magnified in interpretation in his brain. Unable to concentrate on the contest, he should be given a rest until the intensity of the pain stimulus subsides. Competitive spirit is a quality which comes under the heading of learned behavior and, as such, should be taught by the coach, using all the concepts for good teaching and learning which he has at his disposal.

Test Questions

1. Explain the contrast between objective and subjective differences in individual athletes.
2. How does home environment affect the progress of the young athlete?
3. What factors other than speed may determine an athlete's fitness for a position?
4. List some reasons for variations in performing athletic skills.
5. Define style in athletic performance?
6. Explain the difference between motives and incentives.
7. How do personality traits affect the learning of certain athletic skills?
8. List some favorable and unfavorable attitudes for learning found among athletes.
9. How are motivation and meaning related in the acquisition of skills and knowledges?
10. What are the physiological responses to a rise in emotions?
11. What is meant by mental stance?
12. What types of fear are found among young players?
13. Name and explain a few methods of controlling fear.
14. From the standpoint of permanency, what is the best method of breaking a fear habit?
15. Is temperament easily changed? Does self-understanding help?
16. Which of the temperamental types might be considered problem athletes?
17. How does the "threshold for pain" affect the player's performance?
18. How would you describe a "craving for crisis"?
19. Can competitive spirit be learned?
20. Is competitive spirit a part of athletic instinct?
21. How might a high emotional state cause a loss of efficiency in a highly emotional player?

Discussion Questions

1. What effect, if any, does ethnic background have on athletic performance?
2. Will gold stars and other symbols of outstanding play have a motivational effect on college athletes?

3. What kind of temperament would you look for in a quarterback, a catcher, a two-miler?
4. Some coaches select and post a list of teams before the start of the season or on the first day. How does this affect competitive spirit?
5. Are the same types of fear found among older, experienced players as among youngsters? What are the implications for coaching?
6. Can the performance of a player with a low threshold for pain be altered by telling him that the pain is only in his mind?
7. How could a defeatist attitude develop from practice situations?
8. While youngsters are being coached, do they actually become more self-assured, confident, and emotionally stable, or is this an illusion created through the survival of the fittest?

Suggested Readings

BOOKS

1. Berkowitz, Leonard. *Aggression.* New York: McGraw Hill Book Co., 1962, pp. 299-300.
2. Bernard, Harold W. *Adolescent Development.* Yonkers: World Book Co., 1957, Chapters 3, 4, and 12.
3. Cattell, Raymond B. "Some Psychological Correlates of Physical Fitness and Physique." *Exercise and Fitness.* Chicago: The Athletic Institute, 1959, p. 145.
4. Conrad, Herbert. *Studies in Human Development* (Jones). New York: Appleton-Century-Crofts, 1966, p. 247.
5. Davis, Elwood C., and Lawther, John D. *Successful Teaching of Physical Education.* Englewood Cliffs: Prentice Hall Inc., 1948, Chapter 13.
6. Griffith, Coleman. *Psychology of Coaching.* New York: Charles Scribner and Son, 1932, pp. 13, 115-116.
7. Haas, Kurt. *Understanding Ourselves and Others.* Englewood Cliffs: Prentice Hall Inc., 1965, p. 29.
8. Hamrin, Shirley, and Paulson, Blanche. *Counseling Adolescents.* Ann Arbor: Edwards Brothers Inc., 1960, Chapter I.
9. Jersild, Arthur T. *Child Psychology.* Englewood Cliffs: Prentice Hall Inc., 1960, pp. 255-285.
10. Lindgren, Henry C. *Psychology of Personal and Social Adjustment.* New York: American Book Co., 1953, pp. 60-84.

11. Massey, Harold, and Vineyard, Edwin. *The Profession of Teaching.* New York: The Odyssey Press, 1961, pp. 110-137.
12. Nelson, David M. *Football—Principles and Play.* New York: The Ronald Press Co., 1962, pp. 28-32.
13. Pinter, Rudolf, and Ryan John. *Educational Psychology.* New York: Barnes and Noble, 1962, pp. 39-41.
14. Reidman, Sarah. *The Physiology of Work and Play.* New York: Holt, Rinehart and Winston, 1950, pp. 549-557.
15. Sorensen, Herbert, and Mahn, Marguerite. *Psychology for Living.* New York: McGraw Hill Book Co., 1964, pp. 113-135.
16. Secrest, Lee, and Wallace, John. *Psychology and Human Problems.* Columbus: Charles E. Merrill Book Co., 1967, pp. 341-344.
17. Stagner, Ross. *Psychology of Personality.* New York: McGraw Hill Book Co., 1948, p. 429.
18. Wyburn, G. M., Pickford, R. W., and Hirst, R. J. *Human Senses and Perception.* Toronto: Toronto Press, 1965, pp. 17-22.
19. Young, P. T. *Motivation and Emotion.* New York: John Wiley and Sons, Inc., 1961, pp. 22-23.

Suggested Readings

ARTICLES

1. Blount, Joe M. "Letter-Award Point System," *Scholastic Coach.* Vol. 31-5, 1962, p. 48.
2. Borgotta, Edgar J. "Mood, Personality and Interaction," *The Journal of General Psychology,* Vol. 64:105-137, 1961.
3. Broughton, Bob, and Nelson, Dale. "Verbal Conditioning in Selected Skills," *Scholastic Coach,* Vol. 37-3, November 1967, pp. 38-39, 44-46.
4. Carron, Albert. " Motor Performance Under Stress," *Research Quarterly,* Vol. 39-3, October 1968, pp. 463-469.
5. Carron, A., and Leavitt, J. L. "Effects of Practice Upon Individual Differences and Intra-Variability in a Motor Skill," *Research Quarterly,* Vol. 39-3, October 1968, pp. 470-475.
6. Carter, J. Lindsay. "Somatotypes of College Football Players." *Research Quarterly,* Vol. 39-3, October 1968, pp. 476-481.
7. Casady, Donald. "Relationship Between Written Test Scores and Performance Skills in Sports," *Proceedings Annual Meeting of National College Physical Education Association for Men,* January 1964, pp. 43-46.

8. Cox, James J. "The Tall and the Short of Growth," *Today's Health,* Vol. 46-4, April 1968, pp. 27-29, 72.
9. Davis, William E. "The Meaning of the Athletic Letter," *Scholastic Coach,* Vol. 35-2, October 1965, p. 72.
10. Donelli, Aldo. "Incentive and Individualism Afford the American Athlete the Edge in the Sports Race," *Amateur Athlete,* Vol. XXXVI, No. 7, July 1965, pp. 671.
11. Duback, Harry. "Creating Interest," *JOHPER,* Vol. 39-4, April 1968, p. 71.
12. Edwards, M., and Neal, R. "Competition: Why Should I Strive? What More Could One Ask?" *JOHPER,* Vol. 37-1, January 1966, pp. 28-29, 61-62.
13. Fales, Edward D., Jr. "What Makes the Athlete?" *Science Digest,* Vol. 32:57-9, October 1952.
14. Frymier, Jack R. "Motivating Students to Learn," *NEA Journal,* Vol. 57-2, February 1968, pp. 37-42.
15. Gieck, Joe. "Psychological Aspects of Athletes," *Athletic Journal,* Vol. XLVIII, February 1968, pp. 23, 77-78.
16. Gibson, Vince. "Kansas State's Organization and Drills for Defense," *Scholastic Coach,* Vol. 37-1, September 1967, pp. 14-5, 80-87.
17. Goldfarb, J. M. "Motivational Psychology in Coaching," *Scholastic Coach,* Vol. 38-6, February 1968, p. 54.
18. Hanebutt, Elmer. "Obligations of an Athlete," *Athletic Journal,* Vol. XLV-10, June 1965, p. 41.
19. Hatch, William H. "Playing the Percentages," *Athletic Journal,* Vol. XLIV-7, March 1964, p. 20.
20. Hoitsma, Harry H. "Coaches Dilemma," *JOHPER,* Vol. 32-9, December 1961, p. 25.
21. Howell, Maxwell L. "Influence of Emotional Tension on Speed of Reaction and Movement," *Research Quarterly,* 24:22:32, March 1953.
22. Johnson, Warren. "A Study of Emotion Revealed in the Study of Two Types of Athletic Contests," *Research Quarterly,* 25:484-485, December 1964.
23. Johnson, W., Hutton, D., and Johnson, G. "Personality Traits of Champion Athletes as Measured by Two Prospective Tests: Rorschach and H.T.P.," *Research Quarterly,* 25:484-485, December 1964.
24. Jordan, Dayton. "Emotional Fitness for Track and Field Competition," *JOHPER,* Vol. 32-2, February 1961, pp. 29-30.

25. Kipnis, D., and Wagner, D. "The Interaction of Personality and Intelligence on Task Performance," *Educational and Psychological Measurement*, Vol. XXV-3, 1965, pp. 731-744.
26. Kressler, Raymond. "Motivation for Track and Field Athletics," *Athletic Journal*, Vol. XLV-5, January 1965, pp. 46-47.
27. Leeper, R. W. "A Motivation Theory of Emotion to Replace Emotion as Disorganized Response," *Journal of Genetic Psychology*, December 1954, 85:289-304.
28. Marsh, Richard L. "The Beginning of Sports Psychology in Distance Running," *Coach and Athlete*, Vol. XXIX, April 1967, pp. 20-24.
29. Nelson, Dale O., and Langer, Phillip. "Getting to Really Know Your Players," *Athletic Journal*, Vol. XLIV-1, September 1963, pp. 39, 88-93.
30. Ogilvie, Bruce C. "What is an Athlete?" *JOHPER*, Vol. 38-6, June 1967, p. 48.
31. Sexton, D., and Dooley, J. "Game Day Psychological Devices," *Scholastic Coach*, Vol. 35-9, May 1966, pp. 74, 82-83.
32. Schreiber, V. R., and Herman, M. "Why People Play Football," *Science Digest*, Vol. 60-3, September 1966, pp. 12-16.
33. Skinner, Charles and Krupa, Thomas. "High School Wrestlers Need Motivation," *Athletic Journal*, Vol. 41-4, December 1963, pp. 46-48.
34. Slusher, Howard. "Personality and Intelligence Characteristics of Selected High School Athletes and Non-Athletes," *Research Quarterly*.
35. Stoops, Emery. "Keys to Leadership," *Phi Delta Kappan*, Vol. 45, October 1963, pp. 42-43.
36. Veller, Don. "Problem Children in Athletics," *Athletic Journal*, Vol. 45-3, November 1967, pp. 36, 72.
37. Veller, Don. "Praise or Punishment," *Athletic Journal*, Vol. 48-6, February 1968, pp. 40, 78-80.
38. Wolfe, Herman. "Picking the Team," *Scholastic Coach*, Vol. 34-2, October 1964, p. 30.
39. Word, E. Larry. "Reasons for Recent Popularity of Wrestling," *The Physical Educator*, Vol. 25-1, March 1968, p. 26.

Chapter VI
COACHING THE SQUAD

"Take advantage of the social implication of team play."

MEETING THE SQUAD FOR THE FIRST TIME

First impressions often turn out to have a quality of permanence. The coach's general appearance will create some sort of effect, so it is important that in this first confrontation between a new coach and his team the players will like what they see and hear. Proper dress, good grooming, and articulate speech give an immediate impression of sharpness. Carelessness about such personal practices could indicate sloppiness about other factors. For the first meeting with his players, a coach might well follow the slogan of the razor blade company to "look sharp—feel sharp."

One's self-image will serve as a guide in adjusting to this important social situation. People adjust to any social situation and to the individuals in it on the basis of the way they feel about themselves. The coach should exude quiet confidence. He must have been sure of his ability to function well in this new setting or he would not have accepted the position; therefore his self-confidence should manifest itself in everything he says and does during the meeting.

The initial contact between a coach and his team preferably should take place somewhere other than a playing field, gymnasium or locker room. To wait until the first practice session to hold this important but time consuming meeting would be a woeful waste of valuable time. Practice hours are too precious to be used for anything but action, not sitting and listening, which is called for in this situation. Because a degree of formality will prevail, the meeting should take place in a classroom, club room, or a meeting hall in the Student Union where the atmosphere is better suited to produce the social outcomes desired, namely:

For the coach:

1. To gain some knowledge of the type of squad he has inherited.

2. To establish a relationship between himself and the players which will develop into a fine rapport.
3. To discover potential leaders among the squad.
4. To impress the players with his and his other coaches' fitness for the job.

For the player:

1. To understand the coaches' philosophy of coaching.
2. To understand their responsibilities for the success of the team.

Ordinarily a new coach will not be totally unaware of the type of squad he has inherited. Some facts about the individuals and the type of game they have been playing over the past few years will be ascertained before the meeting takes place. In fact, much of it should have been gathered before he applied for the new position. Interviews with coaches left over from the old regime, examination of the squad personnel records, viewing of game movies of the past few seasons, and chats with faculty members, townspeople, and interested alumni will serve to acquaint the coach with the following facts:

a. the number of lettermen returning,
b. the minutes of actual game experience for each player,
c. the ages of the players,
d. the intelligence of the players,
e. the apparent morale of the team,
f. the extent of discipline exerted on the team,
g. the attitude of students and faculty toward the team.

The team will already have some knowledge of the coach's background, but a brief survey of his past record delivered by him in a modest, matter-of-fact manner, bringing out some facts about his past that might not be widely known would be appropriate. He should lead from this discourse into a few words concerning his present task. At this point, he might invite comments from the group concerning their past season or seasons, their opponents, and their analysis of the reasons for the team's success or failure. Team leaders usually will emerge during this session, but it will not be until later, when these individuals actually perform in game situations, that a coach can validate his impressions of the speakers. At some time during the discourse there naturally will arise an opportunity for the coach to comment on the past performance of the team as it appears to him at that point. Only favorable comments are in order. The good points should be categorized as the strong foundation upon which the new team will be built. Care must be taken not to speak of the former coach in disparaging terms for, regardless of how successful or unsuccessful he has been, there are sure to be some squad members or assistants present who have a fondness for him and will resent any uncomplimentary reference to him.

A presentation of the coach's philosophy is next in order, so that the players may understand the "what" and "why" of the program they are to follow. His attitude toward such factors as offense, defense, conditioning, study, individual counseling, conduct, training rules, punctuality, appearance, individual skill practice, and many other problems must be clear to the squad. He will explain his long range goals and objectives, followed by a clear concise plan for attaining them. His ambitions for the program, such as strengthening the schedule, additions to the coaching staff, improvements and control of financial aid, tutorial methods, and publicity should be presented not as vague, abstract ideas, but as clear, concise, definable plans, invaluable in every respect. They must be reasonable, practical, attainable objectives, not beyond the coach's personal and material resources for fulfilling them.

The squad will be anxious to learn the coach's attitude toward such items as the athletic scholarship program (if any), the degree of opportunity for starting positions, rules of behavior and disciplinary action for infraction of rules. These are only a few of the factors of the program, but they are paramount in the minds of the players because of their personal nature. Financial aid often decides the question of whether or not an athlete can remain in college. A change in regime introduces an element of uncertainty about his retention of the scholarship in spite of rules covering the problem. Assurances that the institution will live up to its obligations to all students should be given.

All athletes are ambitious for a starting position, but it is difficult to win one over a player who has been a starter for one or more years. Often substitutes feel that they deserve the starting job over the men selected by the coaches. Under a change in the coaching staff, they see the chance of proving their worth without having prejudice affect their chances. An announcement that all starting berths are open will fire their enthusiasm.

Rules of behavior on and off the field must take into consideration the age and maturity of the players. Adolescents can be expected to act like adolescents, while adult behavior can be demanded of adults. Unreasonable restrictions should be avoided, for they will breed infractions, and every infraction should call for disciplinary action. The coach could assure the players that infractions will bring penalties, but in each case he will take into consideration extenuating circumstances.

It should be pointed out to the squad that the success of the program will depend upon real cooperation among a wide range of agencies, such as players, coaches, faculty, alumni, parent and booster clubs, managers, trainers, etc., all discharging their duties as a single structure in a unified effort known as the program, be it football, basketball, baseball, track, soccer, swim, or whatever. Unlike a truly democratic organization, there must be a concentration of power, of decision making in the hands of one man, the coach. He will expect to receive guidance, advice, and counsel from each agency listed above but, above all, the major determining factor will be the quality of effort coming from the players. It will call for the marshalling of all their health and skill resources to fulfill their responsibilities. He should close the meeting with a wish that they now regard themselves as partners with him and other agencies of the institution to bring about the ultimate goal of becoming a winning team, expressing confidence in their capabilities to get the job done supremely well. It is of deep concern to all of them to assist each other in improving their contributions to the joint effort. With all concerned parties, agreeing on goals, diligently pursuing the planned activities, accepting a concentration of power in the coaching staff, there will be generated the necessary social action to produce a winner.

THE CONCEPTS OF GROUP ACTION

Athletics call for much individual performance; it also calls for the individuals to blend their deeds and acts with those of their companions in a group enterprise. It is difficult to consider concepts of group action without reference to socialization. A coach is faced with the problem of not only imparting skills and knowledges to his players but also getting them to understand and appreciate their dependence upon one another, to recognize the strength of the team as a group. The concepts of group action as discussed here will refer not only to the player's activities in the sport but also to the coach's relationship to the players and the learning situation.

Authorities have mentioned guidelines for group action; some of them seem modifiable to the practice periods of athletic squads situation.

1. Make optimum use of the practice time for player activity, and keep coach participation at a minimum. Many coaches are guilty of talking too much. The players stand and listen while he goes into a lengthy and involved discussion of the many details of the act to be practiced. Players learn by doing and should be given every opportunity to be the actors and not the audience.

2. Distribute skilled and unskilled players in such a way that the activities are stimulating, challenging, and safe. When skilled players work against the weak, inexperienced scrubs for long periods in rough contact sports, neither group profits much and the activity ceases to be fun. Injuries may be sustained by the weaker boys because they are overpowered and do not have the skill or knowledge to protect themselves when fatigue sets in. Short periods may be of some value, but as soon as the more advanced group has exhibited its mastery the activity should be stopped and stronger opposition supplied, in order that the learning situation may more closely assume that of game conditions. In any sport, mixing the players so that the unskilled have an opportunity of performing with the skilled sometimes stimulates and inspires the former group to greater efforts than are usually displayed. One method of learning is through imitated behavior, and among the classes of persons who are imitated are the superior technicians in any field.

3. Help the player understand that certain skills are a vital need for an excellent performance. Many boys may recognize the importance of the skill to their own playing, but the need for the skill is not as strong as the desire to loaf, so they are satisfied to remain mediocre; however, players who fully adopt the idea of improving will supplement the regular practice sessions with self-directed practice. In fact, many of the finest basketball players have spent hundreds of hours at individual practice in working against another player in unsupervised play. The touring golf professionals may be cited as examples of devotion to practice in the quest for perfection. The best of them put in long hours of practice whenever their critical self-analysis indicates that their proficiency is slipping.

4. Make sure that the young inexperienced player has an opportunity to be successful in his first experiences at learning an athletic skill. When a boy first reports for a sport, he should not be expected to perform the same skills as the older,

experienced players. His activities should be modified to coincide with his ability in the simple movements learned first. As he gains in skill, he can be introduced to the more complex movements of the game. Football coaches have sometimes been guilty of putting a big, strong, unpolished boy, reporting for the first time, against a group of well-trained varsity players. The green player, having nothing but strength and size to aid him, finds that it is not enough against speed, finesse, and knowledge. He usually gets very fatigued and acquires, along with numerous bruises, a healthy dislike for football in general and the coach and his players in particular. It would have been far better to wait until the boy had more insight into what was expected of him, gained some knowledge and skill, and had become eager to try his prowess against the better boys.

Another point for coaches to remember is that it is always better to suspend an activity while the boys are still eager to continue rather than to wait until it gets to the point where they are hoping to quit.

5. Stress the fundamental importance of the contributions of each skilled performer to the success of the team as a whole. Many men are involved in every offensive or defensive play in a game, and the degree to which each man carries out his assignment is summed up in the total performance of the team. The contributions of each player are by no means equal, because all do not have equal ability; but each has a duty which is, theoretically at least, within his power, and he is expected to perform it. Players should be made to understand that on every offensive play the key maneuver, or those maneuvers made at the point of attack, are most important, and the entire team is depending on those players to perform the key maneuvers perfectly or nearly so.

While the key moves are the most important, they are by no means the entire answer to a successful play. Each little detail has a meaning, and the player responsible for carrying it out must do so correctly. For instance, the football player who carries out a fake has a great deal to do with breaking the ball carrier into the open. The basketball player who takes his guard away from the "key hole" opens the pathway for a teammate to score unmolested. All players should acquire the attitude that to share in the glory one must share in the responsibility for gaining it. Encourage the feeling of group responsibility for victories and defeats. Both must be acknowl-

edged, as natural outcomes of competition as defeats usually
are the fault of more than one player.

6. Recognize the value of self-sacrifice for the good of the team,
as well as the topnotch performance for the good of the team.
Linemen are often regarded as the forgotten men on the
football team, but it is not necessary that they be so regarded.
Most football players of today realize that a lineman has to be
not only a good, fast blocker but also a quick thinker to
diagnose the defensive alignment and adapt his performance
to it. An excellent shooter is invaluable to a basketball team,
but without a good backboard man a team cannot effect
victories. A splendid pitching performance can be wasted
unless the hitters can produce enough runs to insure the
victory. With knowledge of the game comes mutual respect
for the contributions of all players to the success of the team,
but the coach should hasten the process by visible commendation for all sincere efforts toward team success. The similarity between situations in team-sport activities, and in life,
should constantly be pointed out by the coach. It seems
reasonable to expect that there will be some transfer of
training from the playing field to other situations.

7. Although most coaches prefer to have more than one player
competing for a starting berth, it is not always a good plan to
keep this spirit of competition at a high point. Individuals
differ in their reactions to it. Some are not affected at all,
while others become so emotionally upset that their efficiency
is impaired. Most players are stirred to greater effort, and this
is probably why most coaches prefer it. Care must be taken,
however, that individual motivation does not lead to a loss of
team loyalty and friendly personal relationships.

8. Beware of animosity between playing partners. This is not to
say that two players who are unfriendly should not be played
side by side. Close friends probably would tend to cooperate
more, but the situation may require that the two unfriendly
boys play beside each other. The answer seems obvious. The
coach should make every effort to iron out the differences
between the two and strive for mutual respect and admiration
for each other's ability.

Enthusiasm should be kept at a high point, cooperation
encouraged, mental and physical growth stimulated, and
genuine friendships established in a sound program of sports.
Participation in athletics is a voluntary action engaged in by

those who are satisfying an inner urge for physical strife on a sportsmanlike basis. Care should be taken that this need be gratified in activities that are stirring, clean, and wholesome.

DISCIPLINE

Discipline has long been a matter of concern for educators and others interested in the training of youth. The history of education in the United States shows an early regard for the problem of discipline which resolved itself into a question of whether or not corporal punishment was necessary to establish the teacher's authority and maintain order. Although the term discipline has broader implications today, it still refers to the guidance and control of behavior. In an ideal sense, discipline strives for the achievement of self-discipline by the student as a result of positive motivation. In other words, the players act in an acceptable manner because they want to do so. This desire to conform and to be an asset to the group can be developed in young athletes if the coach will concern himself with ways and means of bringing it about.

Sports-learning situations are characterized as semidemocratic and probably will remain so for many years. Most modern coaches are not arrogant, domineering individuals, but are friendly, sincere men who believe in strict discipline. If there is one matter in which the learning situation of the classroom and that of the athletic field differ, it is in the matter of pupil participation in planning. A sport season has many features that are similar to a military campaign, and the successful conduct of both types of enterprise seems to call for a line and staff organization with orders emanating from the top. As in a military group, the assistants (staff members) share in the planning, and the orders are made as clear and understandable as possible to those who are carrying them out. This is not to imply that players' feelings are unimportant. Players should not be prohibited from asking questions and making suggestions concerning their program, for such prohibition would create resentment. Their comments can be passed along to the head coach during the staff planning sessions and given due consideration. Athletes apparantly accept this centering of authority, and unless the coach becomes unduly overbearing they go about their designated tasks without resentment. It is not unusual for players to appreciate some forms of constraint. They openly laud the coach who is a "stickler for details" and who insists on their adherence to training rules which aid their health. So, for the sake of order and cohesion as opposed to chaos and confusion, it seems safe to say that athletic coaching is carried on in a semi-democratic atmosphere in which the "consent to be governed" plays an important part.

A coach should strive to promote a relationship of mutual confidence and sincerity between himself and his players. He must display genuine interest and sympathy in the personal problems of his boys. He must be fair, ready with encouragement, quick to praise, and hesitant to censure. His players should discover that the coach is competent, reliable, intelligent, a man who stimulates faith and self-assurance.

It is sometimes difficult for a coach to hide his fondness for a certain player. Deepseated and long-established attitudes may make the coach biased in favor of one type of boy. Perhaps he himself was a rough, aggressive youngster, and he looks with favor upon this type. He may even be opposed to the shy, quiet type of boy. A coach should never let his emotions interfere with his coaching and show favoritism.

A coach should not overlook insubordination or infractions of rules. To do so will result in a loss of respect for him. Coaches should not predict certain punishments for definite infractions, because circumstances may alter cases. A better plan is to take care of each situation as it arises. Disciplinary cases should be handled wisely. An entire practice period should never be assigned as punishment. The purpose of a practice period is to gain knowledge or improve one's technique in some skill and not as a disciplinary measure. The causes and not the symptoms are the important factors. The coach should endeavor to find out why a youngster fails to conform. The reason may be a deep one, calling more for correction than punishment. The objective is to bring about improved behavior by whatever method seems best.

The chief concern of the coach is the establishment of a spirit of willingness to work within the group. The ultimate aim of all discipline is to bring about unified action and insure that it will occur spontaneously. Teamwork is very important, and teamwork implies friendliness, cooperative endeavor, spontaneous offering of aid, and the acceptance and giving of constructive criticism without involving personalities. The coach must be a part of the group and still maintain control of the group. Sound, meaningful learning is the foundation for desirable relations with learners. They must be convinced that what they are doing is worth doing and that, for them, the chosen method of doing it is the best. When the boys are allowed to ask questions, make suggestions, and are encouraged to discuss methods with the coaches, they are more likely to enter into the practice experiences with enthusiasm. This need not detract from the coach's control of policies; it is merely a matter of acting human with human beings.

A coach should believe in himself and in the boys. If he acts as though he expected them to be alert, attentive, cooperative, friendly, and eager, the chances are that those responses will be forthcoming.

MORALE

Morale is an attitude or state of mind which may have a physical foundation. It can be defined as a person's approach to problems with respect to self-assurance, persistence, and retention of principles. This implies that morale is a personal factor, but individuals usually associate themselves with others and so morale involves an identification of self with some group purpose. When identifying high morale in an individual, the term most often used is courage; the most expressive word for high group morale is spirit.

From the individual standpoint, the term courage is not used in the sense opposed to cowardice but in the sense opposed to discouragement. Courage is the carrying out of a difficult course of action in spite of extreme difficulty or recognized danger with all thoughts and actions on a single goal. When courage is interpreted thusly, it is possible to associate it with either positive action or endurance. Positive action involves persistent endeavor in the face of resistance and inertia while a person seeks and chooses a method of attack. The persistent endeavor continues as the method is carried out. Endurance refers to physical and mental lasting power. It means resistance against attack while at the same time carrying the intention to go on the offensive whenever the occasion may permit. It is not merely a matter of being able to stand up under fatigue and hurt without whimpering, but of "carrying on" when circumstances combine to make it easier to give up than to continue the struggle. Such then is personal courage.

Most human endeavor is associated endeavor, so morale also has its social aspect or group spirit which refers to a firm and united will to work together. This social aspect introduces new requirements. Men must be loyal to one another, respect one another, agree on a common objective, feel its collective importance, have faith in one another's ability, and bear with one another during periods of physical stress and nervous tension. Seeing morale in the light of this social dimension makes its enemies quite obvious; jealousy, irritability, selfishness, distrust, prejudice, and dissension. They cause an individual to put personal or factional interests above the common cause and instigate warring against his partners instead of the common foe. Collective courage, then, is a state of mind which constitutes high morale while discouragement and disunion, or both, characterize low morale.

Is it possible that this state of mental animation can be instilled in an athlete through a process of good teaching? If the answer is yes, a brief study of the factors which affect morale, high or low, seems to be in order. The causes may be classified as physical, psychological, ideological and rational.[1] All of them may play an important part in determining the quality of mental spiritedness which permeates an athletic team.

Physical causes stem from such factors as heat, cold, hunger, sanitation, fatigue, injuries, medical care, equipment, and the like. Teams will lose their "pep" and enthusiasm when forced to drill for long hours in extreme heat or to stand around idle on a cold afternoon. Poor food or the lack of ample food at the training table will promote disunity and bickering. Dressing and showering facilities which are dirty and limited, worn and cheap equipment, and lack of medical care will tend to lower the spirit and desire of a group of youngsters. On the other hand, a team that is well equipped, well fed, and soundly trained is no easy prey to discouragement.

A team's morale may be heightened psychologically through stimulation of instinctive reactions such as fear, hate, anger, pride, imitation, and friendliness. Popular belief has it that most coaches are past masters at this form of morale stimulation. In rare cases, a coach may find it possible to inspire a boy by making him angry or by getting him to hate an opponent. Wild tales about the bestiality of the rival team are ridiculed by most players. Tradition, history, or hard-won victories in the past, slogans, band music, yelling squads, and pep rallies tend to raise morale. The difficulty with most of these forms of psychological stimulation is that they are superficial. They lack a good, solid base to withstand the shock of long, hard combat. When the pressure of an important game bears down on a team, when injuries pile up, when fatigue inhibits the action of muscles, when the chances of victory start to fade—then is when the psychological reasons seem unimportant and the team resigns itself to its fate.

Ideological causes of morale affect the will through specific beliefs. The members of a team may gain courage from their convictions. They may be convinced that they have the best team in

[1]Ralph Perry, "The Meaning of Morale." *The Educational Record*, 22:446-60, July, 1941.

the conference, that their coach is the smartest in the business, and that they are destined to be winners throughout the season. Perhaps the team has decided that it will have the trickiest attack among the school teams of the league. In spite of the fact that some individuals on the team believe that the group would be better off running a more deliberate-type of attack they will subordinate this personal interest in favor of the group interest. The common goal is so important to them that its achievement, no matter how difficult, exhausting, and delayed, far overshadows the inconveniences it demands.

Rational causes of morale, the last and best type of morale builder, resemble ideological causes in that they are based on belief, but unlike the ideological, they appeal to reason. A rational cause is one in which men believe not merely because their hearts so dictate but because their minds and intellects tell them so. The proof is in their experiences. Players may accept a certain method because of their love and affection for a veteran coach. If this coach is ridiculed, and if his job is threatened because of the team's failures, the boys may band together and put out an extra effort in an attempt to win a game for their beloved coach. This is an ideological cause of high morale. If that same team could be convinced that their coach's knowledge and his methods were the best for them, the cause would be rational.

It would be necessary for the players to have had the experience of trying the coach's methods and finding them successful. When a team has tried out a certain method of attack based on fundamental moves by the individual players and found that the method is highly successful, the members of that team will work long and hard to perfect the necessary maneuvers for proper execution. Their minds tell them that the method is right because their experiences confirm the belief. A team that is sure they are using the best methods because they have seen those methods work is hard to discourage. They realize that failures are due to their own inadequacies or carelessness, and they can be subjected to long and arduous practice sessions in an endeavor to improve. When in the course of a game this team meets one bad break after another, it will refuse to quit because the players firmly believe that their methods are sound and that sooner or later they are bound to click for the winning combination.

THE DESIRE TO LEARN

When team members believe they have reached such a point of excellence in their performance that all they need to win is to line up and put on their exhibition, they are ripe for a crushing setback. Perhaps a defeat would be a good thing. It would uncover their shortcomings, erase the feeling of satisfaction with their present level of achievement, and incite greater efforts toward learning. Of course, defeats are not to be sought even for so lofty a purpose, but the problem of intent or desire to learn is a consideration for all teaching.

Some psychologists believe that the will to learn is the first and essential law of learning. On any athletic squad, there is no learning where there is no will to learn, and the desire to learn will be centered around the learner's goal. Learning will never take place unless the player has a desire to learn. This depends upon an understanding of definite and explicit instructions which the player may have received from a coach or imposed upon himself. So long as the player knows what he intends and wants to do and understands his method of proceeding, he has a good chance of accomplishing the act.

As an individual meets a situation time and time again, it becomes a sort of game between himself and the situation for mastery and success. Through a gradual process of elimination and adjustment, the learner's methods of dealing with the situation become more and more efficient and satisfactory to himself. The experience of success thus leads to increased mastery by promoting within the individual a positive, assured attitude and a feeling of mild exultation over his newfound abilities. This stimulates him to further trials for increased ability. We see this point operate in a boy learning to throw a curve ball. When he finally puts together the ingredients of proper grip, arm angle, and wrist snap, the ball will break. There will be no need for the coach to exhort the boy to renewed efforts to improve the curve. In fact, the young pitcher will have to be advised against overworking his arm.

The individual members of a team must be stimulated to work—so a goal is a necessity. To win all games may be the goal, or merely to win the next one may be enough. If victory is the goal, it is a remote goal in contrast to the more immediate goals such as the mastery of certain plays and techniques necessary for winning. If the desire or the need for victory is strong enough, the players will work hard during the learning experiences. It is essential, though, for the players to see some chance of accomplishing their goal. If the team is to be hopelessly outmanned in the contest, or if the plays designed by the coach are well beyond their abilities, the team will lose its desire to learn because of the utter inaccessibility of the goal.

American sports are fascinating games for most youngsters, containing a great deal of intrinsic interest; that is, the activities themselves afford much satisfaction for those participating in them. Psychologists maintain that it is the task of education (as well as other agencies) to develop and strengthen certain interests as more or less permanent features of a person's makeup. The task of the coach is one of keeping and strengthening the intrinsic value in the game for the players. This he may accomplish by getting them in fine physical condition for enjoying the strenuous elements of the game, getting the team to agree on goals for accomplishment, and seeing that the team has a reasonable chance of attaining the goals.

When a group can agree on what is to be accomplished and what each member's contribution is to be, it will enter into the task of accomplishment with a great deal of enthusiasm. A coach may desire to put in a certain type of offense for his team, or he may want to use a defense which calls for a high degree of coordination between players. In either case, the team will have to work hard and conscientiously to master the intricacies of that style of play. The coach must convince the team, first, that the new material is sound; second, that they are capable of mastering it. With enthusiasm for the task aroused, goals firmly established, and methods clearly outlined, the group will almost drive itself without any further stimulation from the coaches.

THE WILL TO WIN

Probably no phase of American sports has been criticized and maligned more than the desire for victory or the playing to win. Authorities have bemoaned the fact that coaches overlook the social and educational values of athletic competition in their striving to win records. This may have been true in the early history of college and secondary school sports and, in some instances, may still be true today; but with the advent of the well-educated coach has come a better understanding of the place of sports in American education.

Winning is an American tradition. The history of the nation abounds with incidents of triumph over hardship and suffering. Americans are a confident people who attack problems with the intention of solving them successfully. The educational system is designed to prepare for future as well as present living, and its evaluating methods are based mainly on achievement. The determination to succeed or the will to win seems quite appropriate in this sort of organization.

The will to win grows out of high morale. In order that a team's determination to succeed be valid, it must be based on energy, physical conditioning, skills, knowledges, habits of perseverance, and be focused on one goal—victory. All of those qualities and factors are derived from a good program of learning experiences, plus the leadership of the coach. The attitude of the coach is reflected in the conduct and thoughts of his players. No matter how well trained a team may be, if the coach lacks the power to inspire the players, the team will be colorless, listless, and spiritless. A coach who is confident, alert, assured, courageous, and dynamic can convince his players by his actions that victory is theirs if they work for it. The high morale which comes from their experiences and associations with such a man will stand them in good stead when the fight becomes difficult.

A coach who teaches to win must also prepare for the eventuality of defeat, for in defeat will come a test of the will to win. A coach must teach his boys the art of losing graciously, as well as of winning modestly. Boasting of one's own success and ridiculing of an opponent's defeat is not a part of American sportsmanship, and neither is whimpering nor alibiing in defeat. Winning opponents should be congratulated by the losers, but the losers should possess determination to turn the tables at their next meeting. Players can be taught to diagnose the reasons for defeat, to study their own weaknesses and failures in a contest. A postgame recapitulation of the events leading to defeat should always be made by the coach. He should climax it with an appeal to the players to use the lessons learned in that contest for making them more efficient in the next.

Coaches believe that sports are educational and that the development of proper habits, attitudes, and appreciations are outcomes of participation in the game. The will to win or determination to succeed is important in life, for without it a man lacks ambition. It seems probable that there can be a transfer of training from the learning situation in games to that of other life situations. Surely, there are times in a man's life when he needs the determination to succeed in the face of obstacles, to overcome handicaps, and to win over strong opposition. When failure is a man's lot, he needs the determination to use the experiences not as reasons for pity but as references for a new attack.

The will to win and the wish to win are not synonomous. A team should be made to realize that the will to win is more of a will *to prepare for winning.* Wishes for victory will not be gratified unless persons prepare to win by working hard. When the capacity to win has been developed, the will to win has meaning.

OVERCONFIDENCE

Confidence is a mental attitude resulting from the acquisition of ability to perform a task. True confidence is associated with high morale, for it stems not only from belief in one's self but also from proven skill. The mere conviction that one is right is a valuable asset, but to have a background of proof for that conviction has an even more far-reaching effect. To have the skills and knowledges which enable one to perform brilliantly and thus to prove one's ability requires thorough preparation—whether it be winning a game or performing a heart transplant.

When confidence is created soundly in an individual, it is likely to breed similar feelings in those about him, especially if they are concerned with a common cause and are all striving toward similar ends. Moreover, confidence grows within the individual himself with each added success. The winning team seems to win more easily so long as confidence is sound, that is, well founded on proof of methods.

A confident person is one who knows his own ability and who respects the skill of an opponent or realizes the difficulty of tasks that lie ahead. A person may express confidence in his own ability before he is aware of the enormity of a job, only to have his confidence fall when the difficulty is appreciated. A rookie entering the professional ranks is a good case in point. No matter how brilliantly he performed in college, invariably he suffers a rude awakening when he pits his skills against the seasoned professionals. Confidence will return later on a firmer basis, as the tasks are better understood and mastered.

When a person or a team experiences easy victories or a long string of successes, they may overestimate their ability or underestimate their future opponents. This form of delusion or false security is known as overconfidence. There is no way of knowing how many games have been lost as a result of overconfidence, but the large number of "upset" victories scored by supposedly inferior teams each season makes it seem likely that the number is tremendous.

A team suffering from an exalted opinion of itself is heading for disaster, for its members will not exert the necessary effort to prepare properly for the game. The players will show an utter disregard for detail. Their timing and precision become sloppy because individuals who are certain that they can better their past performances are likely to use inferior methods to complete the task. The players, feeling smug and satisfied, fail to complete the techniques required for a good performance and pay little or no attention to good form. They are not willing to push themselves near to their potential limits but are satisfied to stop at their practical limits of performance. An easy schedule or lack of competition in practice may result in a loss of perspective for a team. The strength of their opponents may have been so low that the team ran up top-heavy scores with little effort, and so they come to expect that the same degree of effort against all opponents will bring similar successes. A team that scrimmages against a weak group of scrubs or an average freshman squad is very likely to develop a false sense of superiority. Moreover, the players become satisfied with mediocre performances that have been adequate for those situations. The boys become so fascinated by their present achievements that their past failures are forgotten; they become blind to any future engagements which require more skill than they now possess.

Too much publicity for a team or for its individual members is often blamed for the development of overconfidence. The coach is in a position to control much of the publicity given out; but, as a team or an individual member gains prominence, more and more lines are written about their achievements, and radio and television commentators dwell on their prowess. Publicity is a valuable asset from a financial standpoint and some schools, unfortunately, have to depend upon gate receipts to support their entire athletic program. Young players, however, may take seriously everything that has been written or said about them, and if the publicity has been too laudatory it can lead to feeling of smugness, security, and superiority.

An overconfident player may feel that he is safe in disregarding teamwork in an attempt to live up to his publicity, and so he may ruin the spirit of cooperation among the team members. A team that enters a contest expecting to gain an easy victory will not go about its tasks with zest and enthusiasm. The basic fundamental techniques will be sloppy, ball handling poor, and the running halfhearted. When such a team suddenly finds that its efforts are fruitless against an inspired foe, they may become disorganized. To snap out of such a mental attitude which has persevered for a week or longer is very difficult, especially in the heat of a game. It takes a mighty good group of players figuratively to lift themselves by the bootstraps and begin playing the game as they should.

There are methods of preventing overconfidence and of remedying it when the symptoms appear. To prevent it, the coach should attempt first to control the publicity his team receives. If he is afraid that too much praise will react against the best efforts of the team or an individual member, he can request the press and radio men to ease up. Second, the coach can have the scouts dwell long and loudly on the prowess of the coming opponent. If the opponent is woefully weak as a team, the scouts may emphasize the skill or strength of one or two members and may exaggerate their concern over the ability of the team to stop these stars. Third, the coach can use as many players as possible in the games so that the first string players do not come to think of themselves as indispensable.

When a team has become overconfident, the surest but least desirable method of remedying it is through defeat. A week of hard work is another device for curing the attitude of complacency when it appears. A team that is driven hard to accomplish something during the week may take seriously the coach's apparent concern over the coming game. The coach should demand excellent performance from his players every once in a while and, when the team shows signs of overconfidence, he should be a stickler for details. The coach can afford to be hard to please at this time. A change in the lineup will sometimes aid in snapping a team out of its lethargy, especially if a known loafer has been demoted. This method will lose its effectivenes unless the coach sticks to his decision and actually starts the new man in the game.

The coach should realize that overconfidence is a mental attitude that is built up over a period of time and that it has definite symptoms which can be observed. Upon their emergence, steps must be taken to remedy the condition. Knowing the causes of overconfidence, the coach should also be on the alert to prevent its occurrence through some of the steps mentioned above.

THE MENTAL LEVEL OF THE SQUAD

If a classroom teacher confronts a pupil with a task for which he is not ready, with the implication that he should succeed, it will give the pupil a feeling of frustration and undermine his security. Instead, the teacher should guide the pupil into learning situations that he can encounter confidently and with enough success to afford him gratification, stimulation, and growth. This principle holds true for athletic activities. To insist on a highly skilled performance from a young athlete whose physical development is far from complete could bring on a serious emotional upset. Athletic coaches, like classroom teachers, are faced with the problem of offering their learners tasks which are within their physical and mental capacities.

Mental capacity involves such characteristics as imagination, memory, and reasoning, although they are thought of as being used in a total integrated effort and not as separate entities. Team games call for the exercise of all three of these characteristics, and the degree to which they are developed within the squad will largely determine the type of game which the team can play. The higher the mental level of the squad, the more involved brand of ball the members are capable of playing. A team made up of individuals below the school average in mental capacity would be wise to use a system that is simply devised and easily executed. The number of offensive and defensive formations and plays should be kept at a minimum, so that more time can be allotted to the learning of each necessary task.

An average high school squad will be composed of boys of different mental abilities because of the fact that these abilities mature at different chronological ages. A college team will also have differences in mental ability within the squad, because in mental development like physical development there are wide individual differences and some of the boys may still be in the process of growing mentally. As a rule, college teams are capable of playing a more involved type of game than high school teams because of their experience and age level. As a youngster grows older, he increases in his ability to remember, to heed, to persist at an intellectual task, and to solve problems. These factors of experience and age, however, work for both high school and colleges, for there are differences in age and experience within both groups.

A team made up largely of sophomores generally has difficulty in winning over teams on which older, more experienced players are performing. The sophomore team is usually guilty of misunderstanding, forgetting instructions, and failing to envisage a situation. A coach who burdens a young team with numerous plays, intricate patterns of offense, and defenses for any and all offenses in courting trouble. He would be far better off to concentrate on his basic system with enough variation to keep his players interested and give his system "color." The following year, with their mental abilities matured, the boys should be capable of handling more intricate material and of remembering more details. Naturally, one or two slow learners on a team can handicap the entire group, especially if they are key players on the team. A boy may be an excellent performer in a phase of the game involving only one or two techniques but woefully weak in remembering game plans or diagnosing an opponent's maneuvers. The coach is then faced with the problem of deciding whether the boy's strong points outweigh his weaknesses in the total pattern of team play.

Even though motor ability is not related to intelligence, the smarter team usually learns more skills and learns them faster. This is because of the intelligent person's capacity to understand instructions and to envisage the situation in which the skill is to be used. If a coach has boys who are above the average in intelligence, he may offer them not only more material but also more intricate and involved material. A system that calls for imagination, daring, and interpretation has appeal for smart, alert youngsters and keeps them inspired.

SUMMARY

No person can learn to play football, basektball, or baseball by himself, for they are team games and call for concerted group action; therefore the sociological aspect of teaching must be taken into consideration by the coach. Players must be taught to respect the abilities of their teammates and recognize and accept their own responsibilities for the success of the team. The type of discipline for which the coach should strive is self-discipline. The creation of policies may remain within the coaching staff, but if the players are to enter into the activities with enthusiasm, the coach must maintain an open and receptive mind to their discussions and suggestions regarding methods. High morale based on well-founded beliefs in themselves, their coach, and their system will stand the members of a team in good stead when the tasks facing them are difficult. The knowledge that what they are attempting to learn is right for them is a stimulant for that learning. Enthusiasm for learning may be instilled in a squad if the players can be convinced that the material is sound, that they need it, and that they are capable of mastering it.

The will to win needs a foundation based on the capacity to win. The players can secure this by learning the skills and knowledges which make a team good. Defeats should serve to whet the appetite for victory by pointing out to the team the areas which need improvement. Overconfidence can ruin a team's desire to improve; so the coach should be alert for symptoms of this state of mind after a team has experienced several easy victories. He should never allow the players to become smug and satisfied with mediocre perform-

ances but should demand enough effort to carry out their assignments in proper fashion. The type of assignment which a team is able
to carry out will depend upon the degree to which the mental
abilities of the members have matured. Older, more experienced or
more intelligent teams are capable of handling an intricate and
involved system, whereas such a system would be a handicap to a less
intelligent or less matured team. Team intelligence also affects the
degree to which a team can take advantage of the breaks, the game
opportunities that are offered to the alert players. Success usually
comes to the smart team.

Test Questions

1. Where should the initial meeting between the new coach and his
team take place?
2. What means might a coach employ to insure that he creates a
good impression during his first meeting?
3. What type of information about his team could a coach gather
before his first meeting?
4. What are the desired social outcomes for the coach and players it
is hoped will develop from the first meeting?
5. With brief statements of each, list the eight concepts of group
action.
6. Why should young players be allowed to be successful in their
first attempts at a new skill?
7. Define discipline. For what does it ultimately strive?
8. Why is it not a good plan to have standard penalties for certain
infractions of rules?
9. Should a coach occasionally overlook insubordination or infraction of rules?
10. What are the most expressive terms used in describing high
individual morale and high group morale?
11. Explain the relationship of courage to morale.
12. List some destructive influences on morale.
13. Explain the four types of causes of morale. Which is the best?
Why?
14. How does having a goal affect the desire to learn?
15. How does the possibility of attainment affect learning?
16. Why are the will to win and the wish to win not synonomous?
17. Why must a will to win have a foundation in high morale?

18. What are some symptoms of overconfidence which a team may exhibit?
19. List some ways in which a coach may combat overconfidence.
20. What is involved in mental capacity?
21. Why does a team made up largely of sophomores have difficulty in winning over teams on which older, more experienced players are performing?

Discussion Questions

1. Why is a concentration of power in a coaching staff acceptable in a democratic society?
2. Should a coach try to impress on his team the idea that all players contribute equally to the success and/or failures of the team?
3. How can a strong will to win in sports transfer its habits to later life?
4. If motor ability is not related to intelligence, why does a smarter team usually learn more skills and learn them faster?
5. How much influence should athletes have in determining which position they will play?
6. How would you combat overconfidence after your team has beaten an opponent badly and will be playing them again later in the season?
7. Is it true that a winning team requires less discipline than a losing one? Explain.
8. How does a superathlete affect team morale?
9. Should the captain of a high school team be allowed to handle minor disciplinary problems?
10. How would you attempt to develop a feeling for group action?

Suggested Readings

BOOKS

1. Beaumont, Henry, and Macomber, Freeman. *Psychological Factors in Education*. New York: McGraw Hill Book Co., 1949, pp. 81-82.

2. Blair, G., Jones, R. S., and Simpson, Ray. *Educational Psychology.* New York: The Macmillan Co., 1962, pp. 305-342.
3. Brown, Edward J., and Phelps, Arthur T. *Managing the Classroom.* New York: The Ronald Press Co., 1961, pp. 130-132.
4. Bryant, Paul. *Building a Championship Football Team.* Englewood Cliffs: Prentice Hall, Inc., 1960, p. 5.
5. Buros, Oscar K. *Tests in Print.* Highland Park, N.J.: Gryphon Press, 1961, p. 731.
6. Cofer, Charles N., and Appley, Mortimer H. *Motivation Theory and Research.* New York: John Wiley and Sons.
7. Commins, William. *Principles of Educational Psychology.* New York: The Ronald Press Co., 1937, p. 448.
8. Conrad, Herbert. *Studies in Human Development* (Jones). New York: Appleton-Century- Crofts, 1966, p. 447.
9. Crow, Lester, and Crow, Alice. *Adolescent Development and Adjustment.* New York: McGraw Hill Book Co., 1956, pp. 137-163.
10. Davis, E. C., and Lawther, John. *Successful Teaching in Physical Education.* Englewood Cliffs: Prentice Hall, Inc., 1948, pp. 505-508.
11. Miller, Neal, and Dollard, John. *Social Learning and Imitation.* New Haven: Yale University Press, 1941, pp. 194-196.
12. Ogilvie, Bruce, and Tutko, Thomas. *Problem Athletes and How to Handle Them.* London: Pelham Books, Ltd., 1966.
13. Pressey, Sidney, and Robinson, Francis. *Psychology and the New Education.* New York: Harper & Row., 1944, p. 192.
14. Rupp, Adolph. *Championship Basketball.* Englewood Cliffs: Prentice Hall, Inc., 1960, p. 179.
15. Shetzer, B., and Stone, S. *Fundamentals of Guidance.* Boston: Houghton Mifflin Co., 1966, p. 3-29, 362-379.
16. *United States Naval Academy Training Manual.* "Football," Annapolis: U. S. Naval Institute, 1943, p. 9.
17. Wrenn, C. Gilbert. *Student Personnel Work in College.* New York: The Ronald Press Co., 1951, pp. 455-473.

Suggested Readings

ARTICLES

1. Baer, Roger. "Rules of Conduct for High School Athletes," *Athletic Journal,* Vol. XLVI, February 1966, pp. 54-55.

2. Bergman, Robert. "The 44 Defense and Adjustment to Varied Offensive Situations," *Athletic Journal,* Vol. XLVIII, March 1968, p. 16.
3. Bliss, Gary. "Coaching Techniques That Build Team Unity," *Coaching Clinic,* January 1967, pp. 17-18.
4. Cornicella, Ronald. "Psychology of Winning," *Proceedings* 45th Annual Meeting of American Football Coaches Assn., January 1968, pp. 75-79.
5. Duk, Frank. "The Coach in Time of Social Crisis," *Athletic Journal,* Vol. XLVIII, March 1968, pp. 68, 99.
6. Duncan, Raymond. "It's Important to Win That Game," *Illinois Educational Journal,* Vol. 37, January 1949, pp. 161-162.
7. Edward, Marigold. "Why Should I Strive?" *JOHPER,* Vol. 38-1, January 1966, pp. 28-29.
8. Eldred, Vince. "Coach and Player Relations," *Coach and Athlete,* Vol. XXX-1, August 1967, pp. 16-17.
9. Gieck, Joe. "Psychological Aspects of Athletes," *Athletic Journal,* Vol. XLVIII-6, February 1968, pp. 23, 77.
10. Goldfarb, Joseph. "Motivational Psychology in Coaching," *Scholastic Coach,* Vol. 37-6, February 1968, pp. 54-59.
11. Hanebutt, Elmer. "Obligations of an Athlete," *Athletic Journal,* Vol. XLVI-6, June 1963, p. 41.
12. Harring, Roger. "Building a Winner in Football," *Scholastic Coach,* Vol. 36-8, April 1967, pp. 17-18, 79.
13. Hiers, H. L., Jr. "Developing a Winning Attitude in Track and Field," *The Coaching Clinic,* Vol. 4-13, November 1966, pp. 22-23.
14. Johnson, Donald, and Rhoades, Charles. "Measurement of a Subjective Act of Learning," *Journal of Experimental Psychology,* 18:90-2, January 1941.
15. Karabetsas, James D. "The Psychological Aspect of Coaching," *Coach and Athlete,* Vol. XXIX, March 1967, p. 26.
16. Lewin, Kurt. "Experiments in Autocratic and Democratic Atmospheres," *Social Frontiers,* July 1938, 4:316-319.
17. McClay, Charles. "A Preliminary Study of Factors in Motor Educability," *Research Quarterly, May 1946.*
18. McWhirter, Jeffrice J. "The Application of Sociometric Technique in Basketball," *Athletic Journal,* Vol. XLIV-3, November 1963, pp. 32, 48.
19. Mills, Chuck. "Conducting the Team Briefing," *Athletic Journal,* Vol. 44-1, September 1963, p. 38.

20. Morrill, J. L. "Address," *Proceedings* of the Twenty-Fourth Annual Meeting of the American Football Coaches Association." January 1947, pp. 21-4.
21. Reninger, Grady. "The Winning Spirit," *Athletes in Action,* 2:10-11, September 1968.
22. Rowan, Vic. "Psychological Gimmicks in Coaching Football," *Scholastic Coach,* Vol. XXXVII-1, September 1967, p. 62.
23. Rowan, Vic. "Mental Aspect of Pursuit," *Athletic Journal,* Vol. XLVIII-3, March 1968, pp. 85-6.
24. Sexton, Dennis, and Dooley, Jay. "Game Day Psychological Devices," *Scholastic Coach,* Vol. 35, No. 9, May 1966, pp. 74, 82-8.
25. Slusher, Howard. "Overt and Covert Reactions of Selected Athletes to Normative Situations as Indicated by an Electronic Psychometer," *Research Quarterly,* Vol. 37-4, December 1966, pp. 540-552.
26. Veller, Don. "Praise or Punishment," *Athletic Journal,* Vol. XLVIII-6, February 1968, pp. 40, 78-81.
27. Witthuhn, Bill. "Motivation for Winning Teams," *Scholastic Coach,* Vol. 38-2, October 1968.

Chapter VII
EVALUATION

"What kind of a job are you doing?"

PURPOSE OF EVALUATION

The improvement of a sports program depends upon the extent to which a measurement can be made of the changes produced by the present coaching procedures and methods. In classrooms and on playing fields, teachers and coaches are constantly trying new methods in an effort to aid and improve the learning process. Unless they can tell what improvements are produced by different procedures, they cannot discover which methods are best. Evaluation is a valid and discriminating study of a job of learning.

Confusion exists between the meaning of the words evaluation and measurement. To differentiate between the two, we might say that to evaluate is to judge the importance of, to determine the value—the soundness or unsoundness—of some process or thing. Measurement means the counting of a numerical expression for something. The implication for education in these definitions is that through measurement teachers have more appropriate and more dependable information upon which to evaluate, that is, upon which to pass judgment on the degree of worthwhileness of some teaching process, learning experience, or manner of performing some act. For example, a coach may keep an accurate record of the number of times each play succeeds, the amount of time spent in practicing each fundamental, and the number of trials necessary before the players grasp the fundamentals of some movement. By contrasting these results with those of some other play and method, he will have some basis for evaluating their worth.

The three main purposes for evaluation in coaching are (1) to discover present abilities, (2) to determine progress, and (3) to make future plans. Evaluation should be an integral part of every teaching and learning situation such as is found on every athletic field. It will involve a general diagnosis of present conditions and a detailed diagnosis of the causes of defects in learning. A general diagnosis may call for classifying the squad according to ability or intelligence, in order to make sure that the material offered is capable of challenging their interests but is not beyond their physical or mental capacities. A detailed diagnosis of defective learning among players might point to such causes as insufficient practice, improper methods of work, deficiency in fundamental skills, absence of interest, physical defects, and subnormal intelligence.

Constant evaluation will enable the teacher (coach) to discover wrong responses soon after they appear, and corrective measures can be immediately instituted. For example, a basketball player may be pulled out of position on a zone defense by some move of the offense. The mistake must be pointed out with a minimum of delay and the proper technique demonstrated. In this way, incorrect habits can be prevented from becoming firmly established, and the learner can be redirected to a new and more profitable method of performing. From a teacher's standpoint, this is the chief value in evaluation.

The coach's responsibility is to produce a number of specific changes in the types of response of the players, or to enable them to respond correctly to new situations. Evaluation is a process which allows the coach to know whether the desired changes are taking place. If the learning has developed, then further learning can be provided; but if the desired learning is not taking place as it should, new devices and procedures must be employed. The players will have a part in this process in that they will review the goals they set for themselves in the beginning and then estimate their progress. In this way, they can help evaluate the methods used to gain the new learnings and discover their own shortcomings, if any are present.

The coach is concerned with evaluating not only to appraise the rate of progress of individuals and the team, but also to determine the value of certain methods of teaching and the effectiveness of his system of play. It may be that his system, consisting of certain offensive and defensive patterns and plays, is not appropriate to the present squad. A complete study of the individuals making up the squad will often reveal the reasons why a certain type of offense is doomed to failure in their hands. Physical, mental, emotional and social factors play a significant part in determining the success of a style of play. An offense built around one player will work like a charm one year, but the following year with new players on the squad it will be hopeless.

In a recent season, John McKay, the Southern California football coach, in evaluating his personnel decided that the bruising type of attack they had been running would be too difficult for any fullback on the squad. Also, Coach McKay had the good fortune to have on his team O. J. Simpson, the best running halfback in America. A drastic change in the Trojan's offensive pattern was made with Simpson doing practically all the ball carrying. The team proceeded to win the national championship, proving the validity of Coach McKay's evaluation of the team's potential.

An examination of the time spent on certain practice methods in comparison with the degree of proficiency attained may reveal the inefficiency of these methods. The number of shots actually gotten off from a particular basketball offensive maneuver, or the amount of ground gained by a football play, in comparison with the time spent in practicing them may reveal their worth in the system.

The progress of the team toward meeting the objectives for the day and week will call for revisions of the master plan for the week. This means that an evaluation by the coach and his assistants should be made each morning when drawing up the plan for the day's work.

Evaluation should also determine how well the learning has been retained and how readily it can be transferred to other situations. These can best be determined through games, but the coach will use a scrimmage or drill as a means of finding them out for himself and the players before putting them to this final test.

Evaluation might be said to be an integral part of any teaching situation, for to separate teaching and evaluation—that is, to teach without evaluating, or to evaluate without regard for the objectives, content, and methods of teaching—is an artificial process, and the results are bound to be misleading. The essential function of evaluation is to provide data which will serve to determine readiness for learning, progress and difficulties in learning, final attainment, and the extent of retention and transfer. Out of this the coach will find data for a critical analysis of his particular system of play and his methods of teaching it.

CHARACTERISTICS OF GOOD EVALUATION

An evaluation of a job of coaching or teaching might be done in different ways by different people. The differences would be due to the emphasis that each one puts on some phase of the job. Evaluation may concern itself with direct results, transfer of learning, or a direct examination of the learning process itself; however, any scheme chosen must be related to and help along the athlete's purpose. His purpose is that compelling need which motivates him to strive for skill or knowledge so that he can control some situation.

The most commonly emphasized feature of learning is that of direct result. How well can a boy tackle? How often does a batter hit safely? How fast can a sprinter run? How many free throws can a basketball player make? How many times can the passer connect with his receiver? This emphasis on direct result is understandable. The coach is looking for improvement, and the players expect to get better as they practice, but what is the effect on the learner when direct results are emphasized? The learning process is supposed to proceed best when the player realizes how well he is doing without being told, but the effect on his purpose may be detrimental if the decree of failure is imposed by someone other than the player, or by dictatorial standards beyond his control. The player should not have to depend on the coach to tell him whether or not he is making good. The practice experiences should be so well planned that the learner can intelligently judge for himself just how well he is doing and how he stands in comparison to his fellow players.

A prime example of an arbitrary standard over which the player has no control is a coaching decree that no sophomore shall be in the starting lineup. Faced with such a situation, a sophomore can be expected to lose his zest for improvement.

Fortunately, most of the laboratory situations of playing sports lend themsleves admirably to an important point—that is, that the learning should be organized in such a way that the learner is made aware of the results he is achieving while the job is going on. Players are aware of their prowess and knowledge before the crucial test of Saturday's game. They know from their practice drills just how well the learning is going.

The results of which the player is made aware must be the type that he desires, or else the awareness of the results mean nothing to him. For instance, there is no sense in testing a tackle for his speed in pulling out of the line, if he never pulls out of the line in a game. The results mean nothing to him. An extremely tall basketball player who spends most of his playing time under the backboard will not be concerned about his inability to hit the long shot, because he rarely will take such a shot in a game. A defensive end could not care less about his lack of skill in pass receiving, for none will ever be thrown to him. Other cases, however, may be involved with a morale factor. Suppose that a baseball player is not a good bunter and does not care to become one because he likes to hit and prefers taking a full swing to sacrificing. He is not concerned about his poor rating in bunting because he feels no urge to improve it. The obvious job for the coach in this case is to make the player feel the *need* to become a good bunter.

The process of evaluation may concern itself with the problem of transfer. The real test of whether a sport skill has been acquired or knowledge gained is whether or not it can be transferred from the practice field to actual use in a game situation. A team that looks like a championship group in scrimmage on Wednesday but acts stupid in the game on Saturday may be the victim of spurious learning—that is, the players learned how to act in the specific situation which was practiced on Wednesday but gained so little insight into the total picture that, when confronted on Saturday with a new situation not exactly like that practiced, they were not able to recall and transfer the obvious maneuver.

Coaches might be surprised if they gave their squads some practical tests on the meaning of information in the scouting report. Players have been known to memorize an entire report, including such items as "Blank, No. 24, runs from the slot-back position and does the passing on reverses." When asked to demonstrate just what this means out on the field, the players cannot do so. Basketball players may also memorize the offensive rules against defensive formations, but recognition of the formations is another thing. When actually confronted with a formation, they will not be able to react correctly. They can recite the rule that applies but not fit the action to the words.

Evaluation of results that involve transfer serve two purposes. First, it makes apparent to the coach just how meaningful the learning is for the players. Second, it shows the learner how well he can apply his learning to a playing situation. His success or failure helps him better to understand and guide his future learning.

Evaluating a job of learning by observing the direct results may determine whether or not the learning was successful but, to be of the most worth, evaluation should follow the plan or scheme that the coach has set up as his own guide or concept for learning. Taking the organization of the concepts of learning as outlined in this book, the evaluation could attempt to answer the following questions:

How well is the stage set for learning? Is there any attempt made to orient the learner in the situations so that he has a clear understanding of what is expected of him? Are the experiences planned and offered in a way that will promote continuous improvement? Are the principles of individual differences recognized and provided for? Are the social factors involved in the team situation recognized?

Each of these concepts has a more or less direct relation to the learner's purpose, and the evaluation must be in terms of whether or not it fosters and stimulates that purpose. It seems proper again to emphasize that evaluation should be carried on while learning experiences are being offered. An evaluation that takes place at the end of the season may reveal many strong and weak points in the system or organization which the coach set up for teaching and the learning of his sport, and the results may serve well to aid in planning for the next season. However, it does nothing to aid and abet the purposes or goals of the learner while the activity is in progress. Constant attention by the coach to the concpets of learning which he deems important will improve the effectiveness of his system.

METHODS OF APPRAISAL

It would be ideal if a coach had an accurate measuring device for determining the strong and weak points of his squad before subjecting them to such a critical evaluating process as a scheduled game. Persons vary in efficiency from day to day. If there were some way to measure the curve of efficiency in a player, as far as his playing ability is concerned, it would be easy to select the five best, nine best, or eleven best men on a given day. Unfortunately, there is no known scale or measuring instrument available, at least none which can be quickly and easily applied. The results of games (won or lost) are not an accurate indication either of improvement or of loss of skill because of the conditions under which the game is played. The strength of the opponents, for one thing, can cause a team to look very good or very bad. Weather conditions, travel, lack of rest, and digestive troubles are just a few of the factors which play an important part in the performance of a team. However, the coach must use some form of evaluation to determine which players are the more skilled, how well the learning is going, and which methods are best for teaching.

A certain sequence must be followed in organizing a program for evaluating or measuring the efficiency of athletes. We suggest:
1. The coach and player should agree on the general phase of the sport to be evaluated, i.e., offense, defense, strategy, rules, etc.
2. The coach and player should agree on the specific knowledges and skills (objectives) to be measured.
3. Design a drill or other test which will allow the learner to be judged on how well he is meeting the objectives.
4. Develop a method of scoring the results.
5. Use the evidence to grade the player's performance.
6. After determining the causes of successes and failures, follow with a plan for improvement.

If a coach is attempting to determine the defensive ability of his players, his first step should be to define just which part of defense he intends to measure—fielding bunts, tackling, footwork, pass defense, rebounding, charging, or other specific skills. Each should be treated separately, and the player should be informed as to just what he is expected to display.

The specific objectives are those items in the player's behavior which are indicative of the fact that he possesses the quality or skill looked for. A football coach testing a man for pass defense should watch the way the defender gives ground with the receiver, how he maintains his balance, keeps his legs uncrossed, keeps the passer and receiver in his line of vision, and how he plays the ball after it is in flight. The method of evaluating just described, known as observation, is probably the most widely used method of evaluating employed in athletics. When used by experienced coaches, it has a high degree of validity.

The coach may use other means of appraising his players, but the important point to be remembered is that the test of whatever method used must be based on behaviors which truly indicate whether the player has or has not acquired a particular skill or knowledge. For instance, the example given above would test a player's pass defense ability but would be worthless as an instrument for testing his offensive ability or even his knowledge of defense against running plays.

A coach should be interested in appraising not only the degree of skill possessed by his players but also their knowledge of and attitudes toward the various phases of the game. To investigate knowledges and attitudes, he might construct an objective type test covering rules of the game, signals, offensive and defensive assignments, and game strategy. Objective knowledge tests have three important purposes in athletics. First, to discover the player's level of knowledge before beginning a course of instruction on the game. Second, to determine the degree to which the players have grasped the material presented on the field, in lectures, and in scouting reports. Third, to motivate learning.

Acquaintance with their level of ability and rate of progress aids in stimulating the efforts of players. A few standardized knowledge tests for sports have been published, but it would not be a difficult task for a coach to construct his own. An original test would be far better for him because he and his players know what objectives he deems important, and these can be emphasized in the test.

Because the coach is constantly striving to improve and add to the skills of his players, it stands to reason that he should be concerned with some means of measuring those skills. Football achievement tests designed for the purpose of selecting players most likely to succeed as varsity material have been designed. The tests include such items as forward passing at a target, running with the ball, forward passing for distance, blocking, punting, dodge and run, and charging. The players are scored according to their ability in each item of the test, and the results are compared to the judgments of players and coaches regarding the ability of the players. Substantial relationships exist between the achievement scores and player's opinions of the playing ability of one another, and fair correlation exists between achievement scores and coachs' ratings. The latter's ratings seemed to be influenced by a knowledge of a player's previous experience.[1] The results of this test would indicate that a battery of achievement tests could be of great value in measuring the amount of learning, that is, general ability in football skills possessed by players.

Professional teams in all the major spectator sports realize the importance of achievement tests and their close relationship to future success in the sport. Many players report for preseason training during which they are put through a series of performance tests, the results of which are compared to norms established by active players already proven to be successful. The validity and reliability is so high that many rookies are cut from the squad after only a few workouts, thereby saving the club time and money in developing its squad.

The Research Council of the American Association for Health, Physical Education and Recreation is in the process of developing skill tests in the following sports: archery, badminton, baseball, basketball, field hockey (girls), football, golf, gymnastics, lacrosse (girls), soccer, softball, swimming (girls), tennis, track and field (girls), and volleyball. It will be several years before this ambitious undertaking is completed.

To be of optimal value, a battery of tests should include only items which are characteristic to that player's position. For example, an achievement test for a lineman should include only the skills which are important to a lineman and should not include such items as kicking and passing. To go a step further, the tests could be broken down into the acts which are most important for an individual position. The importance of a skill should be based upon the frequency with which it must be used by the player and its

---

[1]David K. Brace. "Validity of Football Achievement Tests as Measures of Motor Learning and as a Partial Basis for the Selection of Players." *Research Quarterly of the American Association for Health, Physical Education and Recreation.* 14:372, December 1943.

relative significance for successful playing. If this principle were observed, there would be little justification, for instance, in picking a first baseman on the basis of his skill in starting the double play rather than of his ability to dig low throws out of the dirt or in selecting a hockey goalie on his ability to skate and shoot, skills that he will not use in a game.

A careful analysis of the plays usually tried in a game will give the coach a good indication of the type of maneuver which the player is most frequently called upon to execute, and if the maneuver is part of a key play the skills connected with it are the most important for that player. In measuring technique in sports, this fundamental of determining the specific techniques to be measured is very important. Other recommended steps are to select valid and reliable tests to measure these techniques, to experiment to determine norms and directions for their use, and to devise definite directions for administering and scoring the tests.

In common practice, coaches do not bother with achievement scales to measure skills, but they usually resort to judgments or simple ratings of the qualities and abilities of their players. When the qualities and abilities are broken down into specific items and scaled, they are quite valid. The illustration of the correlation between a coach's observation and judgments and the Brace Achievement Test illustrates this point. When a coach has decided on specific objectives or traits to measure and uses a scale in which the ratings are carefully made, he can reasonably expect his results to be valid, reliable and objective. A careful rating of a player's ability may reveal to the coach that his overall judgment of a player was faulty. When rating the player for form, each individual skill should be separated and given a rating. The combined rating or judgment may often be higher than the coach's original overall judgment. The player benefits from this method by gaining insight into the specific skills in which he is weak.

No matter what method of evaluation the coach uses, he should record the results in a form in which they can be understood by himself and his players. A single mark of classification means nothing to the boy, but if he understands the criteria upon which the classification was made and the reasons for his particular rating, it becomes more meaningful to him. Some coaches use a squad rating sheet which changes weekly. On it are the names of the squad members with ratings for several qualities or skills which are deemed important in their system of play. Most of these plans employ only the coaches to make the weekly ratings; they would become more valuable if they included ratings by the players.

In making any form of evaluation, coaches should not depend entirely upon practical experience, snap judgment, hunches, and "common sense" but should make an honest effort to appraise the achievements of their players through some valid system which throws more light on the matter. Motion pictures of the games have proven to be a great aid in evaluation. Very often the actual play of a man in the game is vastly different from that which was expected of him according to his rating in practice. The camera keeps a permanent record of that player's achievement in competition, and it may be used to check against his rating in practice tests. When this information has been gathered, some good use should be made of it. Diagnosis of weaknesses should be followed by remedial procedures. It is not enough that evaluation be used only for the purpose of classifying players according to ability. The causes of low scores in performance will indicate to player and coach the specific skills or knowledges to be worked on in subsequent practice sessions. Discovery of these needs should be through a constant evaluative process, not through infrequent testing. Constant evaluation will indicate gains and losses in skills and knowledges which, in turn, will throw light on the matter of teaching and learning methods.

THE PART OF THE PLAYER IN EVALUATION

The testing program in American schools started with testers swarming over the schools and colleges analyzing and classifying whatever was being taught. It was not long before they discovered that in order to make the program more effective, it was necessary to take the teachers into their confidence. As the teachers turned to testing, they, in turn, found that in order to make the teaching more effective it was necessary to take the students into their confidence. At the present time, pupil participation in evaluation is not only accepted but also advocated as a measure to aid in the learning process.

One of the major goals of all education should be to help the learner increase his ability to identify his own strengths and weaknesses and plan accordingly. Any program of education would seem to be in harmony with democratic philosophy if the learner has a major share of responsibility for evaluating his competencies, making plans for improving them, and judging his progress toward the attainment of goals.

An important part of evaluation for the player will be self-analysis. He should be aware of the extent of his speed, strength, skills, and knowledges so that he can compete against himself for constant improvement. He can remember his scores for passing, hits for times at bat, baskets for each try, time for each event running or swimming, and try to better his former marks. Competition offers incentive for improvement, and this applies equally to competition against his former abilities and against his fellow players.

The player should be aware of the importance of physical condition and accept the responsibility for appraising his own health and fitness for vigorous play. Checking the weight chart will tell him something, but his general feeling of health and his reactions to such exercises as fast calisthenics, wind sprints, and other forms of running will tell him whether or not he is up to par.

It is also important for a player to be able to analyze his temperament and his social relationships with his coaches and teammates. Any deviations from the usual rapport should be apparent to him so that he may discover the causes and may remedy the situation if it is within his power. It is not very difficult for a youngster to discover why he is being treated coolly by the other players and coaches. He is usually well aware of the reason and, if he is sincere, he will take immediate steps to put himself back in good standing.

One way in which the young athlete could become more aware of his fitness for the social atmosphere of athletic team competition is through an informal self-appraisal chart in which he rates himself on qualities affecting his readiness for varsity competition. The coach may include as many items as he deems necessary to provide him with the desired insight into the attitudes of his players.

The coach orients the players in a general meeting by explaining the meaning of each item, encouraging them to be frank and assuring them that all responses are held in the strictest confidence. After examining each athlete's appraisal form, the coach can determine the areas in which each boy *thinks* he needs help, so that a proper program of improvement may be instituted between the teachers, coaches, parents, and the athlete himself. Even though youngsters may be reluctant to grade themselves low on the chart, it will stimulate them into self-improvement through a knowledge of the qualities deemed important by the coach. A sample form follows:

Self-Evaluation Chart

Directions: On the scale under each item, place a mark at the point which you feel is the most accurate estimation of the degree to which you possess the quality described. The range is from 0 (Poor) to 5 (Excellent).

1. <u>Diligence</u>: Do you pay proper attention to directions and are you careful about details?

```
    0       1       2       3       4       5
   ┌───────┬───────┬───────┬───────┬───────┐
   └───────┴───────┴───────┴───────┴───────┘
```

2. <u>Honesty</u>: Do you honor the concept of private property?

```
    0       1       2       3       4       5
   ┌───────┬───────┬───────┬───────┬───────┐
   └───────┴───────┴───────┴───────┴───────┘
```

3. <u>Modesty</u>: Do you act quietly confident as opposed to arrogant, boastful, and pretentious?

```
    0       1       2       3       4       5
   ┌───────┬───────┬───────┬───────┬───────┐
   └───────┴───────┴───────┴───────┴───────┘
```

4. <u>Respect</u>: Do you show respect for school authorities, teachers, and coaches?

```
    0       1       2       3       4       5
   ┌───────┬───────┬───────┬───────┬───────┐
   └───────┴───────┴───────┴───────┴───────┘
```

5. <u>Truthfulness</u>: Can your word be accepted without reservation?

```
    0       1       2       3       4       5
   ┌───────┬───────┬───────┬───────┬───────┐
   └───────┴───────┴───────┴───────┴───────┘
```

6. <u>Appreciations</u>: Do you appreciate the efforts of your teachers and coaches to provide you with a good education?

```
    0       1       2       3       4       5
   ┌───────┬───────┬───────┬───────┬───────┐
   └───────┴───────┴───────┴───────┴───────┘
```

7. <u>Cooperation</u>: Are you willing to play your part in meeting team and individual goals?

```
    0       1       2       3       4       5
   ┌───────┬───────┬───────┬───────┬───────┐
   └───────┴───────┴───────┴───────┴───────┘
```

8. <u>Will to Win</u>: Are you unwilling to accept defeats as natural possibilities?

```
    0       1       2       3       4       5
   ┌───────┬───────┬───────┬───────┬───────┐
   └───────┴───────┴───────┴───────┴───────┘
```

9. Spirit: Do you enjoy tough situations more than the easy going?

    0   1   2   3   4   5

10. Conduct: Are you setting a good example for younger players and students in the matter of speech, mannerisms, courtesy, dress, and cleanliness?

    0   1   2   3   4   5

11. Punctuality: Are you prompt in arriving for practice, class, and other responsibilities?

    0   1   2   3   4   5

12. Loyalty: Do you give your coaches and teammates your complete support and backing?

    0   1   2   3   4   5

13. Dependability: Except for your studies, does your team come first in the expenditure of time and energy?

    0   1   2   3   4   5

14. Courage: Can you face the possibility of playing larger or more experienced players without feeling apprehensive?

    0   1   2   3   4   5

15. Work habits: Do you go through a vigorous practice without moaning about it?

    0   1   2   3   4   5

16. Study habits: Do you follow a regularly scheduled program of study time?

    0   1   2   3   4   5

17. <u>Emotional control</u>: Can you hold your temper even if your opponent plays you "dirty"?

    0   1   2   3   4   5

18. <u>Obedience</u>: Do you immediately respond to orders of coaches, teachers, and team leaders?

    0   1   2   3   4   5

19. <u>Responsibility</u>: Do you accept and act in accordance with training rules and other team regulations?

    0   1   2   3   4   5

20. <u>Leadership</u>: Do your actions inspire other players to increased effort for the good of the team?

    0   1   2   3   4   5

The concept of readiness which plays such an important part in learning to read is also significant in evaluation, for it affects the learner's efficiency in self-appraisal. The player's level of maturity and background of experience will largely determine the worth of the evaluation. It would be unwise to expect a youngster with very little experience to analyze his technique in the complex skills of a sport. He will need a great deal of training and guidance before he acquires competence in evaluating his skills and knowledges.

One of the goals of coaching should be the power of evaluation by the players. It would be a great help to a coach if his players had the ability to evaluate wisely the material to be learned, the techniques to be mastered, and the methods used to teach them. Much time and effort could be saved by the early elimination of some materials and methods and the readjustment of others as a result of efficient evaluation of those items by the players under the guidance of the coaches. This may be too much to ask of the average high school or college team, but it is widely used in the professional ranks where maturity and experience allow for critical judgments.

Some people do not have the emotional stability to give criticism objectively or to accept it from others. It is part of self-evaluation to recognize this weakness, make plans to remedy it, and then examine efforts toward reaching the goal.

The learner must not leave the task of evaluation to the coach alone. He must share the responsibility for discovering the crucial features of the fundamental skills of his sport, as well as the key features for the success or failure of the various offensive and defensive formations.

To make his evaluation a part of the learning situation in individual stunts, the player should try to develop the ability to select and utilize proper bodily movements by observing what others did in getting the job done and to detect and eliminate errors. To do this, the player must understand the technique which he is attempting to perform. By paying attention to technique, most players can become systematic and alert to their own reactions and thus increase their ability to learn. Allowing the players to use the movies to study critically their performances in games will aid them in this self-appraisal.

When a player has clearly analyzed and understood a group or team maneuver, his next step is to examine his own movements and contributions to the group maneuver in order to discover strong and weak points. The intelligence which some players display in analyzing the strengths, weaknesses and appropriateness of certain plays is heartening to a coach.

Player evaluation should be constant during the season, with summaries at the end of each week. The players' game reports should contain an evaluation of their own play, including their good and bad points, the salient features of the opponent's attack and defense, the strong and weak points of their own offense and defense, and a constructive criticism of the strategy employed in the game. In this way the coaches and players can gain insight into the type of work necessary for individual and group improvement, and each player and coach can set up goals for the coming week. At the end of the season, the players should cooperate in an overall evaluation of the entire program including such items as the schedule, hours of practice, the training table, care of injuries, methods of travel, type of equipment, the offense and defense, abilities of various players, methods of practice, and many others. Any and all features of the program should be treated.

Evaluation should be a part of the process through which the player is guided to understand what he is doing in the sport. It is a recurring method the coach wants him to employ during his playing career and his subsequent life. It is a method used by any individual who expects his athletic experiences to contribute to his continuous physical and social growth.

THE PART OF THE COACH IN EVALUATION

Evaluation must not be thought of as an ultimate objective but rather as a means for day-by-day improvement through the cooperative give and take of gaining the most from a learning experience. Evaluation is as much a part of each learning experience as the explanation and demonstration by the coach. It must be a continuous process and not used merely for marking a terminal point in individual or group activity. It must be a cooperative activity; that is, it must involve an exchange of frank and helpful criticisms between player and coach, all directed toward the goal of making the learning more effective and meaningful for the individual player.

If evaluation is to be a cooperative affair, it will be necessary for the coach to establish a good rapport between himself and his players. His part in carrying out the purpose of evaluation—that is, appraising abilities, determining progress, and making future plans—is that of a helpful and friendly critic. He should strive to create an atmosphere in which the athlete will be eager to test himself and be eager to seek advice and aid in improving his knowledge and skill. The player must have confidence in his coach's ability to define and recognize an effective performance, and the coach must be able to explain the salient features of the performance, so that both parties will understand the criteria upon which the performance is being judged. When a boy knows *what* the coach is looking for in the way of a proper performance, he can devote his practice to the development of that technique. The coach should encourage and train his players in self-appraisal so that they may judge their progress and be critical of the appropriateness of certain styles for their own performance. The good teacher experiments—and encourages his learners to experiment—with new ways of working which appear to promise improvement.

The emphasis in all evaluating procedure carried on by the coach should be on guidance. The idea is to get the boys to improve; therefore they must be motivated, directed, stimulated, aided, and encouraged to improve. Improvement in athletics comes only through hard work in a program that has been devised to meet the needs of the players as discovered through some form of evaluation.

If the coach is concerned about using evaluation as a means of guidance in athletics, it stands to reason that he must have some method of discovering the needs of the individual and doing something about them. The Self-Appraisal Chart is an example. In order to discover these and other vital needs, he must use some diagnostic tool, such as observation of the player, analysis of the player's explanation of his methods, analysis of the players cumulative record, interviews with the player, rating scales, and physical examinations. The needs may be physical, such as more weight, height, strength, speed, and rest, or they may be in the nature of skills and improved techniques for those skills. The player may need "squad education;" that is, he may need advice and direction about getting along with players and coaches. All of these things can be discovered through evaluation.

There are several types of tests which a coach may employ in following out the purpose of evaluation in sports. He might try to measure the potentialities of his squad. Information comes from the records containing physical examinations, age and experience, and from interviews with the boys. He tests his squad for present ability to see how far along the road of potentiality they have progressed. This is usually done by having the players perform individually and in groups. A coach may also test for diagnosis of reasons in the play of one or two individuals. This is done by breaking the plays down into component parts and watching the effectiveness of individuals or small groups. A coach may test his boys merely for the purposes of motivation. He may feel that they need some stimulation, and a test where players are pitted against one another to see which of them is the better skilled always arouses them. Another means of motivating is to let the player perform by himself and do all of the measuring. Shooting baskets, kicking goals, baseball hitting into certain spots, and forward passing for accuracy are tests of this type. The coach may also evaluate his squad for purposes of classification into groups such as varsity, junior varsity, and scrubs. His basis for this classification is usually the judgment of his staff and himself, supplemented with the recommendations of the players.

A good coach will be skillful in the periodic refinement of his own goals—that is, in discovering whether or not the things he is attempting are necessary and helpful to his system—and he will help his players to use their own growth and understanding to aid in this part of the evaluation. In order for this cooperative process to be successful, it will be necessary for the players to have a complete understanding of the objectives, both personal and team. This means that they must know what is expected of them in the way of skills and knowledges, so that they can judge thir progress toward those goals. They must also understand how these skills and knowledges are supposed to contribute to the team objectives. If the coach encourages his players to evaluate his methods in terms of their worth to the success of the team and to volunteer their impressions frankly and honestly, the players will grow in understanding and will acquire a feeling of mutual responsibility for the success of the team. When the coach has succeeded in selling his team on the idea that evaluation is a cooperative enterprise, the players will feel the need of knowing the results rather than feeling that they are going through a meaningless mechanical procedure. A scrimmage becomes a necessary test of how well the learning is proceeding and how much the new method is contributing to the team's objectives. The emphasis of evaluation (for any educational program) must always remain centered on the learner. Thus, the coach's efforts will be directed toward helping the player make self-appraisals, set his own goals, criticize his techniques, determine the rate of his progress or improvement, and search for new goals upon which to set his sights.

THE USE OF RECORDS

Athletic coaches are credited with having a closer personal relationship with their students than do other teachers. The nature of sports activities allows the coach a good opportunity to see his boys in intimate circumstances and see them behave under emotional strain, thus giving him a fair insight into their personalities. However, a coach would be doing himself and a boy an injustice if he were to base his judgment of the boy's ability, potentialities, progress, and promise of future development on mere observation of his behavior in a few athletic incidents. Coaches need a great deal of information about their players which must be gained from many sources.

Much can be learned about a boy by giving him a chance to play in a scrimmage or game and then watching what happens, but this information necessarily will be limited. It may point out the extent of the learner's growth or readiness for the sport, but it will not shed much light on why he reacts as he does. The coach must know the extent of the boy's previous playing experience, his emotional control, his physical status, intelligence, his interests and attitudes, his plans for the future. A player's behavior emerges from the effect of many psychological situations in and apart from athletics. In order to obtain as adequate a picture as possible of an individual at any given moment, the coach must have some sources of information which will shed light on the player's group experiences in school, his total psychological environment out of school, his learnings from previous experience, and his ability to interact with other people. A true and useful picture of the player's development and of the many factors which affect his ability to learn and play a sport can be secured from a cumulative record.

The guidance departments of many schools and colleges keep cumulative records on each student attending the institution; and separate departments, notably the physical education department, keep records on individual students. Records are a vital part of the evaluation process in athletic coaching and should serve as an aid in the teaching and learning process. To get the most value out of cumulative records, the coach should create his own system of records. Because of the pressures of academic and athletic duties, the coach may assign the task of collecting and compiling much of the data to persons outside the coaching staff. The form should be simple and the method easy to operate. Some coaches use a filing system featuring eight-by-ten-inch manilla folders with items of information entered upon sheets of paper about the same size as the folder. Important items written on smaller sheets and hastily thrust into the folder may later be posted to the regular sheets of paper.

The actual form of the record is not as important as the material that goes into it. All the significant aspects of growth must be considered in any comprehensive plan of records. This calls for data regarding the player's health, physiological needs, and emotional adjustments; his mental characteristics, his talents and aptitudes; his values and attitudes; his social relationships and competencies; his ability to function effectively in the playing field environment; his interests, successes, and future plans.

Each player's record should start with the first item of information that the coach receives concerning the boy. It may be a letter which the boy or some other person has written about the boy, or it may be a newspaper clipping referring to some game in which the boy played. From there, the folder will build up with material shedding light on a wide range of personal factors.

The late Billy Hayes, former track coach at Indiana University, collected an impressive file on each of his athletes. It included information concerning the boy's early life, schooling, work habits, past athletic experiences, health, intelligence, and family backgrounds. Most of this information was compiled even before the boy enrolled at Indiana. The close personal relationship that would develop between Coach Hayes and the boy thereafter produced a great amount of additional information for the file. The records were not compiled as ends in themselves, but rather to enable the athlete and Coach Hayes to better understand the boy's capabilities. Goals were agreed upon which might include even the setting of a collegiate or world's record in a given period of time. The athlete would enter into a training period leading to the goal with the utmost confidence. More often than not the goal was reached in the stated time.

A coach's system of personnel records should include the following items:

1. An elaborate amount of information about the athlete's life interests. Much of this material may have to be gathered through questionnaires, self-appraisals, and biographical accounts. It should be very comprehensive, containing information about the boy's home life, family, work experiences, religious beliefs, ambitions, hobbies, and education to the present time. This is an extremely important part of the record and may serve to offer more understanding of the "whole boy" or total personality than any other possible sources.

2. A record of the boy's participation in that sport and other extracurricular activities. It should also include a record of the achievements of teams on which the boy played and his special contribution, if any, to the team effort. These give an indication of his growth and development into a well-rounded person.

3. A record of the player's academic progress. This means a transcript of grades from institutions previously attended as well as his current program. An examination of this record might indicate trouble in his academic work and allow the coach to make provisions for securing tutorial aid for the player before trouble sets in.

4. Information indicating the mental capacity of the athlete. This means more than a mere Statement of an Intelligence Quotient. The folder should contain notes on other items of interest concerning factors that affect the player's capacity to learn, such as home environment and physical and emotional handicaps. His aptitude for learning sports material as contrasted to academic matter might also be noted. The coach might also discover something about the boy's capacity to learn from watching his working habits. If the player worked hard, long, and diligently to master some knowledges and only succeeded in a mediocre fashion, the chances are that he is scholastically limited, while if he grasped things with but little effort, the reverse is probably true.

5. Incidental items of interest gathered from many sources—family, friends, other coaches, doctors, trainers, girl friends, other players, faculty members, and even campus police. Methods of gathering the bits of information could vary from informal chats to formal interviews. Many important points

regarding his personality which might otherwise be overlooked may come to light in these sessions.

6. A medical history of the player including his present health status, the findings of his physical examinations, records of injuries and sicknesses, and such statistics as sizes for the various items of uniform apparel.

7. A record of the player's reactions to ordinary and extraordinary situations. It should include written notes on the athlete's behavior on the field, in the dressing room, on trips, in classrooms, at parties, or any situation where the coach had an opportunity to see the boy act. The usual method is for the coach to jot down a note referring to the incident and then file it in the folder at the first opportunity. These notes may be compiled, summarized, and pasted on regular sheets of paper at a later date.

Cumulative summaries and appraisals of the above data should be made periodically by the coach. If regular dates are set for this function, it will insure against forgetting. This summary should give as full a picture as possible of this player's personality, development, future possibilities, and plans. It should take into account his strong and weak points, his needs and best means of meeting them.

Much of the material mentioned above may be secured from the school guidance department if one is already established. The coach will probably never feel satisfied with the amount of information gleaned from this source and will make an effort to secure his information from original sources and compile his own summaries.

The importance of a system of records is determined by the use to which they are put in answering questions regarding the learner.

An effective record not only provides data regarding past experiences but is a working tool through which present activities are interpreted. It should show changes as the learner develops, and therefore it must include notes on positive and negative characteristics as they occur. This is necessary if the record is to give an accurate total picutre at any given time. It should shed light on the whole personality covering a wide range of information about the player's strengths; weaknesses; inclinations; attitudes; mental, emotional, and social growth; ability to adjust and solve his problems. Finally, it should serve as a basis for predicting his behavior in various situations.

MEASURING THE EFFECTIVENESS OF COACHING

A common practice among coaches is to have a scout watch the team during a scrimmage or early game and make out a complete report on the team similar to those turned in for regular opponents. The purpose is to give the coach some means of evaluating the strength and weaknesses of his team and system. The report will give him some idea of where he is failing and in what respects he is being successful. If he should wait until the end of the season, a glance at the win-and-loss column would give him a fair idea, but the coach prefers to have some indication of which things he is putting across and which he is failing in before the team tests its prowess against strong opponents.

To judge the effectiveness of coaching on the win-and-loss columns is tantamount to marking progress in the classroom on tested achievement and nothing else. Effort, attitude, good and bad behavior, differences in ability, personal pleasantness or unpleasantness, cooperativeness or noncooperativeness, and similar factors are supposed to be disregarded; but teachers usually refuse to adhere to tested achievement alone, and the above considerations do creep in. Because teachers recognize that they are dealing with human personalitites, they feel justified in taking into account more than tested achievement. The teaching and learning of sports involves teachers and students who are affected by factors making for good or bad learning, just as in any academic subject. It seems that the same fallacies that affect the marking of pupil success on tested achievement alone could also apply to judging effectiveness of coaching only on winning and losing.

If any attempt were made to instill in the players such attitudes as cooperation, perseverance, courage, and other desirable qualities, why should not the degree to which they were acquired by the squad be measured?

Learner accomplishment alone is not a valid instrument for measuring coaching efficiency, for there is no way of knowing the good or bad influences exerted on the players by such factors as maturity, intelligence, physical efficiency, family, home, and social environments. Obviously, they have some effect. Therefore, it cannot be said that achievement in athletic performance is the only objective to be attained by a good coach, for to teach proper habits, attitudes, ideals, and appreciations is equally as important as imparting skills and knowledges.

It is not proper to regard winning or losing as unimportant. On the contrary, they are important to players, coaches, and everyone connected with the institution. Winning is an exhilarating experience, losing is depressing.

The win/loss record can be a definite means of measuring the effectiveness of a job of coaching if it is kept in proper perspective. The type of schedule played should be considered in conjunction with the record. If the schedule calls for a team to play the majority of games against opponents above its class, it can be expected to lose the majority of its games. Among the factors that determine the class of a team are the size of the student body, the size of the coaching staff, facilities and equipment, the number of athletic scholarships available, the emphasis on recruiting, and the institution's admission standards and eligibility rules. Institutions that are similar in the above features and activities are in the same class. To be absolutely fair in the appraisal, it must be determined whether or not the team really is in the same class as its opponents. When a coach cannot match the preparations of his opposition on an even basis, he should not be expected to win, for the circumstances are beyond his control.

Time is another impotrant factor. Over a period of several years, a team playing in its own class should win its share of the games. Anything better than an even break indicates a good job of coaching and, conversely, anything less than an even break cannot be considered good. One or two losing seasons are not proof that a coach is failing, but a four- or five-year record of consistently losing in his own class indicates that a coach is just that—a loser.

Rating scales as a form of evaluation of teaching efficiency have attained wide popularity, but they have slight claim to the quality of objectivity. A wide variety of rating scales have been developed; but the essential feature of most of them is a list of traits, qualities, or attributes which the creator of the scale deems essential to successful teaching. The person rating the teacher is supposed to give his estimate of the degree to which the teacher possesses each of these traits, qualities, and attributes. The basic reason for variety in rating scales is that no one has been able to determine by a scientific procedure just what the essential attributes of a good teacher are, to say nothing of the relative importance of the attributes. However, a list of desirable qualities for coaches was listed in Chapter I under Personality Traits of Coaches.

The evaluation of teaching or coaching is a very complex activity. The efficiency of teachers depends upon many different qualities, abilities, attitudes, understandings, and auxiliary competencies. It is possible to list several types of devices for measuring teaching success: check list, rating scales, appraisals, anecdotal records, films, measurement of qualities commonly associated with teaching success, interviews and questionnaries, and observations of changes in pupil growth, learning, and achievements. Each of these methods serves its own particular purpose and is limited by its own peculiar limitations, but any job of teaching should come under some form of evaluation by somebody interested in the effectiveness of the teaching, preferably the teacher himself.

The most alert person to good and poor teaching should be the teacher. There are no devices available at present for measuring the effectiveness of athletic coaches, but many of the instruments mentioned above could be used by a coach in evaluating his own efficiency. It may be necessary for him to seek assistance in recording the happenings of some segment of the athletic program, but the coach can take the data collected by an observer and evaluate it in terms of its effect on his coaching success or failure. We can suggest several methods of self-analysis which might give the coach some insight into his strengths and weaknesses: rating scales for personal inventory in which the coach would rate himself in the degree to which he possesses qualities generally associated with good coaches; questionnaires in which the coach would answer pointed questions dealing with his personal and professional qualities and actions; analysis of the results of his coaching by measuring the progress of his players in such objectives as the fundamental skills and knowledges of his sport; a checklist of expected outcomes which would be checked off as each of the outcomes appears to have been attained; brief summary records of each workout made at the end of practice which can be summarized and analyzed weekly for indications of progress; and, finally, standardized tests for measuring the coach's ability and aptitude for educational work.

The questionnaire method of self-appraisal could be used to indicate to a coach many of his personal and professional strengths and weaknesses. In such an evaluation, the coach might answer these questions for himself:

1. Do you observe the concepts of good teaching by adjusting and revising your system when the quality of material (their intelligence, skill, maturity, experience and temperament) dictates the advisability of change?
2. Are the practice sessions well planned and effectively carried out? Are the objectives for each day and week clearly explained to the squad? Are the plans flexible enough to be quickly adjusted when proven to be ineffective?

3. Is your discipline a matter of wholehearted cooperation with an atmosphere of friendliness, eagerness to learn, and pure enjoyment of the sport pervading?
4. Do you "set the pace" for the coaching staff in industry and enthusiasm for the entire program, not just during practice time?
5. Do you know the game well enough to recognize the need for supplementary material in your system as well as to recognize the presence of superfluous material?
6. Do you give a full measure of attention and devotion to your job, or are too many outside interests interfering with your effectiveness?
7. Do you regularly attend the national and local meetings of your coaches' association? How much reading have you done in the technical aspects of your sport in the past year. Have you been asked to serve on a panel for the program of any coaches' meeting in the past five years?
8. Are the daily and weekly schedules of practice sessions well organized? Are you now using a wider variety of instructional aids than in past years?
9. How many different coaching jobs have you applied for in recent years? Is your unhappiness in your present position so pronounced that it is interfering with your coaching?
10. Do the players and assistant coaches thoroughly understand your philosophy? Are your objectives clearly defined?
11. Do your personal characteristics enhance or detract from your coaching effectiveness? (See Personality Traits of Coaches, Chapter I.)
12. Do you welcome any and all boys in the school or college to come out for the team and encourage them to persist in their efforts to make a varsity position? (This must be done within reason, for no teacher is at his best when the class load is too high—thus the number of assistant coaches available for instructing will determine the maximum number with which the coaches can operate effectively.)
13. If you have a recruiting program, are your best recruiters your players, past and present?

In evaluating player *improvement* as the season progresses, the coach might make use of a rating scale or a checklist, either completing it himself or having some person outside the coaching staff recording data to answer questions such as these:

Specific Examples for Baseball
1. Are the batters getting more base hits?
2. Are the pitchers allowing fewer walks?
3. Are the infielders making more double plays?
4. Are we working the sacrifice more often than not?
5. Are we breaking up the sacrifice more often than not?
6. Is our opposition scoring less runs?

Specific Examples for Basketball
1. Is our shooting percentage improving?
2. Are we making more free throws?
3. Are we committing less fouls?
4. Are the opponents attempting less shots?
5. Are we getting more rebounds?
6. Are we recording more assists?

Specific Examples for Football
1. Are we completing more passes?
2. Is our passer getting off more passes without hurrying?
3. Are the punters improving in distance?
4. Are the place-kickers more accurate?
5. Are we running more plays per game?
6. Are our players making more single tackles per game?

General questions for all sports
1. Do the players interpret situations and react to them quicker?
2. Are they making fewer mistakes in assignments?
3. Are they calling fewer "time-outs" because of fatigue or injuires?
4. Do the players display more confidence, more poise and higher morale?
5. Is the spirit of teamwork more pronounced?
6. Do we appear to be gaining in team speed?

In the evaluation of player *behavior* to measure the effectiveness of coaching, the coach might answer the following questions:
1. Do the players show evidences of liking practice, hating it, or mere indifference?
2. Do the players show interest in school or college affairs other than the sport?
3. What do they do when the season is ended? Do they relax their training altogether or do they spend some of their spare time in exercising?

4. Do they compare favorably with other students, or do they stand out in a detrimental fashion? Do they dress carelessly and appear unshaven in classes?
5. Are the players desirable representatives of the school or college when traveling? Do they leave a good impression with their well-mannered, decorous behavior?
6. Do the players come to the coach with their intimate problems?

A good idea of the effect of a coach's program for his sport can be gleaned from an evaluation of the *attitudes of school or college personnel.*

1. Are the players regarded as ruffians, hired hands, poor scholars, or ideal students?
2. Are the coaches looked up to as examples of social refinement, good taste, and culture?
3. Are the coaches regarded as worthy members of the faculty? Are they asked to serve on administrative committees? Do they attend social affairs? Do their wives mingle with other faculty wives?
4. Are the coaches welcome to join in school or college, community and civic affairs? Are they active members of service or church clubs?

Many of the factors mentioned in the above list seem remotely connected with the actual teaching and learning situation as seen in the athletic arena, but instructional efficiency is indicated by the number of constructive changes in player performance and attitudes accomplished by the coach in the shortest time and under the most harmonious relationship possible.

An evaluation of the data compiled from investigations, such as the few samples given above, will reveal to the coach the effectiveness of his coaching, as well as the sources of strengths and weaknesses, the ultimate uses of which will result in the improvement of teaching and learning in that sport.

SUMMARY

A coach must have some means of judging how well the learning of his sport is progressing. Since he prefers not to gain all of that knowledge through games, he uses various methods of evaluating. The essential function of any of the processes is to provide data which will serve to determine the readiness of players for learning, progress and difficulties in learning, final attainment, and the extent of retention and transfer. Evaluation may be characterized by attention to direct results—that is, how well the players have mastered fundamentals—or it may be judged by the degree to which players are able to transfer their learnings. However, good evaluation will always be in terms of how well the job of coaching fostered and stimulated the learner's goal or purpose.

A coach should have several methods of appraising the worth of his players, such as rating scales, moving pictures of games, knowledge tests, and achievement tests based on the requirements of certain positions. The player should accept a share in the responsibility for evaluating his own and the team performance, the methods of teaching, the system of offense and defense used by the team, and many other features of the program. Part of the job of coaching is to train the players so that they might contribute their efforts to the task of evaluation. Because the emphasis of evaluation must always be centered on the learner, the coach should make every effort to make the players see the value of self-appraisal and to convince them that evaluation should be in terms of how much progress they are making toward their goals. To learn as much as possible about his players, the coach should put into use a system of cumulative records containing enough information to give the coach a good insight into the player's previous experience, his attitudes, physical health, mental capacities, interests and hobbies, and plans for the future.

To measure the effectiveness of his coaching, a coach may analyze his own personal and professional equipment and behavior; he may examine his methods of teaching to determine whether or not he has observed certain important concepts of teaching and learning; he may use a checklist to evaluate player improvement; he may also observe player behavior, and the attitudes of school and college personnel toward the game, the players, and the coaches as a means of evaluating the job he has done in teaching the sport.

Test Questions

1. Differentiate between evaluation and measurement. Show how measurement might be used in a sports situation.
2. What are the three main purposes of evaluation in coaching?
3. How could a personnel study of a squad indicate the suitability of a style of play?
4. What are the strong and weak points of evaluating by direct result?

5. Why must the points upon which the player is being evaluated have meaning for him?
6. Evaluation of results involving transfer serve what two purposes?
7. Why is it important that evaluation be carried on at the same time that learning experiences are being offered?
8. What are the six sequential steps that should be used in measuring the efficiency of athletes in some phase of the sport?
9. Can mere observation of a player's performance by a coach ever be a valid measuring tool?
10. Does a rating scale have any use other than classifying players according to ability?
11. How could a program of evaluation be in harmony with a democratic philosophy of education?
12. How can players measure their social fitness for athletic team competition?
13. What are the values of players' game reports and end of season reports?
14. If evaluation is to be a cooperative affair between coach and player, what role should the coach play?
15. How can evaluation be used to motivate?
16. Why are athletic coaches credited with having a close personal relationship with their players? Is it always valid?
17. What can a cumulative record indicate about an athlete?
18. List some important items which should be found in a cumulative record.
19. Is the win-loss column always a valid instrument for measuring coaching efficiency?
20. Under what circumstances would a win-loss column indicate coaching efficiency?
21. What are some important questions a coach might ask of himself in a self-appraisal questionnaire to determine personal and professional competency?
22. List some items which would indicate improvement in player performance and player behavior.
23. How could the attitudes of institutional and community personnel indicate success or failure of coaches?

Discussion Questions

1. In a private conference, a player bluntly states that he cannot understand why he is not in the starting linup. What are the implications for evaluation?

2. In a self-appraisal chart, a star athlete who is definitely of the irritable type rates himself extremely high in all categories. How would you handle this situation?
3. In the matter of performance, should a coach be more demanding of a highly skilled athlete?
4. Some institutions have a system of teacher evaluation by students. Should athletic coaches be evaluated by the players?
5. Should you expect the same amount of diligence from an athlete whose family is wealthy as from one who is classed as underprivileged?
6. What would you include in an end-of-season evaluation?
7. Evaluation of skill and team success (wins and losses) is not difficult, but how does one evaluate the abstract areas of coaching such as leadership, courage, decision-making, etc.?

Suggested Readings

BOOKS

1. Barr, A., Burton, W., and Bruecher, L. *Supervision.* New York: D. Appleton-Century-Crofts, Inc., 1947, pp. 380-381.
2. Bovard, J., Cozens, J., and Hogman, P. *Tests and Measurments in Physical Education.* Philadelphia: W. B. Saunders Co., 1949, pp. 189-220.
3. Burton, William H. *The Guidance of Learning Activities.* New York: D. Appleton Century Company, 1944, p. 160.
4. Cameron, Peter, and Smithells, Phillip. *Principles of Evaluation in Physical Education.* New York: Harper & Row., 1962, p. 110.
5. Cattell, Raymond, and Stice, Glen F. *Handbook for the Sixteen Personality Factor Questionnaire.* Champaigne, Ill.: Institute of Personality Ability Testing, 1951.
6. Clarke, H. Harrison. *Application of Measurement of Health and Physical Education.* Englewood Cliffs: Prentice Hall, Inc., 1967, pp. 300-337.
7. Cowell, Charles C., and Schwenn, Hilda M. *Modern Principles and Methods in Secondary School Physical Education.* Boston: Allyn & Bacon, 1964, pp. 265-302, 366-368.
8. Latchaw, Marjorie, and Brown, Camille. *The Evaluation Process in Health Education, Physical Education and Recreation.* Englewood Cliffs: Prentice Hall, Inc., 1962, pp. 130-150, 190-215.

9. Massey, Harold, and Vineyard, Edwin. *The Profession of Teaching.* New York: The Odyssey Press, Inc., 1961, pp. 192-197.
10. McCall, William A. *Measurement.* New York: The Macmillan Co., 1939, pp. 385-387.
11. Meyers, Carleton, and Blesh, T. E. *Measurement in Physical Education.* New York: The Ronald Press, 1962.
12. Murray, Thomas. *Judging Student Progress.* New York: Longmans, Green & Co., 1954, p. 9.
13. Neagby, Ross, and Evans, N. D. *Handbook for Effective Supervision of Instruction.* Englewood Cliffs: Prentice Hall, Inc., 1964, Chapter 12.
14. Scott, Gladys, and French, Esther. *Better Teaching Through Testing.* New York: A. S. Barnes & Co., 1945, Chapter 8.
15. Shertzer, B., and Stone, S. *Fundamentals of Guidance.* Boston: Houghton-Mifflin Co., 1966, Chapter 9.
16. Strang, Ruth. *Every Teacher's Records.* New York: Bureau of Publications, Columbia University, 1942, p. 11.

Suggested Readings

ARTICLES

1. Barrow, Harold. "Test of Motor Ability for College Men," *Research Quarterly,* Vol. 25-3, October 1954, p. 253.
2. Black, Allen. "Quick and Easy Method of Player Evaluation," *Athletic Journal,* Vol. XLV-7, March 1965, p. 70, 116-118.
3. Brace, David K. "Validity of Football Achievement Tests as Measures of Motor Learning and as a Partial Basis for the Selection of Players," *Research Quarterly,* Vol. 14, December 1943, p. 30.
4. Bridges, Foster. "Why Game and Practice Limit?" *School Activities,* Vol. 38, February 1967, p. 3.
5. Broer, Marion R. "Evaluating Skill," *JOHPER,* Vol. 38-8, November 1962, p. 22.
6. Cowell, C. C., and Ismail, A. H. "Validity of a Football Rating Scale and It's Relationship to Social Integration and Academic Ability," *Research Quarterly,* Vol. 32, December 1961, pp. 461-467.
7. Gallon, Arthur. "For More Efficient Coaching—A Weekly Time Chart," *Athletic Journal,* Vol. 3-3, November 1951, p. 13.

8. Griffin, J. H. "How Do You Rate With Your Players?" *Scholastic Coach,* Vol. 32-10, October 1962, p. 58.

9. Hainfield, Harold. "Photography in Sports," *JOHPER,* Vol. 38-8, October 1967, pp. 83-84.

10. Harvey, John H. "Organize to Practice to Win," *Coach and Athlete,* Vol. XXIX, August 1966, p. 22.

11. Heilbrun, Alfred B. "The Social Desirability Variable," *Educational and Psychological Measurement,* Vol. XXV-3, 1965, pp. 745-756.

12. Hendrickson, R. and Stevens, K. "Know Your Athletes Through Periodic Self-Appraisals," *Coach and Athlete,* Vol. XXIX-10, May 1967, p. 26.

13. Malone, Wayne. "A Checklist for Evaluation of Coaches," *Coach and Athlete,* Vol. XXVIII-2, October 1966, pp. 42-43.

14. Manoil, A. "The Place of Appraisal in Education," *Journal of Education,* Vol. 146-1, October 1963, pp. 14-29.

15. McClendon, J. B. "Coaching to Win," *JOHPER,* Vol. 29-10, October 1958, pp. 25-26.

16. Megrath, E. J. and Washburne, V. Z. "Teaching Evaluation," *Journal of Educational Reserach,* Vol. 40, September 1966, pp. 63-9.

17. Nedde, Nelson. "Baseball Statistics and Their Analysis," *Athletic Journal,* Vol. XLVI-8, March 1966, pp. 26, 69-70.

18. Prinz, James. "Testing the Potential in Future Athletes," *Athletic Journal,* Vol. XLV-10, June 1965, pp. 22-23.

19. Richards, James M. "A Factor Analytical Study of the Self-Ratings of College Freshmen," *Educational and Psychological Measurement,* Vol. XXVI-4, 1966, pp. 861-870.

20. Rosinski, Edwin and Husted, Frank. "Components of the Evaluation Process," *Physical Therapy,* Vol. 44-1, January 1964, pp. 51-54.

21. Sayre, Joel. "The Once and Future Pro Football," *Holiday,* Vol. 44-4, October 1968, pp. 40-45, 102, 111-112.

22. Sims, Verner M. "Educational Measurement and Evaluation," *Journal of Educational Research,* Vol. 38, September 1944, pp. 18-24.

23. Singer, Robert N. "Athletic Participation—Cause or Result of Certain Personality Factors?" *The Physical Educator,* Vol. 24-4, December 1967, pp. 169-171.

24. Stoup, Francis. "Relationship Between Measurement of Field of Motion Perception and Basketball Ability in College Men," *Research Quarterly,* Vol. 28, March 1957, pp. 72-76.

25. Veller, Don. "Get the Right Boy in the Right Job," *Athletic Journal,* Vol. XLVI-8, March 1966, pp. 46-50, 85.

Chapter VIII
CONDITIONING THE ATHLETE

"You cannot win with the lame and the halt."

WEIGHT TRAINING FOR ATHLETES

Perhaps the most important innovation added to coaching methods in the past twenty-five years has been that of weight training for all athletic teams. The major portion of work done in weight training takes place in the off-season or during the weeks just prior to the regular season. The emphasis during the off-season period is on increasing strength and, if combined with proper diet, on gaining weight. Just prior to the opening of the regular season, the emphasis rightfully should be on increasing endurance, especially in those muscle groups used extensively in the specific sport. It has been an accepted fact for many years that working with increasing weights would develop strength, but it also believed that such a program would make athletes "muscle bound," make them slow to react, make them lose their coordination, or would cause a hernia or an enlarged heart. Lately, these theories have been proven false. As a matter of fact, studies show that a proper program of weight training can produce an increase in speed and coordination.

Muscle boundness can occur if an individual exercises one set of muscles without compensating exercise for its balanced set. For example, and athlete might exercise his pectoral muscles (front of chest), anterior deltoid (front of shoulder), and biceps (front muscles of upper arm) and not work the muscles of his back, rear shoulder, or back of his arm. Graudally the first muscle groups on the front of his upper body become bulkier and shorter, while those of his back would be extended and would lose their tone. The athlete would become partially stooped and would experience difficulty in making quick and powerful backward movements of his arms. Under proper direction, this situation should not occur. Before embarking on his weight training program, the athlete should be clearly aware of what muscles are to be exercised and why.

It might also be wise to explain to him something of the nature of muscles. A muscle is made up of groups of bundles, each separated from its neighbor yet bound together by connective tissue (sarco-lemma). A bundle possesses countless numbers of cells called fibers. Each cell contains cytoplasm held within it by its wall, and the wall is the same connective tissue enveloping the bundles (sarcolemma). Skeletal muscle cells have dark bands (striac) running across them. The cytoplasm or body of the cell contains many different elements, and some of them are combined into muscle food which oxidizes during exercise. The voracious appetite of cells resulting from exercise calls for replacement of the oxidized food, and nature is overgenerous in replenishment. The cell wall (sarcolemma) thickens because of the stretching and contracting action. The combination of increased cell content and thickened walls brings about a gradual increase in the mass of the muscle. The ends of muscles (tendons) which are imbedded in bones also become stronger. When muscles are exercised against gradually increased resistance or weight, they grow in size and strength.

The above description is an oversimplification of the process of increasing strength by increasing the size of muscles.

Coursing in between the muscle cells are tiny blood vessels (capillaries) which join the tiny arteries running to tiny veins. Food, oxygen, insulin, and other substances are carried to the muscles by the arteries which become capillaries in the muscles. The lymph, a free fluid found almost everywhere in the body, acts as a medium of exchange between the capillaries and the cells. Food, oxygen and insulin are washed out of the capillaries, passing through the wall of the cells to be deposited inside. After oxidation, the waste material is washed out of the cell by the lymph and brought inside the capillary to be carried back to the heart and eventually excreted from the body.

Naturally, the ease with which the exchange of fresh material and waste can take place affects the endurance of the muscle. Endurance can be thought of as the ability of the cell to respond to a stimulus to act. If the muscle contains an abundance of capillaries working to keep the cell well supplied with food, oxygen, and other nutritive products, and removing the waste rapidly, the muscle cell will continue to respond readily to stimulus. When a muscle is exercised by repeating a movement over and over again without increasing the weight or resistance, the body will adjust to the demand for better service by increasing the number of the capillaries open for business within the muscle.

In short, we can state that *size* and *strength* of muscles is gained by exercising against gradually increasing weights. For example, a muscle group would be exercised first against 50 lbs. As weeks went by, the weight gradually would be increased progressively through 75, 100, 150, 200 etc. To develop *endurance,* the athlete would start with a weight he could handle safely and repeat an exercise movement 10 to 15 times. Over a period of weeks, *without adding to the weight,* the athlete would increase the number of repetitions for the exercise through 20, 30, 40, etc.

Not all authorities agree that endurance can better be improved through the above plan of weight training. There are those who believe that the benefits gained are almost negligible and that if a coach wishes to develop endurance in a runner, he should prescribe more and more running. Yet there are other well qualified individuals who maintain that an athlete, who subjects his muscles to resistance beyond that normally met in his sport specialty, will develop sufficient strength to make the required action of the sport so easy as to contribute to endurance and potential away beyond what could be gained from going through the regular routine of the sport such as plain running.

ISOTONIC vs. ISOMETRIC EXERCISES

Most exercises done with bar bells, wall weights, springs, and other types of movable equipment are the isotonic type in that they call for a complete range of movement for the muscle from extension to contraction.

Isometric exercises are those in which the muscle contracts against resistance (usually an immovable object), but little or no movement takes place. The tone of the muscle increases causing the body to respond by developing the muscle cells to answer the change. Naturally, this is done over a long period of time, although studies show that increased strength develops faster through isometric than through isotonic exercises. However, making a muscle stronger by contracting it against resistance does not increase the joint's range of movement. In fact, it could decrease flexibility through shortening the muscle. Here again, it must be emphasized that both antagonistic pairs of muscles must be exercised whether by isometric or isotonic means. Because of the wide range of movement for the muscle and the flexion and extension of joints, it appears that isotonic exercises are more beneficial for athletes.

Weight training should be thought of as a means to an end, the end being improved performance in sports techniques. The purpose is not to become a proficient weight lifter, or a beautiful physical specimen, but to increase the athlete's level of achievement in his sport. Studies appear to prove that a scientifically sound program contributes to increased strength, endurance, and flexibility, but other concommitant benefits should accrue. Although it cannot be measured, it becomes apparent that a boy experiences an increase in self-confidence as he feels the change in himself. Being stronger, he does more than he previously could do, thus gaining confidence in his abilities. Because the routine of weight training is demanding and often tedious, the athlete may experience a tug-of-war with his conscience, resulting in a fine opportunity for the exercising of will-power and practicing of self-denial and self-discipline. Other benefits that could be listed are reduction of injuries, lower pulse rate, increased heart size, relaxation, and general improvement of the entire circulatory system.

It should be understood that weight training will not make an athlete out of a nonathlete. Strength is not a substitute for skill and ability. Individuals with slow thought processes and dull reflexes, who are inherently slow and awkward, will not be improved through weight training, but any athlete, good or bad, will gain in skill through extra strength.

Because most of the support of joints comes from the muscles originating in and inserted above and below the joint, it is obvious that the chances of injury to it can be reduced by strengthening those muscles. Ligaments also bind the bones of a joint to each other, but they are inelastic and cannot be strengthened through exercise.

Through the use of weights, we build strength, speed, and endurance in the muscles, and these are invaluable qualities for injury prevention. A strong muscle is better equipped to withstand the stresses and strains of athletic movements. It has better tone and reacts more quickly with more efficiency. It contracts and relaxes better, minimizing pulling and tearing. Stronger muscles and tendons provide more security and stability to the joint, reducing the danger of twisted knees, turned ankles, sprained wrists, and the like, which threaten the career of athletes.

Weight training can also be used in the rehabilitation of muscles following an injury. Any injury that causes the athlete to reduce the normal use of any of his muscles will cause some muscle deterioration. This can be minimized with proper nonweighted bearing exercises even while he is incapacitated. All injured muscles must be rebuilt, a procedure calling for extreme caution. The inside of the body is beautifully organized with cells, connective tissue, blood capillaries, lymph vessels, sensory and motor nerve fibers, and bones laid down in a pattern designated to function harmoniously. Any injury destroys the organization, but proper treatment is supposed to restore it. Coaches and trainers should always avail themselves of medical advice from the team doctor before embarking on a program of treatment or rehabilitation. Legally and morally, it is safer to perform under the direction of the doctor.

Weight training requires of the coach the same degree of planning that goes into all other phases of his program He should make it a part of his year-round program, being prepared to offer it to his athletes as a voluntary activity but carried out with some direction and organization. In most institutions, weight training is started out of season with increase in strength as the main objective. If a coach believes that endurance can be improved by weights, that part of the program should come prior to the start of the season.

Some coaches prefer a schedule calling for Monday, Wednesday, and Friday workouts on the exercises to build strength and size. The off days can be used either for rest, running, or some other activity. It is not wise to lift heavily each day, as it would not allow time for muscle cells to rebuild and repair themselves. A reduction in muscle size and strength actually could result. If the weight program is used to lose weight, a daily workout might be used. Unless a coach plans to build up strength in specific muscle groups, he should plan a program including at least one exercise for each part of the body, being careful to cover the antagonistic counterparts for each muscle group. Included for work would be the neck, shoulders, upper arms (front and back), trunk (upper and lower, front and back), thigh (front and back), knee, lower leg, and ankle (front and back).

Most authorities agree that strength and size develop quickest with the use of weights heavy enough so that only a few repetitions can be accomplished. The amount of weight to start with for each exercise will vary with individuals so the athlete will have to experiment at first. Generally speaking, he should tend toward the lighter weight at the start, even if for no other reason than safety. Each of the exercises should be done in sets of three with a short rest period between. Each set should call for four to seven repetitions. Once ten repetitions are possible, the weight should be increased. Where equipment is plentiful, the athlete may exercise several groups of muscles in a row, allowing each group to rest while he is working on another. He can then repeat the exercises until he has done the three sets for each muscle group. When he has done these exercises properly over a period of months, with progressively increasing weights, the athlete will become conscious of a developing body and a feeling of new power.

Some coaches, having analyzed the skills and techniques required of an athlete in a certain position on the team, next design sets of exercises specifically for developing strength, speed, and flexibility in the muscle groups chiefly involved in performing those techniques. In other words, an athlete who throws will have exercises specific for throwing; one who jumps will develop the jumping muscles, one who kicks will work on kicking muscles, etc. There is no question about the benefits accruing to those muscle groups receiving special attention, but general development will suffer, and the danger exists that a single muscle or group will be overdeveloped to the detriment of its antagonistic partner. A better plan would be one for general development with extra work on those muscles most actively engaged in the athlete's techniques.

Coaches disagree on the question of whether or not to continue weight training during the playing season. Some believe that the time required, even for a limited program cannot be spared during the active season. Another opinion holds that weight training tightens the muscles, and a "loose" athlete is preferred. Still another view is that all weight work should not be stopped during the playing season but that workouts should be limited to about twice per week with a few sets performed to maintain strength. Two or three basic barbell exercises, such as the squat, the bench press, and the curl, will suffice to maintain strength. Most coaches who eliminate the weight program and substitute other exercises, such as rope skipping, situps, pushups, throwing medicine balls, etc.

THE PROGRAM OF LIFTING

As previously stated, there are two types of programs preferred by coaches: (1) the general development program that will result in an improvement in strength, speed, and flexibility in practically all muscle groups; and (2) a program to develop specific muscles or groups of muscles used extensively in a particular sport. A combination of the two types is most satisfactory. Therefore, it becomes the coach's problem to design a series of exercises to bring about general development as well as a series to give special attention to those muscles used most frequently by his athletes. For example, a discus thrower, shot putter, and swimmer will do more and heavier work in bench presses and pullovers because their pectorals, anterior deltoid, and triceps muscles are used extensively in their activities. Baseball players will stress arm curls, wrist curls, and lateral arm raises which tend to strengthen the interior aspect of the arms and shoulders needed for throwing and batting. Football players should give special attention to strengthening the hip extensors and the neck with exercises such as squats, rising on toes, and head lifts with straps.

Weight training programs usually consist of the following types of exercises with barbells:

1. Arm curl—for developing biceps and forearms.

   Stand straight, arms hanging straight down, grasping bar with palms upward. Raise the bar to the chest and lower it with slow motion.

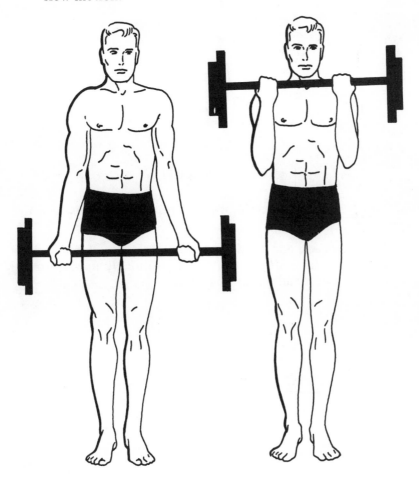

Figure 1. Arm Curl

2. <u>Wrist curl</u>—for developing flexors of the forearm.

Sit with forearms on thighs, wrists at knee joint. Hold bar with palms upward using only the wrists, raise and lower the bar.

Figure 2. Wrist Curl

3. <u>Bench press</u>—for developing the pectorals, triceps, and deltoids.

Lie with back and head on bench. Hold bar at nipple level with shoulder width grip. Press arms directly upward to full length. Lower and repeat.

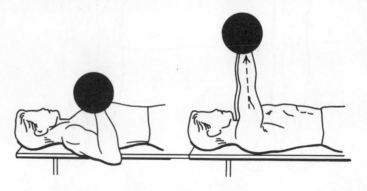

Figure 3. Bench Press

4. <u>Lateral arm raise</u>—for development of pectorals and expansion of chest.

Lie with back and head on bench holding a dumbbell in each hand, palm upward. From extended position straight upward, slowly lower the arms laterally as far as possible. Raise the arms in slightly bent position to starting position and repeat.

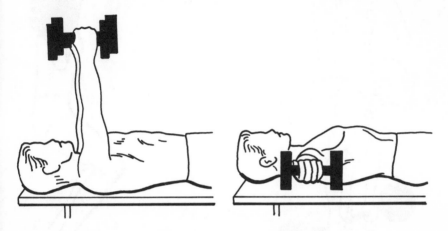

Figure 4. Lateral Arm Raise

5. <u>Dead lift</u>—for developing upper back erectors, legs, hips, and hand grip. (See page 210)

Assume comfortable standing position with barbell at feet. Lean forward, grasp barbell with palm backward. Straighten body to erect position. Lower weight to floor and repeat.

6. <u>Squats</u>—for developing the hips and thighs. (See page 210)

Stand upright, heels resting on 2" board holding barbell on shoulders. Squat to about 90° flexion of knees, keeping back straight as possible. Rise to erect position and repeat.

7. <u>Pullover (bent arm)</u>—for developing muscles of upper body, chest expansion, and flexibility of thorax. (See page 210)

Lie with back on bench, head off the edge. Hold barbell up as in bench-press position. Move barbell back over head and lower to the floor bending the elbow. Bring barbell back up to starting position and repeat.

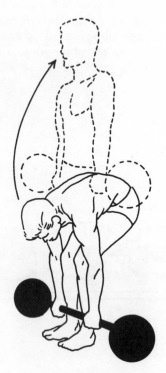

Figure 5. Dead Lift

Figure 6. Squats

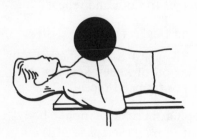

Figure 7. Pull Over

8. <u>Lateral dumbbell raise</u>—for developing posterior deltoid.

Stand bent forward 90° at the hips, arms, extended down-ward, holding a dumbbell in each hand. Swing arms upward and sideward to horizontally extended position. Lower arms to starting position and repeat.

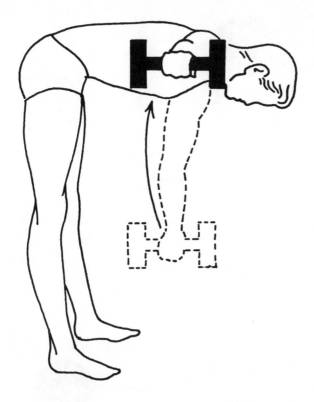

Figure 8. Lateral Dumbell Raise

9. <u>Rowing (bent)</u>—for developing posterior deltoid, rhomboid, and other muscles of upper back. (See page 212)

Stand with feet apart comfortably, with barbell on floor in front. Bend forward and grasp barbell in wide grip. With hips bent about 90° and back straight, raise and lower barbell from extended position to the chest.

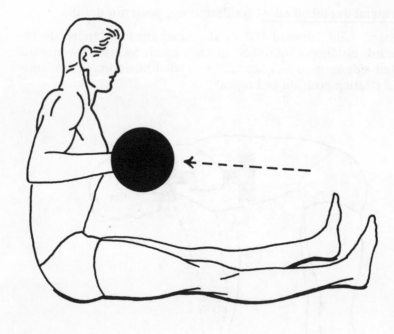

Figure 9. Rowing (Bent)

10. Rowing (upright)—for developing the trapezius, deltoids, and upper back.

Stand upright with barbell held at front in extended arms. Use close grip, palms toward body. Keeping body straight, raise barbell to neck level, where elbows should be higher than the bar. Lower barbell to starting position and repeat.

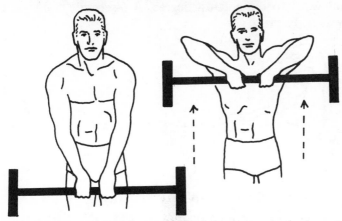

Figure 10. Rowing (Upright)

11. Sit-ups—for developing abdominal muscles.

Lie flat on floor or mat with feet anchored beneath a barbell. Clasp hands behind head and sit up, coming forward as far as possible. Return to staring position. For further development, weights may be held behind the head during the exercise.

Figure 11. Sit Ups

12. <u>Sit-ups (V Style)</u>—for developing abdominal muscles and firming all loin muscles.

Lie flat on floor or mat. Raise head and shoulders clear. At same time, raise extended legs about 10 inches from floor and hold the position. The exact point of elevation for the head and feet will be that which taxes the muscles of the abdomen and waist to the greatest degree. A 6-second "hold" is about average. Repeat.

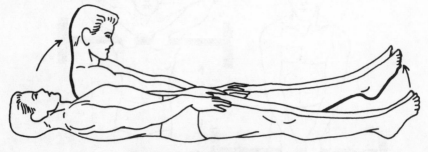

Figure 12. Sit Ups ("V" Style)

13. <u>Back extension</u>—for developing the lower back and hips.

Lie face down on bench with upper body clear of bench from hips up. Have partner anchor lower legs. Clasp hands behind head, lower upper body to the floor. Raise upper body up to starting position and extending beyond if possible. Repeat.

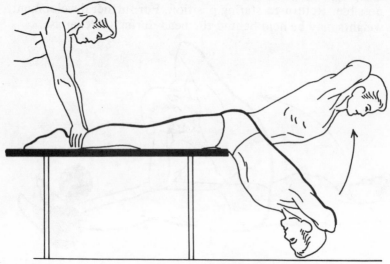

Figure 13. Back Extension

14. <u>Straddle lift</u>—for developing upper thighs and overall body strength.

Straddle barbell with feet spread 2' apart. Bend legs to squat position until hands can grasp the bar, one hand in front, the other in back. Use wide grip, rise to standing position. Lower the barbell to the floor and repeat.

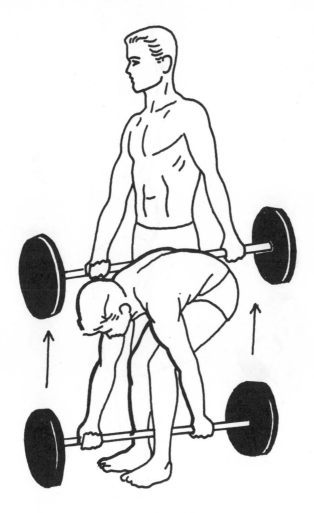

Figure 14. Straddle Lift

15. <u>Leg curls</u>—for developing hamstring muscles.

Work one leg at a time. Attach boot weight to sneaker. Stand upright. Raise weighted leg to rear about 90°. Lower it slowly to floor. Repeat. Do same routine for the other leg.

Figure 15. Leg Curls

16. Toe raise—for developing calf muscles.

Place barbell on shoulders behind the neck. Place feet shoulder width apart with toes resting on 2" board. Raise up on toes as far as possible and hold for 2 seconds count. Lower heels slowly to the floor. Repeat.

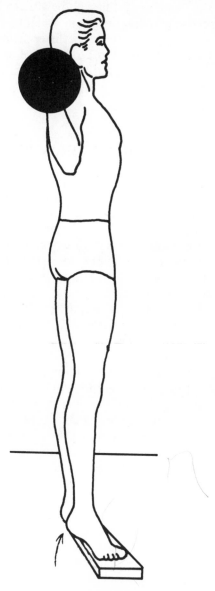

Figure 16. Toe Raise

The exercises listed are only a few of those which might be done, but they include challenges to all the main muscle groups of the body. If they are done with 8 or 10 repetitions in sets of 3 during each workout, a general development of the body will result. The amount of weight lifted in any exercise will vary with the individual, his size, and degree of progression in the program. The longer he participates, the more weight he will be able to handle.

Proper breathing is important in weight lifting. Deep inhalation and forcible exhalation protects the lifter from rupture and abdominal strain. Most lifters develop a rhythm of exhaling on the forceful part of the lift and inhaling during the return to starting position, or just before starting the forceful lift.

CIRCUIT TRAINING

Originally circuit training consisted mainly of a series of weight-lifting exercises done to improve fitness in one of two methods: an athlete might include more and more work on each of the exercises, or he might do the same amount of work in a progressively shorter period of time, accomplishing it by working faster and shortening his rest period. The workouts might consist of ten or twelve exercises performed three times, or three laps within 30 minutes. After five workouts, either the resistance or the number of repetitions would be increased. Circuit training became popular with football coaches because the exercises were designed to develop the muscles used in performing the techniques of charging, tackling, blocking, and warding off blockers.

In today's type of circuit training, all sports athletes find an effective and stimulating method of conditioning because many innovations have been added to the "circuit." Any coach using his imagination and creative powers can devise a series of exercises not only for general development but also to increase power, flexibility, and speed in the muscle groups most important for his athletes. Use can be made of hallways, stairways, and almost any other bit of open space within a gymnasium.

Included in the circuit, in additon to the normal events of weight lifting, could be running, backward and sidestep running, running up stairs, running up stairs carrying another athlete piggyback, rope climbing, dips on parallel bars, medicine ball throws, and jumping. With a little ingenuity, a coach can lay out a circuit of events best designed to accomplish results for his players.

On the basis of scientific evidence, one must conclude that weight training can produce physical growth, increased power, better flexibility, and muscular endurance. Claims of cardiorespiratory development are still unfounded because of the relatively light demand on the circulatory-respiratory system during the lifting. When circuit training is employed and oxygen debt occurs while the athlete is engaged in some of the events, there is no question about cardiorespiratory improvement. The endorsements for weight training come from an impressive list of sports champions and outstanding performers in other fields, such as rodeo riders, musicians, and singers.

Any discussion of athletic conditioning will, like charity, cover a multitude of factors. The day is past when conditioning was regarded merely as "toning up" muscles. The modern coach realizes that proper conditioning for athletic competition will result from a regimen of exercise, rest, nutrition, mental concentration, and avoidance of debilitating activities. The combined effect will promote within the individual a spirit of eagerness to test his mettle in competition. It is true that the desire to compete may run high in a physically untrained person, but the psychological structure will stand only as long as the physical foundation is able to function, and that will not be long. Most athletes, realizing the physical demands put upon them in a sport, attempt to get into fairly good condition before the regular season starts. In fact, it has become common practice for coaches to demand "voluntary" preseason conditioning as a prerequisite for participation. When players report in good physical condition, it is easier to keep them in that state through long, vigorous practice sessions on the skills of the sport. Good condition plus proper training should make the athlete stronger, faster, more skillful, more alert, and more enduring.

Motivating the players to work hard and enthusiastically has been adequately covered in other areas of this book, where it was pointed out that athletes will even punish themselves in a long, grinding program if they believe it is helping them to improve. Facilities, equipment, individual coaching, and meaningful drills promote zeal, spirit, and self-confidence. Above all, however, is the unquestioned necessity to ready the body for the demands to be put upon it.

NUTRITION

In order for the athlete's body to function at its best, it requires a ready and continuing supply of nutrient material derived from the

foods eaten. Whereas the ordinary person can carry on a program of moderate activity in spite of nutritional deficiencies, the athlete's performance would suffer markedly without proper nutrition. Foods serve three purposes in the body for everyone:
1. They furnish energy.
2. They build and repair tissue.
3. They act as body regulators.

In addition to the above, the athlete, if properly fed, will gain the following benefits:
4. Foods may offset the chemical changes taking place which bring on fatigue in the cells.
5. They may speed the energy-producing reactions.
6. They may assist in reducing fat tissue in the body.

To carry out such a program within his body, the athlete must continually be supplied with nutrient material balanced in proper ratios of proteins, carbohydrates, fats, minerals, and vitamins, varied enough to sitmulate his appetite. The benefits will accrue over a long period of time, not in a few days or a few hours prior to a contest. There are no shortcuts to dietary habits. They must be practiced every day during the season, varying only in precontest meals.

The amount of food taken into the body is measured in calories, the same unit used in measuring heat energy. A calorie is the amount of heat required to raise the temperature of 1 kilogram of water 1° Centigrade. The various nutrients found in food produce differing amounts of nutrient calories. For instance, water, vitamins, and minerals, for all practical purposes, produce no calories, but fats yield 9 calories per gram. Carbohydrates and proteins yield 4 calories per gram. In other words, fats produce 2-¼ times as many calories as do equal amounts of proteins and carbohydrates. The daily needs of athletes, measured in calories, will range between 3,000 and 6,000. Age, body size, and the severity of practice work determine the needs. The type of sport evidently has no great effect on the total intake requirement. A general rule is that the amount eaten should maintain the athlete at his optimal body weight for maximal performance and must furnish the calories, amino acids, vitamins, and minerals necessary for growth, development, and bodily functions.

For athletes, the major part of the caloric requirement for body growth and function is furnished by carbohydrates, with proteins and fats playing a secondary role. Some authorities point out that the percentages of carbohydrates and proteins needed may vary with the type of exercise or event practiced. For example, an event calling for *endurance* could require twice as many carbohydrates as a *speed* event but only half as many proteins. More research is needed to firmly establish the relative effects of carbohydrates, proteins, and fats on muscular efficiency. However, it seems safe to conclude that a high carbohydrate diet will yield approximately a 5% greater efficiency than the high-protein or high-fat diet.

Carbohydrates should make up about 60% of the athlete's diet. They may be found in bread, cereals, rice, crackers, cornmeal, grits, oatmeal, spaghetti, sugar, noodles, potatoes, and bakery products. Carbohydrates are changed to sugars and eventually broken down into glucose, the energy food of muscle cells, by the enzymes of the digestive system. It also may be stored in the cells and in the liver in the form of glycogen, which can be readily transformed into glucose when the body needs it. During prolonged physical acitivity, a decrease in glycogen occurs, usually accompanied by an increase in the symptoms of fatigue. When the athlete's blood-sugar level falls to any marked degree, exhaustion will follow. As an emergency measure, heavily sweetened tea with lemon may be taken to restore some energy. Theoretically, a diet heavy in carbohydrates should hold the blood-sugar level high enough even during prolonged, heavy workouts. Therefore, it appears safe to assume that carbohydrates should make up the greater portion of the training diet.

Protein, especially meat protein, usually is regarded as basic to a proper athletic diet. The only argument with this idea is in the amounts necessary. The quantity of protein actually needed to bring about a high capacity for work is undoubtedly much less than the amount ordinarily consumed. Protein molecules, like fat molecules, are large and complex. Through digestion, they are broken down into simple units termed amino acids (NH_2) and absorbed into the blood. They provide nitrogen which is indispensable to the body's structure and function. After using the amount necessary for tissue growth and repair, the excess amino acids are broken down into nitrogenous wastes and excreted from the body in urine. Proteins are not stored in the body as are carbohydrates. Within four hours the body rids itself of the nitrogenous excess of dietary protein. Too much protein could put a strain on the kidney function. Generally, protein foods are deficient in alkaline-producing substances, and therefore a high-protein diet should be balanced with alkaline fruits and vegetables.

Animal proteins are considered to be better for athletes than vegetable proteins. Perhaps it is because of the vitamins and minerals they contain, but they are regarded as more "complete proteins." Dietary proteins furnish growth and repair products, not only for muscles but also to glandular tissue and blood plasma. Of interest to coaches is the fact that they may enhance the development of resistance to infections, the healing of cuts and abrasions, and the functioning of the liver. Its contribution as an energy-producing nutrient is insignificant, but its other values as stated above call for protein to make up about 15% of the athlete's diet. Chief sources are lean meats, fish, eggs, liver, poultry, milk, cheese, dried peas, and beans.

Fats can produce heat energy just as do carbohydrates, but they are not as readily absorbed into the bloodstream. In fact, they have their own special channels (lacteals) in the villi of the small intestine, into which they are absorbed after being broken down into glycerol and fatty acids. Glycerol oxidizes readily to furnish heat energy. Athletes engaged in heavy muscular work can consume a good quantity of fat nutrients. Foods high in fat content are digested slowly and remain in the stomach longer than other foods. Most digestive difficulties with fats result from overcooking them to the point where they become too hard.

In a well-nourished individual, there is always a layer of fat stored as reserve fuel. When dieting properly be reducing the food intake, this fatty tissue is oxidized, resulting in a loss of weight. Fat is also used to protect organs (kidneys and heart) and to cushion joints. In addition to the above virtues, there also appears to be present in fat a factor necessary for the normal metabolism of carbohydrates; therefore a complete reduction of fat intake could result in a loss of energy from faulty oxidation of sugars. Fats should make up about 25% of the athlete's diet. Chief sources are butter, lard, margerine, oils, meat fat, bacon, nuts, cheese, and cream.

Vitamins act as body regulators. They are necessary if the full value of nutrients in the foods eaten are to be gained by the body They are absolutely necessary for proper functioning of the body, yet they do not produce energy or repair tissues. However, they make it possible for the digestive system to garner the valuable nutrients from the digested foods. Because all the vitamins necessary for proper performance by the body are found in an ordinary training diet, supplementation with synthetic substances is unnecessary. Yet there are many coaches who emphatically state that supplementation with Vitamin C tablets improved their athlete's resistance to bruises and colds.

Vitamins are stored in the body. If a diet failed to include certain vitamins, the body's stored vitamins of those types would be depleted. A reduction in work capacity would result, as well as other deficiencies depending upon the type of vitamin depleted or lost.

The most common types of vitamins and their effect are as follows:

<u>Vitamin A</u>	Affects vision.
<u>Vitamin B</u> (Riboflavin) (Thiamine) (Niacin)	They are necessary for proper muscular functions. A deficiency results in a reduction of muscular efficiency.
<u>Vitamin C</u> (Ascorbic Acid)	Prevents deficiency diseases. Assists in repairing bruises. It does not store well in the body and needs to be replenished almost daily.

There are about a dozen other well known vitamins and about twenty less well known that have been discovered since 1911 when the first one was recognized. Their value is unquestioned, but one need not be concerned if a broad and varied training diet is consumed.

The most important minerals used by the body are calcium, phosphorus, iron, sodium potassium, copper, and iodine. They act generally to assist the regulation of metabolism, but some of them have specific functions such as iron for hemoglobin in red blood cells, iodine for thyroxin, sodium and potassium for water balance, phosphorus for fat and carbohydrate metabolism, and calcium for irritability of the neuromuscular system. The chief sources of minerals in the athlete's diet should come from leafy green vegetables, although dried beans and peas, cheese, liver, fish, and eggs also are good sources.

EATING ROUTINES

The worst eating habit of Americans is omitting breakfast. For an athlete to do so is a cardinal sin, for breakfast supplies most of the fuel he will use during the day. Omitting breakfast will lessen work output and increase reaction time, and it could induce muscle tremor. A proper breakfast for an athlete should provide about one-third of the total daily calorie intake.

Lunch may vary in quantity among individual athletes, but it is unwise to skip the meal. Energy production will fall to a low point in late afternoon unless there is some fuel for replacement. Lunch should include variety and balance in essential foods and make up about one-fourth of the daily calorie intake.

Dinner, the heaviest meal of the day, should replace the nutrient material of cells used up during practice. The meal should contain an abundance of proteins, vitamins, and minerals. If an athlete is underweight or maintaining a proper even weight, he could be allowed a bedtime snack. Because of the slowed body processes during sleep, there is a reduced demand for energy, so that much of the food taken before retiring will be stored in the body as adipose tissue.

A precontest meal should be eaten two or three hours before competition. Some athletes beg off eating before a contest because of their nervousness. Their performance will usually suffer, because the empty stomach will send out hunger pains, and the stored supply of glucose and other energy substances will be depleted early in the contest. Uncoordination, weakness, and early exhaustion follow.

If a normal meal is eaten within an hour or so of a contest, the stomach may not completely empty when the athlete goes into action. A distended stomach may impede the movements of the diaphragm, interfering with breathing. If the meal produces gas, the upper bulge of the stomach may press upward against the under surface of the diaphragm, where the heart rests, restricting its action.

The meal should consist of foods that leave the stomach without too much delay. The most common pregame meal consists of bouillon, beef, a green vegetable, toast, fruit, and tea or coffee. Recent reserach indicates that spaghetti or macaroni would provide more energy than beef. Without the appetizing but gas-producing sauces common with those dishes, the athletes find them unpalatable.

The "liquid meal" has found favor among many coaches as a pregame meal because it can be consumed at a time closer to the start of the contest. This meal contains energy-producing nutrients which are readied for use in the body shortly after drinking them. If a coach plans to adopt liquids as the regular pregame meal, he should try them out on the team a few times before scrimmages to determine their effect on individual players.

WATER

Water is an absolute essential to life and must constantly be replaced in the body. It is utilized in all physiological processes and makes up about two-thirds of the body weight. Because of increased intensity and tempo of practice sessions in modern athletics, it is imperative that coaches understand the importance of water balance.

It is not uncommon for athletes to sweat off a gallon of water during a single workout in a hot environment.

When large amounts of water are lost by sweating, the amount excreted through kidney action is decreased. There is also a loss in body salts, due to heavy sweating, especially by untrained individuals. Ordinarily, salt loss can be made up in the diet, but if it is insufficient, salt tablets should be taken. A daily intake of 20 grams of salt is considered sufficient even for active athletes. When salt loss is not made up, retention of water in the body is diminished and dehydration occurs. Dehydration lowers athletic efficiency by reducing blood volume and the velocity of blood flow. Cramps and muscle weakness usually result.

Coaches whose teams must practice in areas where high temperatures are common should take extra precautions not only to prevent cases of sunstroke and heat prostration, but to acclimatize the athletes' bodies to hard work in the intense heat. Some work in the heat is necessary even on the first day of practice, but it should not be too strenuous. Gradually increasing the amount each day for four or five days will acclimatize the squad providing the boys enjoy a good sleep at night. Practicing in early morning or late evening to avoid the hot sun is a mistake, because the squad will not be able to withstand the strain of playing in a hot environment unless they have been conditioned to it. It is also dangerous to prohibit players from drinking water during practice under the assumption that dehydration toughens them. Even thirst is not an accurate guide to the amount of water necessary to replace that lost. Athletes usually deliberately deprive themselves of a sufficient amount and make it up later at meals. The body will not retain water unless there is salt to go with it, so tablets should be available along with the drinking water at practice. Salt tablets should not be taken without the water because they might bring on nausea. Nylon-mesh jerseys have been found practical for use in environments where heat brings on high perspiration. They do not absorb perspiration, and the mesh allows air to cool the body.

A POTPOURRI OF ATHLETIC CONDITIONING

Breathing and Digestion

All systems of the body coordinate their efforts in support of each other. Getting into "shape" involves an improvement in the cardiorespiratory apparatus of the body, so that large quantities of oxygen may unite with red blood cells to be delivered to the cells for oxidation. For each calorie of food burned, the athlete must have an intake of about 200 cubic centimeters of oxygen.

Special Foods

Some athletes become food faddists out of superstition. Even though some of their beliefs may have sound physiological reasons, the effects are more apt to be psychological. Most of the foods taken shortly before contests are made up of simple substances or compounds which are quickly dissolved and digested. Some common substances in the "magic" formulas are honey, wheat germ oil, gelatin, dextrose, beef extracts, fruit juices, sugar, and syrups. Harmful substances are rarely found in these mixtures, so there is no reason to deprive the athlete of the psychological lift he receives from eating them. In fact, his performance may suffer greatly from their absence.

Pep Pills

The use of the so-called pep pills, such as Benzedrine and other amphetamines said to delay the onslaught of fatigue, is prohibited by most athletic regulatory groups. Practically all the drugs are toxic and can result in serious health danger. Regardless of any rationalization on the part of athletes, trainers, or coaches, the athlete absorbing them is performing under the influence of drugs and, therefore, his effort cannot be regarded as a true indication of his ability. The greatest danger lies in the fact that the normal response to fatigue is inhibited and the athlete continues to perform beyond his normal resources, a course which could result in irreparable damage to his tissues.

Smoking

The United States Surgeon General's report on cigarette smoking gave final proof to the generally accepted theory that cigarette smoking added to the susceptibility to cancer infection. Nicotine absorbed into the bloodstream stimulates heart rate but constricts the walls of coronary arteries supplying the heart muscle. Carbon monoxide in tobacco smoke may be absorbed by the red corpuscles of the blood, reducing its oxygen-carrying capacity. Activities requiring endurance suffer when smoking is habitual. In spite of recent discoveries concerning tobacco insensitivity among some individuals, coaches should teach that smoking inhibits athletic performance and is a hazard to longevity.

Making Weight by Drying Out

The only athletes affected by weight restrictions on the interscholastic or intercollegiate levels are wrestlers, lightweight crewmen, and lightweight football players. Losing weight is accomplished through abstaining from food and liquids for a period of time. If an athlete is competing out of his normal weight class, necessitating a period of days without adequate food and water, the practice is deleterious to his health. A heavyweight athlete can very his weight within 7% without much difficulty. If his normal weight is close to what he is trying to reach (within 10 lbs), he can accomplish the weight loss within two days by wearing heavy sweat clothes while working out and spending some time in heat cabinets or saunas. Fasting must accompany the workout regimen. After the weight is made at official weigh-in, the athlete may regain as much as five pounds through eating and drinking his precontest meal. The latter type of "making weight" is considered dangerous to health.

Alcohol

Alcohol taken just prior to or during an athletic contest promotes a false impression of power and security. The feeling soon passes, to be replaced by one of depression. The brain centers controlling wisdom, will, judgment, and fine coordinations are the first affected. The ability to judge speed, depth, and distance are seriously handicapped. Grosser coordinations will be lost if alcohol consumption is continued. In the early stages of intoxication, an individual may appear to perform with a great deal of ease and facility, especially if he normally is nervous and self-conscious. The exhilarating effect will soon wear off, giving way to a feeling of depression. One hears stories of great athletic teams and individuals who regularly used beer, ale, or wine in their training diets with no apparent ill effects. The obvious answer is a question, "How much greater would they have been if alcoholic beverages had not been used?"

SUMMARY

Physical conditioning of players has become a year-round problem for coaches. Strength is a desirable quality for athletes, for it not only affects their play but it also promotes confidence in their ability to perform against all competitors. Therefore off-season training involves improvement· in strength. The weeks just prior to the opening of the season can be devoted to the improvement of endurance and flexibility. Some coaches prefer a system of weight training designed to strengthen specific muscle groups that are used extensively in the performance of techniques associated with a particular sport. Care should be taken to strengthen antagonistic pairs of muscle groups, to prevent imbalance and faulty development. Circuit training which may involve challenging stunts, as well as weight training, is favored by many coaches.

Proper nutrition calling for a wide, varied, and adequate diet for players should be a serious consideration for coaches. Energy production, growth and replacement of tissue, and regulation of body processes are dependent upon the nutrients present in the diet. Energy production and the maintenance of adequate endurance result from the digestion and assimilation of foods rich in carbohydrates transported by an efficient vascular system. Care must be taken to insure that practice sessions and training methods adhere to sound physiological concepts. As a general rule, carbohydrates should make up approximately 60% of the athlete's diet, proteins 15%, and fats 25%. Minerals vary according to individual taste. Adequate amounts of vitamins will normally be contained in a varied, well-balanced diet with resorting to synthetic types. Food fads among athletes are not uncommon, especially with temperamental individuals. The benefits derived from their special mixtures are mostly psychological, but because these can be transferred into an improved physical performance the pet diet should be allowed.

A regular routine of meals is advisable so that the digestive tract may settle into definite periods of work and rest. Breakfast is a very important meal, for it supplies most of the fuel used during the day. Liquid meals have the advantage of remaining in the stomach only a short time. As a pregame meal, it can meet all the energy requirements of the athlete for several hours.

The water content of the body is subject to drastic change when athletes work in a hot environment. It behooves coaches and trainers to be alert to the need of replacing water and salt lost through sweating. Athletes should be allowed "cooling-off" periods during practice sessions in high temperature, but complete avoidance of work during the heat of the day is inadvisable, especially if a team will be playing under those conditions.

The use of pep pills, alcohol, and tobacco should not be tolerated in an athletic program. Enough scientific evidence has been compiled to support their complete prohibition.

Test Questions

1. In a weight training program, should emphasis on strength and endurance change at any time?
2. What is meant by muscle boundness and how is it prevented?
3. How do muscles increase in size through exercise?
4. What is the basic difference between exercising for strength and exercising for endurance?
5. Explain the difference between isometric and isotonic exercises.
6. In addition to increased strength, endurance, and flexibility, what social and emotional benefits should accrue from a program of weight lifting?
7. Why should a trainer perform his duties under the direction of a medical doctor?
8. What is meant by specific weight training as opposed to general weight training?
9. Of what importance is proper breathing during weight lifting?
10. What are the advantages of circuit training over regular weight training exercises?
11. How is physical condition related to morale?
12. What are the three functions served by food in the human body?
13. Which of the basic nutrients is considered the most important for athletes?
14. What is the general rule about the amount of food an athlete should eat?
15. Would an event such as the 100-yard dash require more protein or more carbohydrates?
16. Why might heavily sweetened tea or other sweet drinks be allowed at half time?
17. From a physiological standpoint, which food would be best as a pregame meal, a steak or a plate of macaroni?
18. Why should athletes eat a substantial breakfast?
19. What is the chief value of the liquid pregame meal?
20. How could heavy sweating result in cramps and muscle weakness?
21. Should athletes be allowed to drink water during practice?
22. Should practicing in high heat be avoided at all times?
23. Is it wise to allow athletes to supplement their diets with special concoctions which they believe to have special benefit for them?
24. How does breathing affect digestion? What are the implications for training?

25. What is the effect of most "pep pills"?
26. How do you answer the assertion that many fine athletes have consumed beer and wine during their playing careers?

Discussion Questions

1. You realize that there is a need to build up your players physically. There are no barbells or other weights available in the school. What would you do?
2. A knee must be able to withstand pressure from all directions. Describe the exercises which will build strength in all directions.
3. Your school has no athletic trainer and no funds for hiring one. As a coach, what would you do?
4. You have suspended a player for smoking. His father tells you that tobacco insensitivity runs in his family, and he has allowed the boy to smoke. How would you handle this situation?
5. A new, young team doctor suggests that he be allowed to experiment with a new energy pill that has come on the market. He would like to try it prior to regular contests. How do you react to his suggestion?
6. In order to avoid the dangers of heat prostration and sunstroke, would you have a football team practice during early morning hours and late evening?
7. Is it possible to eliminate practically all serious injuries in contact sports with proper procedures?
8. Should a coach be an expert in diagnosing and treating athletic injuries?

Suggested Readings

BOOKS

1. Clark, Harrison. *Muscular Strength and Endurance in Man.* Englewood Cliffs: Prentice Hall, Inc., 1966, pp. 184-188.
2. Cureton, T. K. "The Value of Hard Endurance Exercises and Tests to Produce Changes in Weight, Fat Metabolism and Cardio-Vascular Condition." *Sixty-First Annual Proceedings College Physical Education Association,* 1958.
3. Dayton, William O. *Athletic Training and Conditioning.* New York: The Ronald Press Co., 1965, p. 6.

4. Dolan, Joseph P. *Treatment and Prevention of Athletic Injuries.* Danville: Interstate Printers and Publishers, Inc., 1961, p. 364.
5. Hooks, Gene. *Application of Weight Training to Athletics.* Englewood Cliffs: Prentice Hall, Inc., 1962, p. 1.
6. Johnson, D., Updyke, W., Stolberg, D., and Shaefer, M. *A Problem-Solving Approach to Health and Fitness.* New York: Holt, Rinehart and Winston, 1966, chapter 22.
7. Jokl, Ernst. *Nutrition, Exercise and Body Composition.* Springfield, Ill.: Charles C. Thomas Co., 1964, Chapters 1-4.
8. Jokl, Ernst. *Physiology of Exercise.* Springfield, Ill.: Charles C. Thomas Co., 1964, Chapters 3, 23.
9. Jones, H., Schutt, M., and Shelton, A. *Science and Theory of Health.* Dubuque: William C. Brown and Co., 1966, pp. 51-80, 193-226.
10. Jones, Harold E. *Motor Performance and Growth.* Berkeley: University of California Press, 1949, pp. 53-57.
11. Karpovich, Peter V. *Physiology of Muscular Activity.* Philadelphia: W. B. Saunders Co., 1965, Chapter 16.
12. Klafs, Carl, and Arnheim, Daniel. *Modern Principles of Athletic Training.* St. Louis: The C. V. Mosby Co., 1963, p. 15.
13. Mathews, D., Stacy, R., and Hoover, G. *Physiology of Muscular Activity and Exercise.* New York: The Ronald Press Co., 1964, pp. 332-341, 351-361.
14. Morehouse, L. E., and Miller, A. T. *Physiology of Exercise.* St. Louis: C. V. Mosby Co., 1967, pp. 201-226.
15. Morehouse, L. E., and Rasch, P. J. *Sports Medicine for Trainers.* Philadelphia: W. B. Saunders Co., 1963, p. 93.
16. Reidman, Sarah. *The Physiology of Work and Play.* New York: Holt, Rinehart and Winston, 1950, pp. 144-172, 405-452.
17. Ricci, Benjamin. *Physiological Basis of Human Performance.* Philadelphia: Lea and Febinger, 1967, pp. 141-158.
18. Rodahl, Kaar, and Horvath, Steven. *Muscle as a Tissue.* New York: McGraw Hill Book Co., 1962, pp. 243-257.
19. Schiffers, Justin J. *Essentials of Healthier Living.* New York: John Wiley & Sons, 1963, pp. 88-94.

Suggested Readings

ARTICLES

1. Allman, Fred L., Jr. "An M. D. Explodes Sports Myths," *Today's Health,* The American Medical Association, Vol: 46-2, February 1968, p. 47.

2. Asprey, G., Alley, L., and Tuttle, W. W. "Effect of Eating at Various Times on Subsequent Performance in the 440 Yd., Half Mile and the Mile Runs," *Proceedings Annual Meeting of National College Physical Education Association*, December 1962, pp. 117-122.

3. Brown, Joe. "Power Weight Training," *Coach and Athlete*, Vol. XXIX-5, January 1967, p. 10.

4. Committee on Medical Aspects of Sports. "Wrestling and Weight Control," *Journal of the American Medical Association*, Vol. 201-7, August 14, 1967, p. 541.

5. Cureton, L. K. "Training Youthful Record-Breaking Athletes," *Athletic Journal*, Vol. XLVI-3, 1965, p. 32.

6. Ellis, R. ("Buss"). "Circuit Training for Basketball," *Coach and Athlete*, Vol. XXIX-5, January 1967, p. 10.

7. Fardy, Paul S. "Preventing Heat Illness," *Athletic Journal*, Vol. XLIX-1, September 1968, pp. 62, 102-103.

8. Goodloe, Mary. "Nutrition for Athletes," *Coach and Athlete*, Vol. XXX-4, December 1967, pp. 22-23.

9. Grieve, Andrew. "Circuit Training for Fitness," *Scholastic Coach*, Vol. 36-1, September 1966, p. 44.

10. Hale, Tudor. "Pressure Training Circuit for Soccer Players," *Athletic Journal*, Vol. XLVIII-2, October 1967, pp. 24-25, 75.

11. Hofacket, "Rusty". "Building Strength and Agility in High School Athletes," *Coach and Athlete*, Vol. XXVIII-7, March 1966, p. 12.

12. Homola, Samuel. "Building Endurance and Power with Circuit Training," *Scholastic Coach*, Vol. 36-8, April 1967, p. 60.

13. Homola, Samuel. "Alcohol and Athletics," *Scholastic Coach*, Vol. 36-3, November 1966, p. 44.

14. Jarnett, Don. "Put a Reason in Weight Training," *Coach and Athlete*, Vol. XXIX-10, June 1967, p. 24.

15. Jenson, Clayne R. "The Controversey of Warm-up," *Athletic Journal*, Vol. XLVII-4, December 1966, pp. 24, 44.

16. Knowlton, Ronald G. "A Discussion of Some Basic Principles of Muscle Training," *Proceedings Annual Meeting of National College Physical Education Association for Men*, Januray 1965, pp. 39-42.

17. McConnell, "Mickey". "Conditioning Exercises for Baseball," *Scholastic Coach*, Vol. 37-7, March 1968, p. 54.

18. McCracken, Herbert G. "The Liquid Pre-game Meal," *Scholastic Coach*, Vol. 31-5, January 1962, pp. 56-57.

19. National Federation of State High School Athletic Associations and Committee on the Medical Aspects of Sports of A.M.A. "Cigarettes and Athletic Fitness," *JOHPER*, Vol. 38-8, October 1967, pp. 12-14.
20. Nelson, Dale O. "Milk and Athletics." *Athletic Journal*, Vol. XL-9, May 1960, pp. 37-38, 43.
21. O' Connor, Bob D. "Scientific Weight Training," *Scholastic Coach*, Vol. 34-3, November 1964, p. 43.
22. Roundy, E. S., and Cooney, L. D. "Effectiveness of Rest, Abdominal Cold Packs and Cold Showers in Relieving Fatigue, *Research Quarterly*, Vol. 39-3, October 1968, pp. 690-695.
23. Sedgewick, A. W., and Whalen, H. R. "Effect of Passive Warm-up on Muscular Strength and Endurance."
24. Veller, Don. "Getting Them to Train," *Athletic Journal*, Vol. XLVII-6, February 1967, pp. 60, 62, 64, 73.
25. Weiss, Steven, and Singer, Robert. "Weight Reduction and Wrestling," *Scholastic Coach*, Vol. 36-6, February 1967, p. 24.

Chapter IX
COMMON PROBLEMS IN COACHING

"A business filled with laughs and tears."

GOOD AND BAD FEATURES OF A COACHING POSITION

A young man desiring to enter the coaching profession must face the experience of applying for his first job.

Later, at some point in the coach's life, he will seriously consider making a change from his current job to a position at some other institution. At the close of any sports season, readers of the sports pages might gather the impression that coaches are nomads, readily folding their tents and moving to new pastures whenever the whim possesses them. The opposite is true, of course, but sometimes a position will appear so attractive that it will induce many coaches to offer their candidacy.

The attractive features usually are: (a) a large institution, (b) a high salary, (c) a major schedule. If these points were sufficient to accurately judge the value of a coaching position, it would be a fairly simple matter to decide whether or not to apply.

A coaching position is either good or bad, depending upon many factors connected with it. Some features are outstanding and easily understood, but others require some investigation in order to ascertain the facts. Some positive features will have to be weighed against the negative before a coach can come to a conclusion about the suitability of the position for him. Everyone doesn't have the same attitude toward things or events. One coach's philosophy calls for him to view a factor such as faculty attitude as extremely important, while another coach practically ignores it. However, it would be well for a coach to be aware of some of the practical problems of coaching positions which he should investigate and consider before accepting.

Type of Institution: There are many schools, colleges, and universities in operation all engaged in the business of educating, but they vary greatly in nature. Ordinarily the larger institutions have extensive athletic programs while smaller ones operate on a more modest basis. Some coaches prefer to work in a small liberal arts college rather than a large publicly supported one for a variety of

234

personal reasons. The lack of pressure and the intimacy of faculty and students are appealing features.

Philosophy of the Institution: The philosophy of an institution in reality is the attitude of the administrative officers toward competitive athletics, manifested in the degree to which they actively support the program through word and deed. Providing facilities, equipment, assistant coaches, as well as allowing class cuts for necessary team travel, reduced teaching loads for coaches, recruiting trips by coaches, and financial assistance for athletes are some of the ways in which an institution indicates it philosophy of supporting athletics. A coaching position in an institution which carries on such practices as those just listed gives a coach an opportunity to meet his opposition on an even basis, but if his opponents should enjoy such privileges while he lacked them, the coaching position ought to be shunned.

Location: A move to another part of the country or even to another town can be a traumatic experience for a coach's wife and family. Differences in customs and traditions require adjustments by individuals. While it may be relatively simple for children to sever old ties and meet and make new friends, adult reserve prohibits easy assimilation into a new social environment. Climatic conditions in various parts of the nation could be either beneficial or harmful to some individuals but, regardless of the effect on one's physical health, radical differences in temperature, humidity and rainfall require mental and emotional adjustments.

Type of Community: Communities, like humans, develop personalities becasue playing upon them are such factors as its industries, commercial enterprises, government, schools, tax rate, churches, public utilities, topography, geographic layout, and its residents. The forces emanating from the inanimate factors have an effect on the attitudes of the inhabitants, so that when one characterizes a town as being dynamic or decadent, friendly or aloof, quiet or lively, one is speaking of the habits of its people. Communities may be appealing or repelling to different individuals, so a coach should consider the effect of living in this new community on himself and his family. But again it must be pointed out that human beings have the power of adjusting to their environment. Many coaches, especially those with families, prefer to work at a high school or college located in a small town. Sociological problems commonly associated with urban communities seem either to be nonexistent or more readily solved in the small towns. Friendships are made more easily, frequent opportunities for public service present themselves and, in general, the atmosphere seems conducive to healthy family living. Often the artistic and social life of the small community centers about the activities of the educational institution, including the athletic events. This brings the coaches and their families into close association with many townspeople. Highly industrialized regions are favored by some high school coaches because they seem to produce aggressive tough-minded youths, while other coaches prefer suburban or even rural areas for the easily coached individuals found there. As was pointed out earlier in this book, many of the identifiable characteristics of the boys from different backgrounds disappear in college after one or two years of working and playing together.

Sports Tradition: Some institutions have, over the years, built up a reputation for producing excellent athletic teams in one or more sports, the reason for which may be simple or complex. Their success might be due to the fact that their system of schooling allows for excellent coaching and participation in the early years, bringing a constant flow of fine material to the senior coaches. Or it may simply be that the coach of a successful sport is a hard-working, intelligent and well-organized individual. Success breeds success, so that in a community where winning in a particular sport has become a habit, the town's interest and support reach down even to the very young children who will engage in that sport more than any other. Motivation is never a problem for a coach in such a community.

Colleges, too, have traditions of winning and losing, but it is not wise to attribute these habits to tradition and let it go at that. There are reasons for continued success in a sport, and the applying coach should know what they are and how much effect he will have in maintaining them. Winning seasons will be expected by an institution or community that has enjoyed them repeatedly, while losers can only hope that a new coach will exert the magic to bring about a delightful change. There are risks involved in both situations.

Interest of Other Coaches: The fact that a school may have a winning team in one sport and be wholly unsuccessful in another suggests that there may be differences in the philosophies among the coaches in the institution. It may be that a coach is successful because of the emphasis placed on his sport by himself and the administration, and neither could care less about the fate of the other sports programs. The status quo could be extremely important to the winning coach, who will resist any attempts to change it, especially if a change in emphasis brings about any lessening of support and interest for his sport. Institutions sometimes are referred to as football schools, basketball schools, swimming schools, etc., in accordance with the emphasis they place on a particular sport.

Sometimes the winning coaches deplore the lack of effort to bring a losing program up to their level of success. This may be because they are genuinely interested in the fortunes of the entire institution, or because they feel that one sport aids another in matters of publicity, playing material, and recruiting. Often an athlete may be skilled enough to become outstanding in more than one sport, and the coaches encourage him to do so, especially if he is a good enough student to spare the time. A happy situation exists where all members of the athletic department recognize the place and value of winning teams in every sport and lend their active support to each other. Conversely, where one or two sports dominate the scene because their coaches resist efforts to improve the quality of the other sports, a bad situation exists and should be avoided.

Material on Hand: Often a vacancy exists because, after experiencing two or three winning seasons, a coach moves on to a more lucrative position. An investigation of the facts concerning his success will reveal that his starting team began their varsity careers as outstanding sophomores, improved each year, became great as seniors and will graduate en masse, leaving a squad of inexperienced players to bear the brunt of the coming season. A new coach coming into such a situation is in a hazardous spot. Normally it will take three years to rebuild a winning combination, so he should ask for a contract covering the rebuilding period. If the former coach's program called for a constant replacement of graduating players via the junior varsity and freshman teams, the situation could be better than it appears. If the administrative officers of the institution recognize the magnitude of the task facing a new coach and so state publicly, it will lessen the pressure on him at least for two years.

Other Duties: Ordinarily coaches are regarded as teachers. In fact, most of them are hired with faculty status after meeting the requirements for certification as teachers. However, it often occurs that a coach will request to be relieved of his teaching load in order to devote more time to coaching. As a rule, such a man is a very successful coach who feels that his future lies in the area of athletics and who anticipates even more success with increased time and energy allotted to it. No man can serve two masters, so it becomes imperative that a coach have only a few demands on his time other than coaching during his season. If he is a college coach, it will also be necessary for him to recruit during the off season, with or without athletic scholarships to offer. He should visit prospective athletes and explain the advantages of a college education, especially at his institution. If an administration thinks so poorly of the task of coaching that it requires its coaches to assume many periods of teaching in addition to the long hours of coaching, it deserves to receive only a half effort in each area.

Not all coaches will agree that teaching assignments should be dispensed with during the active playing season. To some, the classroom experiences give a respite from the mental strain of coaching problems. It acts therapeutically on their nervous systems, delaying fatigue and probably prevents staleness. The number of classroom teaching hours desirable in such cases will vary according to individual preference, so the coach should decide what is best for him and his supervisor should cooperate.

Attitude of the Faculty: One of the worst situations in which a coach might work is in an institution where there exists between the general faculty and the athletic coaches a relationship running somewhere between coolness and open hostility. The feeling may be one of long standing or a comparatively new development but, in either case, a coach should determine his chances of changing the atmosphere before he becomes a candidate for a position in that institution. If the strained relations existed only between the faculty and the coach who is leaving, there is every reason to believe that a new coach could breach the gap of disinterest, bringing about a condition of compatibility between himself and his teaching colleagues. Whatever the reason for the break, it was caused by human behavior and therefore is subject to correction.

Bitterness is often caused because of one or more of the following actions:

Athletes receiving undue privileges with regard to class cuts, housing, food, etc.

Arrogant behavior of athletes.

Pressure put on faculty members to improve the grades of athletes.

Placing and withdrawing athletes in classes in accordance with the reputation of the instructor.

Athletic coaches' salaries in excess of those for the general faculty.

The tendency of the coaching staff and families to remain aloof from the normal social activities of the institutional community.

Jealousy of the athletic coach's prominence in the community.

A distrust of anything muscular on the part of some educators.

In some cases, none of the actions listed above were to blame for the breach of relations but, instead, a single incident between a coach and a faculty member grew all out of proportion, finally involving most of the institutional personnel. Whatever the situation or its causes, if it exists, a coach should be aware of it and decide whether he has the power or the inclination to correct it, because working in such an atmosphere will only add to his problems.

Assistants: When a coaching change takes place in an institution, it is rare that every coach connected with the sport involved leaves with the head coach. Invariably, there will be some members of the staff who have acquired tenure and cannot be removed, or there are assistant coaches who, because of their proven worth, are asked to remain with the institution. In some high school situations, assistants are chosen by the Board of Education without regard to the desires of the head coach. He may recommend individuals, but to no avail because of the vagaries of politics. A head coach coming into a new position should not be asked to surround himself with assistants not of his choosing, for they may be totally ignorant of his philosophy, system, and coaching methods. Moreover, there will exist a feeling of independence on the part of the assistants because they are not responsible to the head coach for their positions. When asked to perform the many tasks of coaching that require long hours away from their families, submerging their personalities in the anonymous world of assistants, they may get a feeling of resentment against the head coach, bringing on a problem of staff morale.

It is always better if a head coach can bring someone with him in whom he has the utmost confidence as a technician and loyal person. Some sports require so many assistants that it would be desirable for him to bring more than one addition. At any rate, the problems of coaching an athletic team have become so numerous, and the techniques of play so involved, that it is impossible for a single coach to adequately do the job. This would be the worst situation; the best would be one in which he had many assistants, all chosen by him. The usual situation is found somewhere between the two extremes.

Chances for Advancement: There are certain coaching jobs that have been known as stepping stones to better positions. Some of them are found in small colleges, others in large high schools where a successful tour of duty averaging two or three years brings the coach offers to move up to positions of major importance paying greater salaries. The jobs are well known to the coaches of these sports, and when a vacancy occurs in one of them it attracts a multitude of applications. This is understandable, for ambition runs high in most coaches, and confidence in their ability to compile a winning record impels them to apply for the opening. On the contrary, some positions are known as graveyards for coaches, because a long line of coaches have met disaster in them. There is an allure connected with such positions because the coach who can reverse the trend will be regarded almost as a miracle worker and is sure to be in demand in any institution that has been experiencing losing seasons. Any applicant for a job that is conspicuous for its disastrous effects should carry out a careful analysis of the causes of such a situation, and if he feels that a change is within his power, he might follow through with the application and, if not, he should withdraw.

A coach applying for the job of assistant coach should always consider his chances of advancement. If the head coach has reached an age where he will be retiring within a few years or is sure to move on to a bigger job, the assistant would be in an advantageous position to replace him. Sometimes a veteran coach bears the reputation of training splendid assistants who move on to head-coach positions in other institutions to produce winners. A young coach would be wise to join such a staff if he is willing to make the sacrifice demanded of an assistant for a number of years, always bearing in mind the ultimate goal of moving on to a head-coach job. A word of caution seems appropriate at this point. The mental picture of the goal should not cloud the responsibilities of the present situation to the point where it interferes with the all-out effort expected of assistants.

Housing Available: A practical aspect of moving from one position to another is that of finding adequate housing. For an unmarried coach or a childless couple, the problem is comparatively simple, but when a few children are involved, the problem becomes more complex. Renting is difficult for families with children, and to purchase a home involves many considerations such as price, location, size, and oftentimes the problem of selling a home already owned. Prices of real estate vary with localities, as does the availability of financing. If a coach already owns a home that he must sell in order to finance the new home, he may be faced with such a financial loss that it would be improvident for him to make the move. Young children in the family almost decree that the neighborhood have children of the same chronological age. Coaches, like all faculty members, are supposed to live at a standard commensurate with their positions, a pseudoregulation that might be difficult if a large house is necessary to meet the size of the family.

Some colleges and universities furnish housing for staff members, a practice that solves some problems but breeds others, such as equalizing the quality of housing for equal faculty rank. Some plans are founded on seniority, and that also becomes a problem when the institution is actively seeking the new candidate.

The cost of moving a household must be considered by a prosepctive coach for, if the distance is great and any delay in moving into a new house requires storage of furnishings for any length of time, the move could be a costly one.

Schools: All parents desire to have their children well educated and, next to providing a comfortable home, the greatest personal sacrifice of parents is made to provide a suitable education for their offspring. The quality of education available for his youngsters is a factor to be considered by a coach before accepting a new position.

Salary: A very important factor in considering a new position is the salary. It seems obvious that a coach would not consider a move unless it provided an appreciable increase in compensation over the one he was currently receiving. This is not always the case, however, for there may be elements of the position which lessen the importance of the salary. For example, the new position may offer security, prestige, or opportunities not provided in his present job. Some institutions have the reputation of retaining their coaches for many years regardless of their win/loss records. Naturally they are careful to select an individual whose qualities make it appear certain that periodic changes would be unprofitable. Some institutions, because of history, tradition, academic distinction, or athletic reputation, offer to its faculty members a measure of prestige. For some young coaches, the opportunity of working on the college level is worth a temporary reduction in pay, when they know that eventually the salary will increase beyond that possible from a high school job.

Unless some of these factors apply, a new position should carry with it a substantial salary raise. In most situations, pay schedules are set up with minimum and maximum annual salaries for faculty ranks based on training and experience. Annual increments provide for regular raises until the maximum salary is reached. In high schools, it has become a practice to provide extra pay for coaching duties with varying amounts for different sports and lesser amounts for assistant coaches. Extra pay seems to be preferred over the practice of reducing the teaching load, but in actual practice some reduction of teaching duties is combined with the extra pay.

In colleges and universities where the athletic program is administered by a department of its own, a salary schedule for coaches may be higher than that for regular faculty members, a situation that may be resented by the faculty. Justification for the separate schedule is based on the fact that coaches are not placed on tenure as are other faculty members; therefore the risk of dismissal is very real during losing seasons. Philosophically stated, it means that hazardous enterprises warrant extraordinary pay.

Tenure: Tenure is the element of permanency granted a teacher who has proved his worth over a certain number of years regarded as the probationary period. Three years is the usual length of the probationary period and, if coaches are serving as regular faculty members under the same salary schedule, they should be placed on tenure when reemployed for the fourth year. Without a tenure system for coaches, there should be a much higher salary schedule to compensate.

Fringe Benefits: Often the factors that make one coaching position more desirable than another are found among the fringe benefits, the extra considerations granted to faculty members to make their living easier. These should always be investigated before applying for a position, becuase the lack of one or two of the benefits which ordinarily are taken for granted could create a problem in living, while the addition of one or two unusual benefits could enhance living for the coach and his family. Types of important fringe benefits are as follows:

1. Medical and hospital insurance. Some institutions pay full premiums for their faculty members, others pay part of the premiums, and still others pay a part of the cost for families as well. Major medical coverage is included in some plans.

2. Life insurance. These benefits vary greatly, for there are numerous plans in operation. Some call for the institution to pay all premiums, and others have the faculty member paying a percentage of them. The amount of coverage varies from a flat amount to figures amounting to double the annual salary of the member. In some cases, the individual may retain the plan upon retirement at a reduced amount of coverage, paying the premiums himself. An option may allow him to receive at retirement a paid-up policy smaller than the amount carried during his active service.

3. Longevity pay. This is a form of inducement toward career service with an institution. The military services and federal government have had such benefits for many years, but only recently have educational institutions added them in the form of lump sum payments paid once or twice a year in amounts determined by the number of years of service compiled by the faculty member at that institution.

4. Personal leave days. This is a practice of allowing a faculty member to be absent from his duties for two or three days per year without penalty. No reason need be given for the absence.

5. Sick leave. Faculty members are allowed to accumulate sick leave benefits for steady attendance to duties. The usual rate is 1¼ days per month or 15 days per year. Should a member become ill, he may use the accumulated days to cover his absence without loss of pay. The differences in benefits lie in the number of days one may accumulate to his credit. They vary from a thirty-day limit to an unlimited number. In some cases, unused sick leave may be credited for retirement purposes and, in others, the retiring teacher may be paid a lump sum for a percentage of the unused sick leave days.

6. Vacations. Colleges and private secondary schools ordinarily have more vacation days per year than public high schools. The difference in the benefits should be judged by whether or not vacation days are paid for.

7. Summer employment. Some coaches find it necessary to work during the summer vacation in order to meet financial obligations. In considering a position at an institution, the opportunity for summer employment should be investigated. Some positions carry with them a guarantee of summer work at the institution, while others are carried out with another agency such as a recreation department.

8. Outside employment. The position of athletic coach offers opportunities for outside employment not found in many other jobs. Head coaches at some institutions, because of publicity and the importance attributed to the position, are considered good personalities for radio and television programs. Speaking engagements are another source of income for an articulate coach with a pleasant speaking style.

9. Free housing. A valuable fringe benefit offered to athletic coaches in some institutions is that of free housing. It may take the form of a single dwelling or a dormitory apartment in conjunction with a position as counselor.

10. Free board. Some positions call for the coach and his family not only to live in a dormitory but to take their meals in an institutional dining hall. The quality of housing in such arrangements varies greatly and should be determined by the coach before applying.

11. Commissary privileges. An unusual benefit, but one that can be extremely important, is that of commissary privileges. It operates only at institutions having agriculture departments or a system of central buying, stocking, and distribution of consumer products, mainly food items.

12. Travel expenses. The practice of paying travel expenses for coaches to attend professional meetings or to carry out the many duties connected with their jobs varies with institutions. The extent to which it extends this privilege to its coaches can be determined merely by asking.

13. Moving costs. Some colleges make it a practice to pay the costs of moving the household goods of a new faculty member to its community from the latter's former location. This can be a considerably important item where great distance is involved.

14. Education costs. This fringe benefit takes several forms. For example, the faculty member may have the privilege of enrolling for credit in any course in the institution without cost. The privilege may also be extended to a spouse and children. One of the best plans in operation is for the college to pay the cost of tuition and fees for any member of the family at any institution in which they are enrolled.

ATHLETIC SCHOLARSHIPS

The problems of athletic scholarships and recruiting may be faced by some preparatory schools, but principally they are confined to colleges and universities. Athletic scholarships are a system of financial assistance in meeting the cost of a college education granted to a student who possesses an unusual amount of skill in a sport. The money figures vary for different colleges, but institutions in the same conference attempt to reach an identical figure in order to balance the strength of the member teams. It has been only in recent years that regulations controlling athletic scholarship were put into effect. Until that time, the open bidding for the services of skillfull performers reached ridiculous proportions. At present, the N.C.A.A. and N.A.I.A. allow financial assistance to athletes who are students in good scholastic standing. A figure of 1.6 out of a possible quality point average of 4 (A) has been given as the minimum scholastic average to be eligible for an athletic scholarship by the N.C.A.A., but not all conferences agree on the 1.6 figure.

The maximum amount necessary is to cover tuition, room, board, required course-related supplies and books, and a maximum of fifteen dollars per month for incidental expenses. Athletes do not have to work for these benefits, and financial need is not a requirement. Conferences make their regulations within the maximum limits allowed by the N.C.A.A. Some may grant almost the limit but base the amounts on individual need. One standard stipulation is that the grant must be given by the regular granting agency of the institution, usually the scholarship committee. Any form of aid offered by individuals or groups other than the official granting committee of the institution is prohibited and can result in suspension and other penalties against the institution and its athletes.

Where an athletic scholarship program operates, a coach usually is allotted a certain number for his sport. He has the responsibility of designating the recipients, although the award actually is made by the scholarship committee. Once it is awarded to a student, it should remain in effect during his college career and not be subject to revocation by the athletic department, regardless of the skill level of the student or even if he quits the squad. Hence, it behooves the coach and his staff to use extreme caution in selecting proper candidates for scholarships.

There are ways, other than through athletic scholarships, for an institution to aid its athletes, such as "workships" in which the athlete is paid for performing some work for the college. To make such a plan acceptable, the athlete actually should perform the service and earn the rate of pay identical with that paid all other students of the college in similar jobs.

The purpose of an athletic scholarship program or any plan of financial assistance is to make it easier to attract good athletes to an institution. The practice has been in effect such a long time that many coaches lose sight of the fact that the system was brought about because of the pressure on coaches to produce winning teams. Institutions of higher learning have always been interested in attracting talented students to their campuses and have not hesitated to offer financial aid to potentially great mathematicians, chemists, musicians, artists, and many others. Such practices are considered ethical and educationally sound, so why not accept the programs of recruiting athletes by offering athletic scholarships? If athletics are educational, if coaches are educators, if the athlete is to receive a college education equal to other students, and if the recruiter is truly interested in the advancement of his institution as an educational establishment, then the answer is Yes. Supporters of this belief see nothing wrong in helping a talented athlete get a college education if he meets all the qualifications of a bona fide student. They point to the many fine young men who would not have received their education had it not been for an athletic scholarship. The program loses its respectability when the recruiting motive is solely to secure playing talent for the college with little or no real interest in the welfare of the boy. In such cases, the scholastic qualifications of the athlete for admission are disregarded, and after matriculation his academic progress is secondary to his athletic growth. Such a system is nothing more than professionalism.

Responsibility for the scholarship program is shared by the coaches, athletic directors, athletic committee members, deans, and college presidents. Whatever the plan for athletic scholarships and recruiting, it must be understood by each individual listed as to limits and methods of administering it. The integrity of the institution and its representatives are at stake whenever a prospective athlete/scholar is approached with the intent of inducing him to matriculate at that school. Anything said to a boy or done for him which is a violation of N.C.A.A., Conference, or college rules should, upon discovery, be dealt with summarily. The violation should be corrected, reported, and the guilty party separated from his connection with the institution. Attempts to cover up the infraction usually end in disaster for all parties involved.

The problem is not strictly unilateral as far as the various institutions are concerned. They may themselves become victims to a mercenary-minded athlete who is "shopping around" for the "best deal" he can make. He will cause one college to bid against another to raise the offer for his services. Whenever a prospective athlete shows little concern about the courses offered at an institution but displays enthusiastic interest in the amount of money and other privileges his athletic scholarship will cover, he should be dropped as a prospect. It may be his immaturity that causes his unconcern for his education and future, but if this is the case he will not be ready to produce in the academic atmosphere of college. Moreover, an institution cannot afford to become implicated in an open auction for individuals whose sense of values is so warped. Coaches who have had this type of athlete on their squads know that problems of morale and discipline centering around these egotists invariably will arise.

When an institution operates an athletic scholarship program to attract good athletes who meet all the requirements for admission and who are genuinely interested in a course of study offered by the institution, there is no need to apologize for the program. There always must be a concern that recruiting practices remain within the rules of the institution, the local conference, and the national body to which it belongs.

RECRUITING

Recruiting has become one of the major responsibilities of a coach and, as such, requires a high degree of organization. It is a year-round operation varying in intensity with the seasons of the year. Ordinarily recruiters are coaches operating under the direction of the head coach, but the organization may make use of alumni, high school coaches, athletes, or professional recruiters. The latter type are the least desirable although they may be the most efficient. It is always better to have the final contact made by a coach who will maintain a personal interest in the student/athlete throughout his college career and beyond. Some of the finest goodwill ambassadors operating as recruiters are a coach's own players. Where good rapport exists between coaches and players, brought about through mutual trust, confidence, and appreciation, it becomes natural for players to assume the role of voluntary recruiters. It will never take place where athletes feel that they have been treated unfairly, where the scholarship program was misrepresented, where their education is inadequate, and where the coaching is substandard.

Recruiting starts with a system of records kept on each athlete from the time he first comes to the attention of the coaching staff. It may commence with a newspaper clipping or an anecdotal account of his introduction to one of the coaches. Thereafter, every bit of information concerning the boy's athletic and scholastic progress should be noted in the record. Formal reports on the prospect compiled by his high school coach, one of the college coaches, an athlete alumnus, or some other qualified observer will be an important item in the boy's file. One member of the coaching staff should bear the responsibility for organizing the lists of prospects. Periodic evaluations of the individuals on the list should be made by the combined coaching staff of the sport, using all the information available up to that time and a priority list made from the group of prospects. Needless to say, there is no static quality to the priority ratings because a boy's position on the list could shift due to an increase or decrease in skill, scholastic difficulties, an injury, a change in vocational interest, and the addition or loss of other prospects for the same position. Because of the limited number of athletic scholarships available, the priority list is extremely important. Naturally, the ultimate objective is to grant the scholarships to boys with the highest priorities, but this is difficult to accomplish with any degree of regularity, and even when it is done there is no assurance that mistakes will not occur. The validity of a priority list of freshman prospects, based on the best information possible, is not very high. Veteran coaches can relate many instances of boys who had the highest ratings turning out to be disappointing failures, while star performers emerged from among the anonymous pack.

The formal report, mentioned previously, should be a printed form summarizing the personal characteristics of the boy as well as statistics proving his athletic prowess. There will be spaces for comments concerning his attitudes, leadership qualities, personality, sociability, personal habits, vocational interests, rank in class, college board scores, and coachability. Other items of interest listed might include his family background, number of brothers and sisters, approximate family income, jobs held, and religion. Under vital statistics would be found his height, weight, age, speed, growth potential, playing experience, record of athletic accomplishments (points scored, batting averages, times and distances recorded, all conference selection, etc.).

One important point about recruiting is that it should be done even by institutions that do not offer any form of financial aid. Most colleges in one way or another seek to attract superior scholars, but many expend their search for talent to include high school students with records of extensive participation in community enterprises, social welfare, church societies, youth organizations, and such extra-curricular activities as glee club, orchestra, band, debate, and drama. The quest for potential is and should be regarded as a proper function of any institution of higher learning. Similarly, if a sound athletic program exists in a college, its operators should be mandated to exercise the same zeal as other college personnel in the pursuit of talent. Without some form of financial assistance, they cannot expect to attract the better athletes who are also good scholars, because they will be vigorously pursued by many institutions granting the maximum aid allowed.

However, coaches should exert every effort to improve their teams, and almost the first step is to gather together the best possible material. Not every potential athlete wants or expects an athletic scholarship or a workship, but any incoming freshman will be impressed and flattered by the attention given him by a college coach. Recognition is a need felt by nearly all youngsters. It is easy to satisfy this need in a boy who may not have reached a point of growth in athletic skill which marks him as an outstanding prospect for college athletics. He may be one or two years away from attaining that point, but he will reach it if only given the opportunity to play in college. Many other good athletes prefer to matriculate at an institution recognized for its academic offerings and purely amateur philosophy of athletics. They will be attracted to a college

RECRUITING REPORT

PART I: PERSONAL DATA

Name _____

Home Address _____ Schools _____

Town _____ Date of Birth _____

Father's Occupation _____ Brothers   Older   Younger

Mother's Occupation _____ Sisters   Older   Younger

Approximate Family Income ____ Telephone _____

PART II: ACADEMIC RECORD

Subject	10th Yr.	11th Yr.	12th Yr.	Rank (Class)	IQ	SAT

Remarks (Guidance Counselor)

PART III: CONTACTS

Date   Person   Remarks

PART IV: SPORTS HISTORY

Sport & Coach   Record and/or Special Contribution

PART V: PERSONAL QUALITIES

Temperament:

Interest in Education:

Practice Habits:

Vocational Interest:

Work Experiences:

Leadership Qualities:

PART VI: VITAL STATISTICS

	Height	Weight		Speed	
Present			Starting	High	Med
Potential			Sustained	100 Yd	

Chest	Waist	Hip	Leg	Shoe Size	Hat Size

Injuries & Operations:

Diseases:

known for these qualities, if someone in the athletic department displays some interest in them.

There are some cautions to be observed in the recruiting program. First, the final grant of the athletic scholarship should be by the scholarship-granting body of the college and not by the athletic department. Secondly, the agreement reached by the athlete and the athletic department regarding his intention to matriculate at that institution should be with either the head coach or athletic director, not with an alumnus or some minor functionary of the college. In some conferences, a written letter of intent is required, and this should not be made public by anyone but a recognized official of the institution. The job of convincing an athlete to cast his lot with a certain institution may be shared by many individuals. Coaches have been known to employ the assistance of politicians, industrialists, girl friends, clergymen, department heads, Booster Club members, and many other characters in the recruiting process. There is nothing wrong in this procedure if the college is operating within the rules of its conference, recruiting only students meeting the requirements for admission and offering the boy a worthwhile college education.

Athletes matriculate at a particular institution for a variety of reasons, so a single approach to all prospects will not work. A good recruiter, like a good salesman, attempts to understand the philosophy of his customer. If the salesman knows the customer's chief interest, his attitude toward the features of whatever is for sale, the value he places upon such factors as price, performance, and service, he will know what to stress and what to play down. A good recruiter should learn as much as possible about the boy with whom he is dealing. Athletes have chosen colleges because of:

1. a particular course of study
2. the social atmosphere
3. the environment (rural vs. urban)
4. the reputation of the athletic teams
5. the reputation of the coach
6. opportunities for religious practices (church or chapel available)
7. co-ed college
8. men's college
9. proximity to his girl's college
10. proximity to his home
11. great distance from his home
12. presence of his friends at the college
13. interest in him displayed by the coach
14. courteous actions of the coach-recruiter

15. similarity of ethnic background of prospect and recruiter
16. similarity of ethnic background of athletes at college
17. influence of a clergyman
18. influence of a college faculty member
19. influence of a high school instructor
20. influence of a respected citizen
21. availability of other recreational facilities (such as winter sports)
22. opportunities for future professional play
23. opportunity for starting role as a sophmore
24. opportunity for admission to postgraduate schools (such as medicine or law)
25. opportunity for employment following graduation (such as investment and banking)
26. parental pressures (parents who are influenced by recruiter or else alumni)

Periodic surveys in the way of questionnaires or checklists among the athletes at a college will reveal important reasons for their choice of that college. The importance of certain factors will be revealed by the frequency with which they occur in the lists. These should be studied to determine if they appeal to all athletes or only to certain types.

If there is a secret to success in recruiting, it is being able to identify the factors rated as most important by the prospect and stressing them through people and agencies having the most influence on him.

In an earlier chapter of this book, we discussed the responsibilities of coaches toward their players. One point mentioned was that high school coaches should accept a responsibility for guidance of their athletes in the problem of selecting a proper college in which to further their education. Many boys are not capable of properly evaluating the opportunities offered them, but a high school coach's educational and athletic background combined with his knowledge of the boy qualifies him to act as an advisor. He should teach the boy how to differentiate between important and inconsequential features of a scholarship offer, how to think in terms of long range values as opposed to immediate benefits. A degree from one institution may be much more important in the long run than one from another, but this fact may not be apparent to a boy dazzled by an image of himself as an athletic hero.

The high school coach can be of service to both the boy and an institution by calling the attention of the college coaches to his player, being selective in his choice of institutions to contact. It is proper to submit a completed form on the boy which includes all the information necessary to give a comprehensive picture of the youngster's potential as an athlete and scholar. Every secondary school coach should devise his own form rather than use those submitted to him by colleges. In this way, he can include personal information he considers to be important, stressing such points as the boy's intelligence, study habits, working habits, personality, athletic strengths and weaknesses, rank in class, college board and other test scores, need of financial assistance, and estimate of success. One final word of caution for coaches—be completely honest in your evaluation of the boy if you wish to maintain the respect and confidence of the college coaches. Moreover, if a boy is directed into a college situation in which he has little chance to succeed, he has no cause to be grateful.

COMPETITIVE ATHLETICS BELOW HIGH SCHOOL

One of the current controversies in education is the problem of interscholastic athletics below the high school level. Many of our nation's foremost educators have agreed that there is no real benefit to such activity. In fact, those who oppose interscholastic competition for youngsters below the ninth grade present many disadvantages which they feel far outweigh the advantages. On the other hand, proponents of organized athletics for the elementary and junior high present strong arguments in favor. The opponents of the program comprise a cross section of the general public, including parents, educators, and medical doctors. Those in favor come from these same segments of society but include more athletic coaches.

One of the chief objections to the early program of athletic competition is its high degree of organization, resulting in rigid game schedules, regular practice sessions, intricate system of play and involved rules, all of which is too confusing and demanding for young boys and girls. However, that conclusion is difficult to prove either by scientific research or through the statements of recognized authorities. Psychologists of adolescents are divided in their views concerning the ability of children and young adults to meet the physiological, emotional, and social pressures of organized athletics.

The interscholastic athletic programs of the elementary and junior high schools have been in operation on an organized basis since World War II. There are staunch supporters of the philosophy that sound, graded, supervised programs of athletics have a place in the curriculum. An examination of literature on the subject shows that there have been a number of studies made with conflicting conclusions, and it is possible to find a study supporting either of the opposing philosophies. Some studies concluded that young participants in interscholastic athletics do not grow as well as those placed in a well-organized physical education program. Other studies showed that the youngsters in the athletic program had a greater rate of growth and physical development. Prior to World War II, the medical profession opposed as too dangerous varsity-type athletics for junior high school students. By 1960, other studies showed a change to the opposite view.

The medical profession at one time frowned upon vigorous athletics for adolescents on the ground that the heart was not capable of meeting the demands of blood vessels during strenous activity. This belief has since been disproved through tests which indicated that the muscular walls of the heart develop just as other regions of the body under a proper training program. The very young teen-agers in the Olympic Development programs who have established world's records are visible proof of the new theory that, with proper motivation, the human body is capable of meeting tremendous demands upon it. Because of individual differences, however, it would be unwise to expect every youngster to safely engage in the vigorous type of training called for in the Olympic competition. Pediatricians also have argued that growing bones may be seriously harmed by strenuous activity, yet they advocate soccer which requires more physical fitness than football or baseball. It has been pointed out that the growth areas of long bones (epiphysis and diaphysis) make them vulnerable to stress and sudden impact, yet some authorities feel that the pliable nature of these same areas actually could protect the youngster.

Regardless of which theory is the more sound, the fact remains that any time a group of youngsters propel themselves at a rapid rate in a limited space in any type of enterprise, there is bound to be a collision and someone is going to be hurt. Fortunately, most youngsters do not dwell on this thought, and mature adults should realize that the definite benefits derived from the activity are far more important than the possibility of injury.

The United States has lagged behind European nations in the intensity of training given to youths in interschool athletics. European competition begins as early as the 4th grade level in school, and for ten-year-olds club activities start and continue through adulthood.

Some high school coaches report that many students possessing athletic talent are not engaging in interscholastic athletics. Actually the same lament was heard from coaches forty years ago, but the reasons given are different today. At present, the question naturally arises as to the part played by prehigh school athletics. Where major emphasis has been placed on athletic programs for youngsters, with great publicity, praise and awards being heaped upon their impressionable heads, the descent from that glorified atmosphere to the austerity and anonymity of freshman or junior varsity athletics is discouraging, to say the least. Only those for whom the game holds intrinsic pleasures will "stick it out" under those conditions.

Another reason for the failure of former star athletes of prehigh school programs to engage in interscholastic athletics is the size factor. Some sports at the younger level restrict the size of the contestants and, in some cases, insist that a certain number of boys of a particular age level and/or size be members of each team. Small boys may find success competing under these controlled conditions. As these individuals grow older, most of them grow larger, but some may not or they may mature at a slower rate, and that puts them at a distinct disadvantage in high school. Hence, they decide not to compete.

The modern high school program offers another reason for the absence of many potential athletes from the squads. There are many extracurricular activities vying for the student's time and energy. It is conceivable that athletics will lose out in some cases. Economic reasons may also explain why some boys are not reporting. Regulations may allow students to drive to and from school. Private transportation is highly regarded, and many boys elect to forego interscholastic athletics for an afterschool job in order to pay for and support a car or a motorbike.

In the United States, competitive athletics for youngsters below high school is firmly entrenched at present. Over 85 per cent of the junior high schools throughout the nation have some form of interschool athletics. Over 75 per cent of the principals of the schools having the programs are in favor of them and, if a change in policy is anticipated, it will be in the direction of expansion rather than restriction. Common sense decrees that the nature of the athletic program for elementary and junior high students should not be identical with that of the senior high school. For the sake of safety, consideration should be given to individual differences in maturity, height, weight, and speed within the same chronological ages. It would be wise to field teams according to size and ability, rather than by grade level alone. A varsity and junior varsity schedule might be necessary if this were carried out, but more youngsters would benefit and better contests would result. It goes almost without saying that the coaches for such age levels should be individuals who not only know the sport but understand youngsters. Their job security should in no way be affected by the win/loss records of their teams, but a supervisor can judge their work by the quality of organization and teaching displayed.

It would be wrong to throw young children into the hot crucible of competition before they are ready, but if the concept of continuity is observed this will not take place. There should be a sequence of competitive experiences offered, progressing from the simple to the complex, having the objective of promoting emotional and social growth each step of the way. For these reasons, inter-scholastic athletics at this early level should evolve naturally from the regular physical education activities required of all, to voluntary intramurals for the motivated and, thence, interscholastics for the higher-skilled, gifted athletes.

PUBLIC RELATIONS

Public relations might be defined as the art of putting the best foot forward, the creation of an appealing image, or the fostering of goodwill, and the stimulation of interest in your program. A coach's chief concern is found in his sport program, but no facet of an institution acts alone; the interests of the entire school or college must be kept in mind. An unhealthy atmosphere exists where an institution is regarded as a stadium with dormitories attached. The academic pursuits of a school or college are the most important activities within its walls and should receive most recognition. This is easy to state but quite difficult to carry out, unless: (1) there is a single public relations department controlling the information ema-nating from the institution, and (2) there is something extraordinary being accomplished within the academic program of the institution.

Regardless of the organizational pattern of the public relations phase of a school or college, there should be at least one person and perhaps several whose duties are solely those of promoting the sports program. Whether they operate as a separate department or as a segment of the central public relations office, their job is to present a sport and its personnel in the best possible manner, bearing in mind that it must always be viewed as a part of the curriculum of the institution. If a school operates without a central information office, the athletic department should promulgate its own program of sports information as a contribution to public relations. In that case, control of the program must be maintained by the director of athletics or, in the absence of such an individual, by the coach of the sport. This is the least desirable situation because it presents another problem to an already overburdened coach; however, he should never divorce himself completely from the publicity phase of his sport. Too often stories and statements that were not cleared by the coach are released by the information department much to the chagrin of the coach. However, if he fails to exercise his prerogative of passing judgment on the type of publicity given his sport, he forfeits his right to criticize.

The list of people and agencies involved in public relations is long:

Players
Coaches
Managers
Trainers
Administrative Officers
Public Relations Directors
Writers
Secretaries
Newspaper Reporters–commercial and campus paper
Radio Commentators–commercial and campus radio
T.V. Commentators–commercial and campus T.V.
Magazine Writers
Columnists
Artists

Although all these listed are involved in the same problem, some will work in opposition to others because of the competitive nature of their agencies; that is, newspaper, radio, and television companies are vying for news. The individual in charge of public relations for the sports program must be knowledgeable enough to recognize the competitive element and refrain from giving one an advantage over another.

Individuals should know what part they are to play in the promotion of the sports program. The best way to accomplish this is through printed directives that can be read, posted, or both. It may be a list of do's and don'ts especially for coaches, players, trainers, and managers. In some cases, it may be wise for the sports information director to establish rigid rules for the activities of outside news agencies, not for the purpose of inconveniencing them but to prevent a chaotic situation for coaches and players. The sports information department is responsible for many services that capture the attention and interest of the public. Some actions are entirely their own, but more frequently they furnish the various news media with information they hope to see presented to the public.

One of the most valuable services performed by the sports information department is the production and distribution of a brochure containing vital information about the athletic teams. These are sent to newspapers, radio and television commentators, and magazine editors who use them as resource material. In some instances, a brochure covering only one sport is issued or, as is the usual case, a single brochure covering the sports for a season such as for fall (football, cross country, soccer), winter (basketball, gymnastics, wrestling, swimming, indoor track, squash), spring (baseball, track, tennis, golf, lacrosse).

Information contained in such a brochure should cover practically every point that might interest a reporter or writer: (a) each player's name, age, class, height, weight, experience, home town, field of study, and position; (b) a schedule of contests, opponent, date, time, and location; (c) a brief history of the sport at the institution, outstanding performances; (d) a resume of last season's record; (e) a discourse on the expectations for the coming season; (f) brief anecdotes concerning individual players and coaches, featuring the outstanding players; (g) feature article about some facet of the sport such as new opponents, new facilities (stadium, track, gymnasium, etc.).

The sports information department is also responsible for disseminating current information about the team, players, opponents, and problems facing the coaching staff. It may be in the form of daily press releases or human interest stories about an individual. The head coach should be given the opportunity to pass judgment on such articles before they are released, lest they contain inaccurate information or statements which could adversely affect team morale. Veteran members of the information staff may reach such a state of understanding with the coach that clearances ordinarily are not necessary, but the veteran writer can sense when a story hinges on controversy, and he will seek the coach's judgment before releasing it.

The sports information department will act as a liaison agency between the athletic staff and commercial news personnel. Reporters, broadcasters, and T.V. commentators welcome interesting news for their readers and listeners. If the coach were to be at the beck and call of each individual reporter or interviewer, he would have a chaotic practice schedule and rarely enough time for daily planning. The institution's sports director should set up the schedule for interviews, picture taking, and the like, after consulting the coach.

During these sessions, it behooves the coach to play the part of a genial host allowing the news group complete freedom.

The athletic contest often calls for gracious behavior on the part of a coach. Pregame, postgame and even half-time interviews are asked of him and his players, together with special requests for locker-room privileges for the gathering of human interest stories. Such procedures require organization and planning beyond what a coach can do and still coach his team. His sports information director or public relations office must work out the details with the news group, relaying the plans to the coach for approval or disapproval. When agreement has been reached, the coach should merely play his part in the production and not attempt to direct the procedure.

Good public relations call for extra service to the news personnel who are working home games. They should have reserved space in the press box, printed programs, and mimeographed dope sheets for instant viewing, a public announcer to relay information from official scorers, a mimeographed resume of each period's play shortly after the end of the period, and refreshments served at their work spaces. The press box itself should be well planned with such features as good lighting, heat, unobstructed views, easy accessibility, and adjacent toilet facilities.

There may be occasions when a coach feels that he is the victim of bad reporting. A critical reveiw of a game or a caustic remark by a commentator could make him unhappy, but he would be unwise to let the incident develop into a feud between himself and the perpetrator. The news media has all the advantages in a controversey and, difficult though it may be, the coach must admit that the reporter has freedom to say and write whatever he pleases. If the coach feels that his tormentor is lacking a knowledge of facts, he should invite the newsman to his office and present him with the correct information. For the sake of his team and his own public image, a coach must keep control of his emotions and play the part of a mature, patient, and well-integrated person.

Mutual confidence is the adhesive substance that cements a proper working relationship between coaches and newsmen. Honesty is a two-way street, and if a coach expects it from newsmen he must practice it himself in his dealing with them. Misinformation or downright lies about his players or plans will result in a loss of respect for the coach's word. Newsmen will not use any confidential information passed to them by a coach speaking "off the record," but they have a right to disclose anything gathered outside the coach's confidential speech. For this reason, the coach should not hesitate to provide the newsmen with a multitude of facts concerning his players, his offensive and defensive strategy, his plans for opponents and any other problems of coaching that fact him. A more factual, sympathetic, and understanding job of reporting will usually result when the newsman has a background of information upon which to draw.

Good public relations calls for more than cordial relations with the news media. The very nature of his position makes the coach an object of interest and places him among the important people of a community. He will be in demand as a speaker at civic organizations, church clubs, alumni chapters, youth groups, sports banquets, and many other gatherings. Coaches should be articulate enough to present themselves in an interesting and sincere fashion.

If a coach is blessed with a sense of humor and quick wit, he will be a tremendous hit, especially if most of his witticisms are turned against himself and his his coaching problems. However, he would be remiss in his duty as a representative of the institution if he did not touch upon the educational values of his sport, especially when talking to parents and youngsters. It is wise to "sense" the tone of the audience to determine which aspects of his coaching to dwell on during the speech. One thing to be avoided is the use of off-color stories or language. To resort to such behavior indicates a limited repertoire and degrades the profession.

College and university athletic departments sometimes sponsor free clinics for high school coaches. The coaching staff of the college presents a program covering many aspects of the sport. Usually these are one day workshops, but they might be longer. If any expense occurs to the high school coaches for attendance, it should be held to a bare minimum, but it would be far better for the college to bear the complete cost and include even a free barbecue. Some coaches are in great demand at coaching schools, coaches' associaton meetings, and other types of clinics. As a rule, not much money is made by the visiting lecturer but, as coaches, they recognize the fringe benefits for public relations and recruiting which accrue from such service.

We have by no means exhausted the topic of proper public relations for a sports activity, but many important facts have been pointed out. Generally speaking, an awareness of the value of public relations is necessary. A sports program rarely can succeed without support in the form of interested spectators. The better informed the spectators, the more appreciative they are of the efforts of coaches and players. Proper public relations creates goodwill, sympathetic understanding, and active interest in the sports program.

PARENTS' CLUBS AND BOOSTER CLUBS

Some volunteer agencies exist for the specific purpose of aiding the athletic programs of a school or college. Parents' Clubs and Booster Clubs are two of this variety and, while they have a common interest in an athletic team, they operate quite differently. Booster Clubs are found at all levels of athletics, but Parents' Clubs rarely get involved above the secondary school. As the name implies, they are made up of fathers and mothers of the players, hence they lack an element of permanence. The majority of parents lose interest in the team and its coach when their sons leave the squad, but during the years when the sons are playing they are actively engaged in supporting the team in many ways.

Enlisting the aid of parents is a good plan for any coach, and if a club does not exist he might initiate the move to form one. The start should be made long before the start of the playing season through a letter to the parents of each player explaining the coach's philosophy, including his attitudes toward study, sleep, exercise, nutrition, behavior, and the place of parents in his program If a club does not already exist, this letter may suggest that one be formed. Periodic meetings throughout the year, and especially during the season, will help tighten the bond between the coach, players and parents. During the meetings, the coach must expect to speak and to answer questions concerning individual players, because the interest of parents naturally centers on their sons.

Not all coaches are enthusiastic about developing a relationship with parents which could lead to interference with coaching technique. When Parents' Clubs are first formed, the degree of formality should be determined. The most highly organized group will adopt a constitution and by laws, together with a declaration of purpose. The more informal type of club may merely elect officers, set dates for meetings and agree on purposes. In either case, there should be a clear statement limiting the activities of the membership to supporting enterprises. There should also be an agreement on practices considered to be in bad form, such as:

questioning the coach's philosophy
criticizing the coach's selection of players
failure to support the coach's training rules
insisting on the coach's presence at all club functions
accusing the coach of favoritism or discrimination
seeking special consideration for any specific boy
offering awards and rewards to players without the approval of
    the coach.

Some high school athletic budgets are so meager that they leave little chance for luxuries. Therefore Parents' Clubs may accept the responsibility of supplementing the budget, subject to the approval of the school administration. Collectively, the club sponsors such affairs as suppers, bazaars, raffles, dances, bridge parties, and many other enterprises for the purpose of raising money to meet the expenses of extra benefits for the team. End-of-season banquets, monogrammed sweaters, gold charms, and sightseeing trips are some examples of the benefits bestowed by parents' clubs.

Understanding, confidence, and respect are the key words in describing the proper relationship of coach and club. The coach must understand the force of parental pride and have confidence in the innate fairness of the people. In turn, the parents should understand the coach's problem in dealing with many different player personalities with varying degrees of skill and knowledge. It should be apparent to them that the coach aims to produce the best possible team, and to do so he will play those who, in his opinion, are the best performers. They should recognize that his greatest satisfaction will come from the improvement of each player's athletic performance and general development. To create this atmosphere of mutual understanding and respect, the coach must convince the parents that he is not only professionally competent in his field, but that he has a genuine concern for the all-round growth of their offspring.

Booster Clubs have the same avowed interest as the parents' clubs, that of supporting the efforts of an institution's team and coaches, but especially the team. There have been instances of a complete loss of loyalty and support for the coach exhibited by Boosters, but as a rule their interest in the team is unswerving. The members comprise a cross section of sports fans, alumni, politicians, and plain "joiners." Like Parents' Clubs, they usually are well organized with elected officers, a constitution, and bylaws. Their meetings may be sporadic except for those held during the active season, which usually are weekly affairs often accompanied by meals, speeches, and movies of games. The head coach is the main speaker at these meetings, narrating the movie of the previous week's game, pointing out good play on both teams. Some coaches make it a practice to present the problems facing the coaching staff in meeting the next opponent, without actually disclosing their plans for solving the problems, but the fact that the members have been taken into the coach's confidence to the extent of understanding his professional tasks excites their egos.

The most important function of a Booster Club is to raise money for support of the many facets of the sports program and especially in the area of recruiting. The money raised may be used to defray some college expenses for athletes, but the disbursing of such funds must be done by the single institutional agency designated for that task.

Extreme care should be taken to see that the above rule is strictly adhered to by the club and its members. In their enthusiasm to assist, they may be tempted to overlook the restrictions on their activities; therefore constant admonitions against such practices are necessary, as well as vigilant surveillance by club officers. The money itself comes from club projects and individual contributions. A frequent practice is to award Boosters with a first choice of reserved seats, for which they pay an amount somewhat above the normal price. The extra money goes into the club treasury. The weekly luncheon or dinner meeting, membership dues, initiation fees, and other club enterprises add to the funds to be turned over to the institutional agency for distribution.

There have been instances of Booster Club involvement in the procurement of coaches. When the salary extended by a college is not high enough to attract a top-flight coach, the club may offer to supplement the regular salary with additional funds, making the coach's annual income sufficient to make the position an alluring one. Offers of housing, automobiles, business enterprises, paid-up insurance policies, and other fringe benefits may be made by the club or by individual members in order to secure an outstanding coach for the college.

The dangers inherent in such a situation are obvious. With such a vested interest in the welfare of the team, it is only natural for the club members to assume some right to its direction. A coach whose salary is being paid, even in part, by an agency other than the college can expect to answer to that agency or a few of its vociferous members. Even with a winning record, a coach will not be free of annoyances from hypercritical members of the club, especially those who fancy themselves as competent coaches, and no club is free of such individuals. His only hope is that the majority of club members entertain no allusions concerning their coaching ability and recognize his professional competency. When adversity strikes and his team suffers a few losses, a subsidized coach can expect to live a miserable existence. The college administration may be willing to overlook one or two unsuccessful seasons, but the coach can expect his relations with the Booster Club to deteriorate, and if losses continue they may reach a state of hostility. When the club decides that it no longer has confidence in the coach, it usually will relay this information to the college administration. If the college administration does not agree to dismiss the coach, the ultimate result will be a withdrawal of the financial supplement to the coach's salary, making his position untenable.

Relations with Booster Clubs need not be miserable. On the contrary, an active club can make the coach's life easier through their efforts to attract and keep outstanding athletes. It must be recognized, however, that it has no official tie with the institution, so neither the club nor individual members can act for the institution. On occasion, their enthusiasm leads to actions, especially in relations with student-athletes, which can embarass the institution, but with proper leadership and supervision these pitfalls can be avoided. In general, the Booster Clubs' effect on the athletic program is more positive then negative.

THE STUDENT/ATHLETE DISSIDENTS

A strange phenomenon occured on many college campuses throughout the United States in the late 1960's and '70's. A coalition of militant students and restless faculty engaged in violent rebellion against the administrative heads of their institutions demanding not only changes in administrative policy but also to be cast as architects of the changes. Their actions range from picketing to sit-ins which sometimes degenerate into destruction of property, equipment and private files. Their purposes usually center around a series of demands such as abolishment of R.O.T.C. programs, cessation of research involving war materials, establishment of a department of Afro-American studies, admission of more minority group students, the addition of minority group faculty, halt to institutional expansion into urban housing areas and more student participation on policy-making committees of the institution. In practically all cases, the militant group makes up only a small percentage of the student and faculty bodies, the majority either looking upon the disturbances with disdain or even open hostility.

Aside from the Reserve Officer Training Corps, the only other single department which has experienced a revolt against its policies has been the athletic department. This fact alarms many conservative individuals who see violence as an enemy of intellectualism and open rebellion against a coach's authority as an attack on the last bastion of discipline in the American college scene.

Protests by athletes have taken several forms. One type has been a revolt by black athletes against what they consider to be ill-treatment by the college in general and the coach in particular. The list of charges include such items as segregated campus housing, meaningless courses of study which follow no degree pattern but are chosen for ease of passage, loss of financial assistance when playing eligibility has been exhausted, assignment to menial and distasteful tasks where athletic workships are in vogue, and a hypercritical attitude of the coach toward the black athlete's performance. To put it simply, the athlete feels that he has not been played but has been "used." If any of the above charges can be substantiated, the coach has only himself to blame for bringing about the situation. The code of proper relationship between the coach and athlete has been violated through a lack of regard for the athlete's feelings and failure to recognize a responsibility for his welfare and education. The college administration cannot be expected to support the coach if he is guilty of discrimination or unfair treatment toward any athlete. If, however, upon an examination of his conscience, a coach firmly believes himself to be innocent of the charges placed against him, he should contest the indictment with all his power.

Some colleges have been presented with demands for the hiring of black coaches. When one considers the number of black coaches in non-segregated institutions, it does appear that consciously or unconsciously, discrimination has been in effect but to demand that black coaches be added to the staff merely for the sake of having minority representation lacks validity. There are many fine black coaches in the profession and many great black athletes with a high potential for coaching. They deserve consideration because of their abilities, not because of their color.

Another form of dissention or open hostility to the coach's authority has been a rebellion against regulations pertaining to dress and personal appearance. Because of the rapport that has existed between the coach and his athletes, he has a tendency to regard them as a special group, above average in personal qualities. He also wants them to be highly regarded by others so he insists that they create the impression of cleanliness and good grooming when they are on public exhibition. The acceptance of his authority and the consent to be governed on the part of the athlete has enabled the coach to set regulations against long hair, beards and off-beat apparel. Most athletes prefer to be neat and clean so there have been few problems. Moreover, the good athlete satisfies his need for recognition through his athletic prowess, whereas other students may find it necessary to attract attention to themselves by a strikingly unusual appearance. However, some athletes, feeling that most of their daily contacts are with people outside of the athletic group, prefer to conform to the standards set by their non-athletic friends thus bringing themselves into conflict with the coach's regulations.

When faced with a challenge to their authority even in matters outside the technical aspects of the job, one coach may unhesitatingly drop the dissenters from the squad. Another, either feeling secure in the belief that the majority of athletes prefer to follow the regulations or that they will back him in any controversey, allow the squad to vote on the question. The coach should realize that in spite of a vote of confidence for him, there is a distinct possibility of losing the rebellious student, especially a strong-willed one.

One may question the advisability of allowing the squad to vote on any question of discipline on the grounds that it could be the initial move in a progressive erosion of the coach's authority. On the other hand, it might be the wisest move. There does not appear to be a single prescription to fit all cases. Each coach must evaluate his own situation. The general atmosphere of the institution is an important clue. If a strong feeling of independence and freedom from conformity pervades the college community, the coach might be wise to allow his athletes to decide on matters outside of actual practice, play and conditioning. He must also be able to recognize the difference between (1) revolutionary anarchism and (2) a legitimate clamor for relief against unreasonable restrictions. In the case of the first, a strong, unrelenting stand is called for, whereas in the second, arbitration should be employed.

A coach could feel safe in putting any matter concerning his authority before his athletes for a vote if the following questions could be answered in the affirmative:

1. Does he feel that he always has acted justly and fairly with the best interests of the athletes and institution in mind?
2. Have the great majority of athletes always indicated an unquestioning willingness to abide by regulations pertaining to conduct and appearance on and off the playing field?
3. Has the morale of the squad been high as indicated by their enthusiasm during practice and games?
4. Is he highly regarded as a fine teacher of the technical aspects of his sport?
5. Have the recent seasons been winning ones?

Some institutional controversies involving students, faculty and administration have been placed before a board or committee which is supposed to investigate the problems in an impartial manner, present its findings and make recommendations to settle the issue. It is quite possible that a dispute between a coach and a group of dissident athletes might be placed before such a board. In such cases, it would be well for the investigators to first establish the following principles that should givern the judgment and action of both parties in any controversy regarding coach/athlete relations:

1. There must be some readiness on the part of coaches to become more flexible in their beliefs about discipline in matters only indirectly connected with actual play.
2. There must be some inclination on the part of student/athletes to be mature in their attitudes toward freedom and/or conformity.
3. Both parties should agree that the rights of the majority must be protected.

The opportunity for real teaching exists in situations of threatened rebellion. The coach should hold frequent meetings with his athletes, individually and collectively, during which exchanges of thoughts and ideas could result in a clearer understanding of each other's feelings, the installation of proper attitudes and the development of acceptable habits of behavior.

SUMMARY

While it possesses many features found in other enterprises, athletic coaching involves enough different facets to be considered unique even in the overall pattern of teaching. Daily, the coach faces problems of organization, leadership, training, teaching, recruitment, public relations, and many others. His knowledge, personality, and judgment will be called upon to produce a smooth-running program. Rarely is a coaching position considered dull and uninteresting. If it is so, it is because the coach ignores his responsibilities or cannot recognize his opportunities for improving his situation.

When contemplating a change in position, the coach should consider the many factors that make a given position good or bad. Among these are location, assistants, administrative support, housing, salary, fringe benefits, material on hand, financial aid, recruiting, and many others. Each coach has his own personal problems that could affect the desirability of making a certain change. The old axiom, "The grass is always greener on the other side of the fence" is as true with coaching jobs as with other situations.

College coaches are faced with the problem of inducing good scholar-athletes to matriculate at their institutions. Recruiting takes many forms and may be done by many agencies or individuals. It is almost imperative that a recruiter be at least a staff member of an institution if he is not a coach. Rules of conduct in recruiting have been drawn up by the regulating agencies, including athletic conferences. Most of the regulations have to do with scholastic standing and monetary awards and should be adhered to strictly. Violations bring drastic punishment, such as suspension from conference championship play for all teams in the college, as well as dismissal from the staff for the offending individual. Stress on the educational advantages of the institution rather than on any financial-assistance program should be a guiding principle for recruiters.

With better understanding of child and adolescent attitudes, as well as the physiological power of youngsters, there has come about revised feelings concerning competitive athletics below the high school level. With properly trained coaches who are more motivated to teach technique than to compile winning records, it is possible to carry on athletic competition at this level which is safe, wholesome, and enjoyable. Youngsters should still be taught to play to win but also to understand the causes of winning or losing.

As in the other levels of education, an interscholastic athletic program should supplement, not replace, an intramural program.

Athletic contests are public spectacles controlled by the institutions fielding the teams. The cost of promulgating sports programs has risen sharply in recent years, to the point where it is impossible to operate without gate receipts. Institutional money may be budgeted for athletics as for other educational enterprises, but usually it will not be sufficient to carry on a complete program touching many students. Hence, it becomes imperative that the good will and financial support of the public be solicited. Presenting the athletic program in its best light is a public relations problem. Agencies such as newspapers, radio, and television become very cooperative when the institution makes a genuine effort to provide them with fresh and interesting news as well as statistical information. The team and its coaches become a part of the image of the institution, so it behooves them to create an attractive one.

Close personal support for the athletic program comes from parents and boosters. The parents have a vested interest because of the presence of a son on the squad. Understandably, their interest centers more on the success of their offspring than in the happiness of the coach; however, the majority of parents can be made to realize the problems of coaching, and this makes them more reasonable in attitude. Educating parents is an important coaching problem, especially on the high school level.

Booster Clubs, like most good things, are splendid when used in moderation. The coach's relationship with the club should be one of courteous enthusiasm, not reluctant toleration. The motivating force behind a booster club is their sincere interest in the team, and that can produce some difficulties for the coach. Close supervision of their relations with players is necessary, a task which cannot be left solely to coaches. The club members, especially the officers, must constantly be vigilant to prevent zealous fellow members from violating rules of support for athletes. Coaches should avoid becoming ingratiated to a booster's club because of supplementation of salary.

In today's rebellious campus atmosphere, the possibility exists that athletes may protest against the coach's rules concerning dress, behavior and other regulations. Where fairness, mutual respect and genuine love for athletics exists, the coach can reasonably expect the majority of his boys to support his stand.

Test Questions

1. What are the usual attractive features of a position which appeal to coaches?
2. How does sports tradition influence the attractiveness of a coaching position?
3. What are some reasons for a faculty having an antagonistic attitude toward an athletic program?
4. What factors of an assistant coaching position should be considered by an applicant?
5. How important is the salary factor in consideration of a coaching position?
6. If athletic scholarships are to be granted by an institution, who should grant them?
7. Basically, what is the purpose of the athletic scholarship?
8. What might cause the scholarship program to lose its respectability?
9. Should recruiting be done by athletic departments which have no athletic scholarships to offer?
10. What are the dangers of having recruiters outside of the institution?
11. List some reasons why athletes matriculate at a particular institution.
12. What, if anything, is the secret to success in recruiting?

13. What responsibility should a high school coach assume in assisting his athletes to matriculate at a proper institution? How could he be of greatest value?
14. Is it bad policy to equip youngsters of grammar school age with uniforms? Explain.
15. Do the physiological limits of junior high school boys and girls prohibit sports activities?
16. How could the concept of continuity act as a guide in developing a good program of athletics below the high school level?
17. Define public relations.
18. Is it best for the coach to direct the sports information program?
19. Why is a sports brochure a valuable public relations tool?
20. List some important items in press-box control.
21. What should a coach do if he feels that he has been treated unjustly by a sportswriter?
22. What is the motivating interest of Parents' Club members?
23. List some actions which could be considered as bad form by Parents' Clubs.
24. What is the most important function of Boosters clubs?
25. Should coaches allow Boosters Club members to make suggestions about coaching the team?
26. Why should a coach object to mediating the direct aspects of his sport?
27. When might a coach feel safe in placing a question of conformity before his squad for a vote?

Discussion Questions

1. You are offered a head coaching position having many attractive features, but the administration informs you that no new assistants may be added because those of the former coach all have tenure. What would you do?
2. If you were to make a priority list of the most important factors to consider in appraising a coaching position, which would you list as the first three items?
3. A student was granted a scholarship to attend a college at the recommendation of the athletic department, but after matriculating he decided not to participate in intercollegiate athletics. As the head coach, what would you do?
4. What is indicated if the most active recruiters for an athletic program are the present and former players?

5. Should junior high school athletes receive a vigorous program or body conditioning, or should the emphasis be on the playing aspects of the sport?
6. In order to retain your services as head coach, five members of the Booster Club offer to supplement your annual salary at $1,000 each. What is your reaction?
7. The institution finds it necessary to eliminate full insurance coverage for athletic teams. What would you as a coach do about this situation?
8. How do you manage the problem of satisfying two local newspapers when one is a morning paper and the other an evening publication?
9. If a coach recruits an athlete who wears a beard and/or long hair, should he insist that the athlete conform to a rule prohibiting such adornment?

Suggested Readings

BOOKS

1. Alley, Louis. "Interscholastic Athletics for Junior High School Boys." *Current Administrative Problems.* Committee Report of AAHPER, Washington, D.C., 1960.
2. Bucher, Charles. *Administration of School and College Health and Physical Education Programs and Physical Education.* St. Louis: C. V. Mosby Co., 1967, Fourth Edition, pp. 301-317, 599-632.
3. Daughtrey, Greyson. *Methods in Physical Education and Health for Secondary Schools.* Philadelphia: W. B. Saunders Co., 1967, pp. 34-46, 476-495.
4. Forsyth, Charles E. *Administration of High School Athletics.* Englewood Cliffs: Prentice Hall, Inc., 1962.
5. George, Jack and Lehman, Harry. *School Athletic Administration.* New York: Harper and Row, 1966, pp. 29-56, 158-159.
6. Graves, Ray. *Ray Graves' Guide to Modern Football Defense.* New York: Parker Publishing Co., Inc., 1966, p. 200.
7. Hackensmith, C. W. *History of Physical Education.* New York: Harper and Row, 1966, pp. 501-502.
8. Havel, Richard and Seymour, Emory. *Administration of Health, Physical Education and Recreation for Schools.* New York: Ronald Press Co., 1961, pp. 287-309.

9. Hughes, W. L. and Williams, J. F. *Athletics in Education.* Philadelphia: W. B. Saunders Co., 1931.
10. Hughes, W., and French, E. and Lehster, N. *Administration of Physical Education.* New York: Ronald Press Co., 1962, p. 82, 273-317.
11. Report of First National Conference on Secondary School Athletic Administration. *Administration of High School Athletics.* AAHPER, 1963.
12. Scott, Harry. *Competitive Sports in Schools and Colleges.* New York: Harper and Row, 1951, pp. 92-100.
13. Tunis, John. *The American Way in Sport.* New York: Duell Sloan and Pearce Co., 1958.
14. Vannier, M. and Fair, H. *Teaching Physical Education in Secondary Schools.* Philadelphia: W. B. Saunders Co., 1957, p. 382.
15. Voltmer, Edward and Esslinger, Arthur. *The Organization and Administration of Physical Education.* New York: Appleton-Century-Crofts, Inc., 1967, Fourth Edition, pp. 450-477.
16. Walker, Bob. *Organization for Successful Football Coaching.* Englewood Cliffs: Prentice Hall, Inc., 1961, pp. 171-226.
17. Weber, Robert. "Public Pressures and Their Effect on Athletics." *Current Administrative Problems.* Committee Report, AAHPER, Washington, D.C., 1960.
18. Williams, J. F., Brownell, Clifford and Vernier, Elman. *Administration of Health Education and Physical Education.* W. B. Saunders, 1966, 6th Edition, pp. 184-215.

Suggested Readings

ARTICLES

1. Alley, Louis. "Report: Standards for Junior High School Athletics," *National Conference on Secondary School Athletic Administration,* Washington, D.C., December 1962.
2. Babbidge, Homer. D. "Student Unrest and College Athletics," *Scholastic Coach,* Vol. 38-5, October 1968.
3. Baker, Paul, M. "Helping the Athlete Get Into College," *Scholastic Coach,* Vol. 35-6, February 1966, p. 48.
4. BeVans, Bonnie J. "The Future of Interscholastic Sports for Girls," *JOHPER,* Vol. 39-3, March 1968, pp. 39-41.
5. Bien, Harry J. "Pre-Game Basketball Ceremony," *Scholastic Coach,* Vol. 38-1, September 1967, pp. 88-89.

6. Brown, Joe. "The Trainer's Role in Mental Attitude," *Coach and Athlete,* Vol. XXIX, October 1966, p. 14.

7. Bucher, Charles. "New Athletic Program for Our Schools," *National Association of Secondary School Principals,* Bulletin 50, April 1966, pp. 198-218.

8. Cope, Myron. "Mossie Murphy's Crusade," *Sports Illustrated,* Vol. 18, January 28, 1963, p. 20.

9. Crossley, J. B. "Goodbye, Mr. Coach. How to Fire the Mentor of a Winning Team," *Clearing House,* Vol. 42-3, November 1967, pp. 152-155.

10. Davis, Michael. "Get Some Public Relations in Your Swimming," *The Athletic Journal,* Vol. 47-2, October 1967, pp. 37, 76.

11. Day, Dick. "Sport Attendance," *Coach and Athlete,* Vol. 28, January 1965, pp. 14, 23.

12. DeBramo, Emilio. "Competitive Athletics at the Elementary School Level," *The Bulletin for the Connecticut Association for Health, Physical Education and Recreation,* Vol. 13-2, December 1967.

13. Fagan, Clifford B. "What is the Purpose of Eligibility Rules?" *School Activities,* Vol. 36, October 1964, pp. 16-17.

14. Fagan, Clifford B. "Administrators Find 'No Promotion' Theory Antiquated for High School Athletic Programs," *The Coach,* Vol. XLIV-4, March 1958, p. 2.

15. Gidden, Paul. "The Scramble for College Athletes," *Atlantic,* Vol. CCXVI, December 1965, pp. 49-52.

16. Gold, Joseph. "Motivational Psychology in Coaching," *Scholastic Coach,* Vol. 37-6, February 1968, pp. 54-55.

17. Graham, R. C. "Plea for Junior High School Athletics," *Clearing House,* Vol. 38, October 1963, p. 79.

18. Griswold, A. Whitney. "College and the Athlete," *Newsweek,* Vol. 53, March 9, 1959, p. 78.

19. Hughes, E. "Surveys of Coaches' Salaries," *Scholastic Coach,* Vol. 34-1, September 1964, pp. 74-76.

20. Kagan, Paul. "Do-It-Yourself Publicity," *Scholastic Coach,* Vol. XXXIII-10, June 1964, pp. 20-21, 30-31.

21. Keller, Irving. "School Athletics—It's Philosophy and Objectives," *School Board Journal,* Vol. 153-2, August 1966, p. 22.

22. Lawrence, Ted. "Selling Your Athletic Program," *The Coaching Clinic,* Prentice Hall Inc., October 1965, p. 32.

23. Moser, C. H. "Our Coaching Profession," *Athletic Journal,* Vol. 45-5, February 1965, p. 34.

24. Masin, H. L. "Scholarship Ahoy!" *Scholastic Coach,* Vol. 35-5, January 1966, p. 80.
25. National Association of Secondary School Principals. "A Survey of Interscholastic Athletic Programs in Separately Organized Junior High Schools," Bulletin No. 42, N.E.A., Washington, D.C., 1958, p. 249.
26. Nelson, J. "To the High School Athlete Headed for College," *Scholastic Coach,* Vol. 32-3, November 1962, pp. 64-65.
27. Oestreich, Harry G. "Extra Pay for Extra Service," *The American School Board Journal,* Vol. 151-3, September 1965, p. 11.
28. Oestreich, Harry G. "Percentage Payment Plan for Extra Services," *JOHPER,* Vol. 37-9, September 1966, p. 40.
29. O'Quinn, Mickey. "Booster Club Boosts Team Through Films," *Athletic Journal,* Vol. 44-10, June 1964, pp. 38-39, 45-47.
30. Santore, Joel and Thurston, James. "Coaching Salaries—Two Approaches," *JOHPER,* Vol. 39-4, April 1968, pp. 30-32, 42.
31. Scott, Calvin. "Should Boys Play Football?" *Parent's Magazine,* Vol. 42-11, November 1967, pp. 84-86, 151.
32. Scott, Harry. "New Directions in Intercollegiate Athletics," *Teachers College Record,* Vol. 58, April-May 1957,pp. 29-37.
33. Sharnik, Morton and Creamer, Robert. "The New Rage to Win," *Sports Illustrated,* Vol. 17, October 1962, pp. 14-17.
34. Shaw, John. "Standards for Junior High School Athletics," *Journal of School Health,* Vol. 34, April 1964, pp. 164-168.
35. Shuck, Gilbert. "Effects of Athletic Competition on the Growth and Development of Junior High School Boys," *Reserach Quarterly,* Vol. 33, May 1960, pp. 288-298.
36. Sobolewski, Eugene. "Recipe for All-Americans," *Scholastic Coach,* Vol. 37-2, October 1967, p. 66.
37. Stuhldreher, Mary. "High Heeled Recruiter and a Mama's Boy," *Sports Illustrated,* Vol. 19, September 23, 1963, pp. 72-76.
38. Tansey, James. "A Sound Approach to the Basketball Feeder System," *Athletic Journal,* Vol. 49-1, September 1968, pp. 90-91.
39. Thurston, James. "A Formula for Extra Duty," *JOHPER,* Vol. 39-4, April 1968, pp. 30-32, 42.
40. Tillman, Ken. "Teaching Load of the College Physical Education Teacher-Coach," *The Physical Educator,* Vol. 25-3, October 1968, pp. 131-138.
41. Underwood, John. "Go Get 'Em Coaches," *Sports Illustrated,* Vol. 19, December 9, 1963, pp. 82-84.
42. Young, George and Paxton, Harry T. "I Serve on the Sin Committee," *Saturday Evening Post,* Vol. 232, April 30, 1960 p. 25.

GLOSSARY

Angle—A charge by defensive football linemen aiming right or left rather than head on.

Athletic instinct—A misnomer applied to habits of performance derived from playing experience.

Boss-man—The individual in complete charge of an enterprise such as an athletic program. The decision maker.

Brush back—Pitching a baseball close to the batter so as to move him back from the plate.

Brush block—A football maneuver in which an offensive blocker lightly brushes by a defensive man.

Buildup—Preparing a player or team emotionally for a contest.

Carrying the fight—Incessant offensive action.

Check him—A football maneuver in which a player momentarily halts an opponent.

Check off—A quick switch of responsibility between players just before or during a play.

Choke up—(a) Shortening the grip on a baseball bat.
　　　　 —(b) A term applied to athletes whose actions are inhibited by apprehension.

Cold storage coaching—Drilling on a skill that has no application for the immediate situation.

Color—A dramatic, spectacular, and dashing quality.

Continuity—Basketball offensive with previously designed moves to produce continuous movement of players.

Cooling off—Slowing bodily processes during a period of reduced activity following a period of intense activity.

Corner man—Football defensive man stationed wide to prevent runs and cover wide receivers.

Cover outside—A football maneuver in which the defensive man protects territory outside of a designated point.

Crawfishing—The act of retreating from or deliberately avoiding bodily contact.

Crowd it—To stand very close to home plate while batting.

Crux—See Nub.

Cut off—A baseball infielder intercepting a throw from the outfield and relaying it to a base to put out a runner.

Dead ball—A point during a contest in which the ball is not in play and time is not counted.

Dig in—A baseball batter's act of firmly implanting his spikes in the batter's box to facilitate swinging.

Double play—The act of making two outs on one play in baseball.

Double team—Assigning two defensive men to guard one offensive player.

Down field block—An offensive football maneuver designed to cut down a secondary defense man in the open field.

Drift—A style of defensive end play in football designed to contain the offensive play to the inside area.

Edge—A high quality of mental, physical, and emotional readiness for a contest.

Even front—A football defensive line employing 4, 6, or 8 men up front.

Flanker—A football backfield man who is stationed wide outside of the rest of the team.

Follow through—Allowing the body to complete an act initiated by muscular contractions in an easy natural manner.

Freeze—Inability to act caused by a high emotional state.

Give and go—Basketball offense where the passer goes either to the basket or to the receiver to screen.

Goal set—The point of accomplishment ultimately to be reached by the learner. His expectation.

Go the extra mile—To readily cooperate. To give more assistance than is expected.

Grant-in-aid—A plan of financial assistance to college students, usually based on need.

Griping—Complaining.

"Guard the dish"—Admonishing a batter to swing at any pitch in or near the strike zone.

Hair brained—Lacking good judgment.

Hand-off—Passing the ball to a teammate by allowing the receiver practically to take the ball.

High post—Basketball offense in which the key man is stationed in front of the free throw line.

Hold him—A baseball expression for keeping a baserunner from taking a big lead.

Inside safety—Football defensive player assigned to deep inside territory.

Jump shot—A basketball shot in which both feet are free from the floor.

Liquid meal—Canned liquid containing calories and nutrients equal to a solid meal but more easily digested.

Loose—(a) A relaxed athlete.
     (b) A style of defense which allows great space between the defensive player and his opponent.

Loosen-up—A series of exercises performed by an athlete designed to stretch and relax his skeletal muscles.

Man-in-motion—A football backfield man who starts moving laterally before the ball is snapped.

Meat hand—The baseball player's bare hand.

Minor sport—A sport considered to have less appeal than some others. This method of classification is disappearing.

Money-in-the-bank—A coach's valuable asset such as an outstanding athlete.

Neuromuscular control—The finely coordinated action of muscles in response to nervous impulses. Skill.

Nub—The most essential feature of an athletic technique which must be understood and executed for a successful performance.

Odd front—A football defensive line employing 3, 5, 7, or 9 players up front.

Off the record—Information and statements issued in confidence and not for public distribution.

Pace—The speed at which athletic skills are performed.

Pep—A high degree of energy.

Pep pills—Amphetamine types of drugs designed to delay the feeling of fatigue. Most are dangerously toxic.

Pick—A method of blocking the path of a defensive basketball player.

Playing for two—Baseball infielders playing deep to improve their chances for the double play.

Play safe—A conservative style of play designed to protect a lead rather than attempt to increase it.

Press—A basketball defense in which the players harass their opponents in all areas of the court.

Protect—A football maneuver in which a player prevents an opponent from contacting a teammate or moving into certain territory.

Push him—Calling for a sacrifice to advance a base runner.

Reading—Quick determination of an opponent's intentions by interpreting his bodily action.

Relay—Retrieving a long hit baseball and throwing it to an infielder for final delivery to the catcher to prevent a score.

Rocker step—(a) A baseball infielder's method of tagging the base and making the throw to first base for the double play.
(b) A fake step in basketball to throw the defensive player off balance.

Screen—To wall off defensive men with the bodies of offensive players.

Set shot—A basketball shot in which both feet are on the floor while shooting.

Short fuse—An uncontrollable temper. Quick to take offense.

Slough off—A basketball defense allowing the players to release from their opponents in certain zones.

Split end—A football end who lines up more than one yard from the next inside player.

Squibb—A kick-off in football designed to make the ball bounce crazily along the ground.

Stuff—(a) A player's repertoire of skills.
       (b) Material to be learned.

Swing man—A football backfield man who runs wide laterally to become open for a possible forward pass.

Switch—Defensive basketball players exchange opponents in order to prevent a pick-off.

Tight—A style of play which has players aligned close together.

Time-outs—Short intervals of rest or inactivity allowed contestants during a game.

Too high—A state of emotional condition beyond the control of the player.

Triangularing—Three-man maneuver in basketball in which each player is either (1) passing, (2) cutting for the basket, or (3) picking.

Twenty-one—A basketball shooting contest done from various areas of the offensive zone.

Upset—An unexpected victory or loss.

Waiting line—A type of defensive play in football in which the defensive line allows the offense to commit itself before moving to meet the play.

Wind sprints—Short runs done at fast speed with little rest between runs.

Yellow—Cowardly.

Zone—A basketball defense in which players are responsible for territory rather than individuals. Also used in other team sports such as football, soccer, etc.

INDEX